# SURVIVING THE MEDIA JUNGLE

David Chagall
July 15, 1996

# SURVIVING THE MEDIA JUNGLE

DAVID CHAGALL

BROADMAN
& HOLMAN
PUBLISHERS

Nashville, Tennessee

4262-63
0-8054-6263-5
Published by
Broadman & Holman Publishers
Nashville, Tennessee
Dewey Decimal Classification: 261.52
Subject Heading: ELECTRONIC APPARATUS AND APPLIANCES\
CHRISTIANITY AND CURRENT ISSUES \ CHRISTIAN ETHICS
Library of Congress Card Catalog Number: 95-23357



**Library of Congress Cataloging-in-Publication Data**

Chagall, David
Surviving the media jungle / David Chagall
p. cm.
ISBN 0-8054-6263-5 (pb)
1. Mass media—Moral and ethical aspects. 2. Mass media—Religious aspects—Christianity. 3. United States—Moral conditions. 4. Manipulative behavior. 5. Christianity and culture. 6. Mass media and children—United States. I. Title.
P94.C44 1996
302.23—dc20 95-23357
CIP

00 99 98 97 96 5 4 3 2 1

# Contents

# Preface

No work that relies to any extent on secondary research can fail to recognize the long ranks of pioneers who, through their dedicated work and zealous pursuit of truth, paved the way for this current exploration. You will find their names, a list too lengthy to enumerate here, in the Notes and Sources section of this book.

I am also indebted to my editor, Vicki Crumpton, who gave me cogent insights and suggestions that helped shape this text through the several phases of its writing and editing. To my wife and life partner, Juneau, go my appreciation and respect for her perceptive observations, encouragement, toughness of spirit, and generous patience she extended all during the researching and writing of this book.

One final note. For the sake of reading ease, throughout this book I have omitted any numbered source references traditionally superimposed above the key words. Whenever I as a reader encounter numbers popping up over a word, I find the flow of narrative, thought, and vision stifled. So for that reason, your reading voyage through the ensuing text will not be impeded by any superscripted numerals.

Instead, at the end of the book you will find an extensive Notes and Sources section. Divided by chapters, it identifies specific pages and line numbers associated with the source references and additional commentaries that apply. So those readers who have a serious wish to follow up the data will find the bibliographical trail laid out.

*David Chagall*
*Agoura, California*

## Introduction

# Tricks of the Trade

*An' the gobble-uns 'll git you Ef you don't watch out!*

James Whitcomb Riley

Americans are arguably the most manipulated people on earth. From dawn to bedtime, and at times even as we sleep, we are prodded, coddled, nagged, terrorized, flattered, and wheedled. Over home television and car radio, at the movies or watching hotel VCRs, day in and night out all kinds of messages penetrate our defenses to shape our actions—until to paraphrase T. S. Eliot, we don't know whether we're alive and the anchorman's dead or if he's alive and we're dead. Or if we're both alive, then the landlord must be dead, and if so, who's been collecting the rent?

For more than two decades I directed marketing and social research studies to discover what makes people react. In the process, I discovered the inside secrets of the "persuasion industry," tricks of the trade—dirty or otherwise—that prompt human beings to dance to somebody else's tune.

Broadcasters, politicians, businesses, and government agencies all exploit this information for their own benefit. They look at the rest of us as viewers, listeners, voters, buyers, tryers, prospects, and just plain suckers. Like it or not, we are all actors in this vast, staged manipulation game.

## The Electronically Wired Planet

Computers and satellite communications have linked the western world into one great electronic village, and it has become even more difficult to define ourselves by geography, history, language, or tradition. Wherever we live, whatever our history or beliefs, we have all become manipulation targets. The only difference between America and the rest of the electronically-wired planet is that it all started here first and thus has developed here into more outrageous, devilishly effective extremes than anyplace else.

But it is simply a matter of time—and not very much of it—before every society on earth will be equally afflicted. Whether we call ourselves Americans, Britons, French, Germans, or Russians—each and every day we are targeted and victimized by "push-button controls." Even if you think you're too discerning to be a victim of any form of mass persuasion think again. Even Christians are vulnerable without the right survival techniques.

Take politics. When we go to the polls to vote, in our own minds we choose candidates we believe agree with us on most important questions. But behind the closed doors of their campaign headquarters, the talk is not about "issues" or "principles" but rather how to put together what the professionals who run the show call the "coalition of 51 percent." More bluntly, the focus is on how they can best manipulate different kinds of voters into believing their candidate speaks for them.

I became friends with top campaign consultant Hal Evry, who ran winning efforts for Senator Ted Stevens of Alaska, Governor George C. Wallace of Alabama and Governor Winthrop Rockefeller of Arkansas. Before he died last year, Evry with brutal honesty told me how our political system works.

"People really don't want to vote," he noted. "It's a chore. They'd rather watch a ballgame or a television movie than drag themselves to the polls. If the media didn't get on their backs the week before an election and say, 'Be sure to vote!,' only a hardcore handful would show up. As it is, most candidates get elected by less than a fourth of those eligible to vote. Since people don't want to vote or read a lot of complicated arguments, you have to make things simple for them.

"Pure emotion is what always works. The higher the emotion, the less people use reason. And the three things that impel people the most are self-preservation, sex, and money, in that order. A candidate has to make the public like him. If the people like him, they'll vote for him. If you're fairly decent, half the people will like you and half won't. If you're an outspoken guy like me, eight out of ten will hate you. But if you appear to be all things to all people, get on television, and don't say anything but make it sound good, you can get three out of four to like what they *read into you*. And that's the secret of a winning campaign."

## Captives in Our Homes

A study by ABC's research department found that two out of every three mothers are accompanied to the supermarket by their small children. One out of three takes her children on *every* shopping trip. Over half the mothers surveyed said their children actually select items to be bought.

So how does that affect you and your family? Very simply, it means that all kinds of manufacturers will aim their messages not only at you but at your more vulnerable youngsters.

For example, a commercial for a popular spray-on disinfectant for cuts and scrapes used a circus clown as their television pitchman. It was an obvious appeal to children, even though the product's own label shouts in bold type: **KEEP OUT OF THE REACH OF CHILDREN**. The label also warns, "Not for use on eyes, mouth, or other delicate membranes." So it is no great surprise when little kids are rushed to emergency rooms for treatment after using these toxic sprays.

As with politicians and clowns, so it goes with the other sensory messages we receive. All through the day in our everyday lives we unwittingly react to words, pictures, colors, symbols, shapes, sounds, and gestures. Nowhere are these responses more effective than when triggered at times and places where we are most relaxed, receptive, and trusting. Where would that be? Why, right in our own living rooms, of course, sitting in front of the family stereos and TV sets.

The coup de grace of electronic manipulation usually occurs inside the sanctity of the American home. There we sprawl on sofas and easy chairs, lulled by beguiling images, cunningly crafted scripts, and seductive musical tones. Our eyes fixate, our brains relax and we slip into a semihypnotic condition where we are vulnerable to a barrage of "targeted messages," designed to make us buy, try, vote for or support the manipulator's products, values, candidates, and worldviews.

How successful are these merchants of mass persuasion? Far more than they will openly admit. The official line of the propaganda industry is to downplay its impact on modern society. But the appalling truth is that they have grown increasingly more ingenious in the art of electronic seduction and mind penetration as they have fine-tuned their techniques over the past half century. Today's mind manipulators can tell within a few percentage points how many of us will be affected and to what degree by their electronic bewitchments.

## Reaping the Whirlwind

The lion's share of their efforts targets those under fifty. These people, born after World War II, represent the dominant new force in this nation's—and the planet's—destiny. These are the children of the electronic village, the first generations entirely weaned while crawling, sitting, and falling asleep in front of the family TV set.

Inhabiting this electronic kingdom, they have forged new patterns of seeing, hearing, and thinking—the very responses that make them more vulnerable than any previous generation to the sights, sounds, illusions, special effects, and belief-systems projected by our modern pied pipers of hype.

Because of the slow-moving way democracies work, a chain of cause and effect has been set in motion that appears to be irrevocable. While some of these consequences may have been unplanned by those who pull the strings, most are consciously calculated. Nevertheless, whether intentional or accidental, the ultimate effect has been the glorification of *me*-ism and the promotion of a feel-good morality—"if it feels good, do it."

In just a few decades, a new kind of planetary barbarian has emerged—a selfish, self-centered electronic addict, inner eyes and ears riveted to a perpetual MTV video dancing across his or her mindscreen. In its latest incarnation, the electronic netherworld has birthed a large crowd of people devoid of traditional loyalties or human compassion. Its extreme elements comprise a highly dangerous, often murderous subclass of mind-blown youth.

*"But how does this apply to me?"* you may ask. "This sort of horror only happens to the poor and ignorant of the inner cities, not to upright families like my own." That is what neighbors of the Golly family thought. Living peacefully in a quiet, middle-class suburb in Los Angeles' San Fernando Valley, Granada Hills is the sort of neighborhood where birthdays, picnics and church potlucks are the hot discussion topics.

Then, late one night in early 1994, the neighborhood awoke to the ominous sounds. Seventeen-year-old Christopher Golly had gone to his room and cranked up his stereo volume with *The End* by the Doors. His father, Steven Golly, went to his son's door and asked, "What's going on"? That was when the neighbors heard the distinct cracks of rifle shots. Someone called 911 and three LAPD squad cars careened to the location. Thirty minutes later, three people lay dead:

Christopher Golly, his father, and a rookie police officer named Christy Hamilton.

Murder and mayhem in Granada Hills? How could this be? High school friends described mild-mannered, bespectacled Christopher as "just a normal laid-back teen-ager." Others said he was a "nice guy" and "good student" who had won his school's Student of the Week award several times. His principal called him "the last student he would suspect being capable of such violence."

But there were other, more troubled signs. Lifelong friends remembered Chris as a bright elementary and junior high school student who changed as he entered high school. He made new friends, skipped school, played video games, and neglected his studies. Finally he developed a passion for "speed metal," a driving, guitar-based music that marries elements of punk-rock to heavy metal.

Like his new companions, Chris favored a hairstyle closely cropped on the sides and long on top. And, like them, he graduated from drinking beer and smoking "pot" to snorting "pink champagne," a rose-colored metamphetamine powder.

Jamie Kushner, part of Christopher's teenage group, recalled that Chris especially loved Pantera, Ministry, and Metallica, rock bands whose loud, aggressive sounds made them a favorite of teenage boys. "We partied, had real good times," he noted. "Teenage stuff, like we drank our beer and smoked our weed. We were supposed to go to the Pink Floyd concert April 17. But Chris just went off, went crazy."

Kushner warned other parents living in similarly affluent, quiet neighborhoods that they may face many of the same problems that one night exploded in Chris Golly. "I hope this wakes people up about places like Granada Hills," he said. "There's a little urban underground hiding out where you least expect it."

## What Sets Us Off?

With Christopher, it was speed metal music, lubricated by beer and speed. With others, it's television, movies, or videos. The Journal of the American Medical Association recently reported a strong relationship between viewing lots of TV violence and the potential of acting out violent behavior.

Another study followed forty-five first- and second-grade pupils in an outlying Canadian town that did not get television until 1973.

These students were compared over a two-year period to children in other towns where television was already available. Over those twenty-four months, the rate of physical aggression acted out by the youngsters who already had television did not change significantly—but among those others who had never had TV, violent behavior rose by 160 percent.

Another study followed nearly nine hundred rural boys over a twenty-two-year span to find that the "degree of viewing violent television acts at age eight significantly predicted the seriousness of any crimes for which they were convicted by age thirty."

In Huntington Beach, California, a thirteen-year-old boy was recently arrested for bringing a machete and loaded gun to school, where he intended to take his classmates hostage. When police sought a motive, they found the boy had identified with the "hero" of a music video called "Jeremy" by the grunge rock group Pearl Jam. This video, depicting a troubled youth who takes a classroom hostage and then shoots himself, was named Best Rock Video of the Year at MTV's 1993 Music Video Awards.

A few weeks earlier, in Moraine, Ohio, a five-year-old boy set his bed on fire with a cigarette lighter. as the fire spread, his two-year-old sister was burned to death. Later, the children's mother told fire fighters that the incident had been inspired by the TV characters Beavis and Butthead, who often discuss burning things, proclaiming that "Fire is cool!" Two months before that, the fire chief in Sidney, Ohio, blamed a house fire torched by three young girls as also inspired by the Beavis and Butthead cartoon figures.

Dr. Brandon Centerwall of the University of Washington estimates that if Americans did not have access to the television programming available in the United States today, there would be 10,000 fewer murders, 70,000 fewer rapes, and 700,000 fewer aggravated assault injuries each year. Just by eliminating television alone, Centerwall believes the U.S. crime rate would be reduced to less than half of its present record levels.

## How Can We Reverse the Tide?

The question remains—have we in fact passed the point of no return? Is there any way to turn back the tidal wave of electronic deviltry that threatens to swamp us? During these last few years of the twentieth century, America—and the rest of the world who follows in our electronic wake—must decide this most crucial issue.

However this global battle turns out, each one of us *can* make a huge difference within the confines of our own homes and families. Even if this great nation, founded under traditional Judeo-Christian principles of western culture, should buckle under to the electronic jungle, as individuals we not only have the option but the sacred duty to fight back and to prevail.

Knowledge is power, and understanding is the doorway to freedom. The father of Christopher Golly should have known, if in fact he did not know, the kinds of music his son favored. Merely by checking out his son's CD and cassette labels, he would have discovered the boy's fascination for poisonous sounds.

Music, like words and pictures, does not exist in a vacuum. Though it speaks its own language, certain kinds of music are invariably associated with "user-friendly" chemicals. "Uppers," "downers," alcohol and psycho-active substances are all linked to their own forms of musical expression. With or without chemicals, music itself fosters a variety of emotions, moods and behavior patterns. As the research shows, violent music does indeed trigger violent behavior.

So how can we combat it? The problem is not so insurmountable as it seems. Once we understand *how* we are influenced by sounds, sights, and symbols, solutions follow close behind. In the words of Solomon, "The mind of the prudent acquires knowledge, and the ear of the wise seeks knowledge" (Prov. 18:15).

Part 1 will first describe how technology exploits our weaknesses through our senses and nervous systems via sounds, symbols, sights, sex, and human emotions. Then it will examine how computerized market research and "psychographics" targets each one of us according to our individual vulnerabilities.

After the early chapters that describe just how manipulators penetrate our defenses by numbing our conscious controls, part 2 concentrates on electronic applications in action—the television industry, videos, TV news shows, motion pictures, and home computers. By the book's end, you will be fully informed on the inner workings of our new electronic village, including the ways it erodes and subverts Judeo-Christian standards—and, most importantly, the ways you can fight back against them and win.

Every magician depends on sleight of hand to work his "spell." As soon as we yank the bandana away from the conjurer's hand, however, we can see how he performs his illusion. And, once revealed, his magical feat is transformed into just another cheap trick that fools no one. To that end, namely exposing all the tricks and traps of the mass manipulators, this book is dedicated.

The stakes are enormous. They involve nothing less than the survival of our nation, our culture, and our values—values that have for over two hundred years sustained the blessings enjoyed by this great nation.

# PART 1

# The Method in Their Madness

# 1

# The Magic of Music

*Music has charms to soothe a savage breast.*

William Congreve

Music is truly a two-edged sword. It can ignite sexual appetites, raise social consciousness, honor the dead, glorify God, and prod people to church on Sundays. In the wrong hands, it can be—and has been—devastating. Used rightly, it can be a blessing as when young David soothed the troubled spirit of King Saul by playing his harp (see 1 Sam. 16:23).

## Music for a Madman

At Pennsylvania's Coatesville Hospital, music therapist Adam Knieste cautiously eyed his next patient, Peter X. The man was so large that several burly attendants had to link their arms together under his armpits to bring him in.

For eight long months, Pete, a former defensive tackle for the Philadelphia Eagles, had babbled incoherently and ripped furniture apart with his bare hands, trying to kill himself and others in the grip of a manic fury. Attending doctors had tried using straitjackets, electric-shock treatments and megadoses of metamorphine to control the murderous giant—all with no effect. So when Knieste asked the attendants to leave the room so he could work with Pete one-on-one, their eyes widened with surprise but they reluctantly complied.

"Pete didn't waste a second," Knieste recounted. "As soon as the aides were gone, he flew through a sea of chairs, grabbed me by the collar, and lifted me off the floor, growling, 'You did it to me, you dirty ______! You, you're the one!'

"Even though I was scared to death, I knew enough not to fight back. I kept talking quietly, trying to reassure him. Finally, he dropped me to the floor and began kicking the chairs around. I moved to the tape player while he bashed his helmeted head against a concrete pole. As he tore a dozen comic books to shreds, I began playing the very loud passages from "The Moldau" by Smetana.

"Peter froze. The music was wild, just like Pete's emotions, and that got his attention. From there I gradually moved the mood, tempo, and intensity to calmer sounds until, after forty-five minutes, I was into some harpsichord things. That was when I spotted him coming for me again, and I figured, *This is it, he's going to finish me off!*

"Instead, he asked for a cigarette and sat down to talk—a man who hadn't spoken one rational word in over eight months. It was a tremendous breakthrough. We proved that by music alone, you could calm psychotics, make them more sociable so they could understand what's been happening to them.

"Most people think that if they feel depressed, the best thing to do is play happy music to cheer themselves up," Knieste explained. "But that's the very *worst* thing you can do. Hyper people who play quiet music to relax end up kicking holes through both speakers. To benefit from mood changes, you have to start right where that person is and establish musical rapport. Depressed people need depressing music. Angry people need angry music. You tell me what kind of music a person listens to and I'll tell you that person's state of mind."

## Music in the Womb

Music both *a*ffects and *re*flects your state of mind. Consider the effects of simple rhythm and "bodybeat sounds" on newborn infants. At Nippon Medical University in Yokohama, Japan, researchers found that the most pervasive sounds a baby hears during its prebirth existence are the steady, pulsating beats inside the mother's womb. Japanese audio technicians then recorded these tones and played them back to a nursery full of newborn infants.

As reported by Dr. Hajima Murooka, head of obstetrics and gynecology at N.M.U., "Our tests prove that this body-beat sound is one hundred percent effective in stopping infants up to four weeks old from crying." Demonstrating his discovery to reporters in the hospital nursery, Murooka explained that as part of the experiment, every baby had been denied its regular afternoon feeding so they would be hungry and irritable.

As the newspeople entered the nursery, all the infants, aged one to ten days, were screaming their heads off. Then Dr. Murooka pushed a button.

The recording came on, a throbbing, pulsating sound that soon filled the room. Incredibly, one after the other, the babies hushed and fell silent. With ninety-three seconds, the last one grew mute.

When Murooka turned the sound off, the first infant began to wail within twenty seconds. Moments later, the entire nursery was shrieking full blast. Murooka switched it on again. This time it took only seventy-six seconds for the room to assume the silence of a tomb.

Subsequent tests show that these womb sounds never fail to work. They are now sold in Japan, Europe, and the United States as an infant pacifier and sleep aid under the label, "Sleep Gently in the Womb." More recent studies in the U.S. combined these womb sounds with women singing soft lullabies on a related recording called "Transitions." The tests found that these mingled sounds comfort premature babies in intensive care.

At the Georgia Baptist Medical Center in Atlanta, seventeen tiny infants were bathed with the "Transition" tones while technicians observed their blood-oxygen level, heart rate, arterial blood pressure, and physical behavior. Whenever a baby was judged to be "agitated," he or she was studied during ten-minute intervals marked by silent periods or bathed with music from nearby tape players.

The results? "Nine of the seventeen fussy infants became either quiet or sleepy during the serenade," reported neonatal specialist Sharon K. Collins. "And while the music played, we saw a significant increase in the oxygen levels of all the babies—a very healthy sign."

## How Music Affects Our Daily Life

From the cradle to the grave, tone power—screaming, subtle or inaudible—works on everyone every day of the week, affecting us at work and at play, in theaters, elevators, supermarkets, and living room entertainment centers. Tests prove over and over again just how susceptible we are to seemingly "innocent" sounds.

In Germany, for example, researchers found that Prussian marches played in car radios trigger so much aggression they can cause serious accidents on the autobahn. Studies with New Jersey high school students find a 30 percent rise in driving errors—as measured by Aetna driving simulators—when students listened to top-40 rock played at high volume than when they listened to Muzak.

Long before children learn to speak, they are conditioned to the special language of rhythms, sounds, and tones. Beyond womb beats and lullabies, the earliest music most kids hear in big doses is tied into cartoon sound tracks. Toddlers crawl, lie, sit, and sprawl in front of TV's flickering *Flintstones* or Disney-type images while music hypes the action.

Car smashups are marked by drum and cymbal crashes. Chases are spurred on by piano runs. Taunts are implied by slide trombones going yeh-yeh-yeh. Happy stories feature flutes and major chords. When the bad guys enter, oboes and organs in minor keys send arpeggios crawling up those tender spines. Children quickly learn a kind of musical shorthand that sets them up for conditioned responses the rest of their lives.

## Musical Magic Sells Products

A top composer of musical commercials, Tony Asher of Asher/Bahler Associates in Los Angeles, explains how he uses music to conjure up television illusions. "When we did the music for Mattel's toy commercials, let's say we were pushing little cars that zip around a track. By using slow, nonmoving music, we made that car look like it was zooming around twice as fast as it really was."

At one point Mattel imported a batch of tiny Japanese dolls. Because of a foulup in delivery, they arrived in Los Angeles a few months ahead of schedule. Since their warehouse was already packed full for the fall selling season, Mattel shipped the dolls straight out to department stores without any backup advertising.

"That's an adman's nightmare," Asher noted. "Account executives lay awake nights worrying that if their clients put their products into the stores without advertising and they sell like mad, the clients will figure, 'What do I need you guys for?'

"That's why Mattel's ad agency came rushing to me screaming, 'We've got to get something on the air and fast!' So we came up with a jingle, strictly a musical sell, and they threw it out over the airwaves. So what happened? Our little song doubled sales in every city it played while in cities without the commercials, sales stayed the same. In a few short weeks, sales of that little doll jumped from 600,000 to 1.3 million."

Musical implants affect us all—old, young, and in-between. Take Ralph and Gerrie Edwards, for example. One Saturday afternoon they took the family shopping at their local supermarket in suburban Pittsburgh. Strolling behind their shopping cart which was pushed by seven-year-old Jason and ridden by three-year-old Carrie, the young couple found their eyes glazing over as they studied the rows upon rows of beckoning attractions.

Suddenly, Carrie pointed to a display and shouted, "Yipes, stripes!"

Her mother's eyes narrowed. "What in the world are you talking about?" she asked.

"Yipes, stripes! Yipes, stripes!" replied her daughter in a rising crescendo.

"She wants the Fruit Stripes, Mom," Jason explained.

"No, she shouted for something called Yipes," Mrs. Edwards said.

"It's bubblegum," Jason explained patiently. "On the Disney Channel. It's a song they sing, "Yipes, Stripes, Yipes, Stripes, Fruit Stripes Gum.'"

"You've already got two packages of gum at home," Mrs. Edwards grumbled at her daughter.

"But I want it. I need it!" Carrie cried. "Yipes, Stripes, Yipes, Stripes!"

Needless to say, she got her wish and another huckstered product found its way into the Edwards' basket. No question that songs, ditties, and jingles work magic at the cash register. That is why the big manufacturers spend hundreds of millions of dollars every year pitching their products over the airwaves.

## Music Banishes Undesirables

Back in the 1970s, jingles and background tunes made up just 31 percent of all television commercials. Today, that figure is well over 75 percent. Since music works invisibly on our nervous systems and emotions, today's TV commercials sell the intangibles—sex, status, and excitement—the yipes, stripes, and kaboom!

"Everybody needs to be different from the competition," Tony Asher explains. "Even if the only difference is a bright green package, music sets you up by a pause in the tempo that says, 'Wait'll you hear this!' Then a prolonged timpani roll transforms garbage copy into a gigantic announcement. The listener feels that importance, even if the product claim is just a lot of bunk."

One recent turnaround story dramatizes the power of musical sell. For many years the 7-Eleven convenience stores were a haven for beer-drinking, late-night young revelers. Then, in the late 1980s—spurred by an anti-pornography campaign launched by family-value groups—management decided to do an about-face. They banned all sales of *Playboy* and other girly magazines, stacked their shelves with soft drinks and snacks, added hotdogs and hamburgers to their line, and remodeled their decor to appeal to the drive-by family trade.

Along with the merchandising facelift, 7-Eleven advertising trumpeted their new role as a tradition-honoring, family-based operation. A highly effective TV-spot dramatized the face-lift.

Onscreen, ordinary Americans were shown working up a sweat—a jogger, a middle-aged man raking his backyard, kids dribbling basketballs and pitching baseballs, young ladies diving for volleyballs, and motorbikers climbing mountain trails. As the visuals flashed by, a gospel-sound handclapping women's choir sang, "SOOOOO—A—THIRSTY, GOTTA PUT OUT THE FIIIIRE! FEEEE-LIN' SOO—A—THIRST-EEEEE, GO DOWN TO THE RIII-VER! GO DOWN TO THE RIII-II-VERRRR!"

A male voice-over said, "For all the ways there are to work up a sweat—" (*visual*: a 7-Eleven logo, then a refrigerator case holding rows of canned soda pop) "Seven-Eleven has over three hundred ways to quench it—" (*visual*: All-American men, women, and kids drinking out of bottles, sports jugs and cups) "No one puts out a fire like Seven-Eleven!" As the choir swelled with a big finish, "OOOOHHHHH, THANK HEAVEN," a screen graphic reinforced the religious sentiment with the slogan OH THANK HEAVEN, while a small logo in the corner identified the pious sponsor—7 ELEVEN.

By using rousing gospel sounds, in the space of thirty seconds the company identified itself with clean-cut Americans engaged in wholesome activities, all of them quenching their thirst at God-fearing 7-Eleven stores. Thus, company advertising galvanized a clientele changeover, with much healthier profits than when 7-Elevens were just all-night beer-and-pretzel shopping sheds.

At some locations, however, the message didn't get through. Near Fort Lewis, Washington, and at North Hollywood and Brea, California, local 7-Eleven outlets continued to attract the old crowds of beer-guzzling, drug-trading youth. Blasting punk-rock through their boom boxes and hanging out until the wee hours, the youngsters promoted all kinds of trouble. Needless to say, the wholesome family trade kept their distance and business suffered. When beleagured managers complained to the police, permissive laws allowed the cops merely to chase off the loiterers temporarily, only to have them return minutes later.

Following the lead of a British Columbia convenience store who used soft background recordings to drive away punk-rockers, management fought back with music. The 7-Elevens mounted powerful rooftop speaker-horns on their buildings and had the Muzak Corporation pump in the light classical channel. Two days of continuous play later, the baroque and chamber music selections had totally banished all punkers and loiterers, their nervous systems tormented by the gentle classical sounds. As an added bonus, losses from theft decreased dramatically.

Since then, the same classical music weapon has been successfully used at a Tampa, Florida, shopping mall where prostitutes and pimps were sent scurrying, against punk rockers at a Salt Lake City shopping center, against pimps and drug dealers at the Port Authority Station in New York City, and at a Cincinnati shopping center where boom-box rock concerts had been plaguing ordinary shoppers. As Muzak's marketing director Leslie Ritter explains, "For years we have been helping our clients with music aimed at customer demographics. Now we are employing those same sounds to repel those whom our customers find undesirable. As weapons go, that is as benevolent as you can get."

## Music Can Make You Angry

Physical sound is measured in decibels (dB). A zero reading is the faintest noise human ears can hear. At 30-45 dB, people start paying attention. By 50 dB, annoyance sets in. At 70 dB, the autonomic nervous system kicks in—arteries narrow, blood pressure rises while blood flow to the heart *de*creases. When the noise level reaches 90 dB, work efficiency falls, and errors abound. Above that level, the adrenaline rush hits so hard that people become openly hostile and belligerent.

In the Conejo Valley suburbs of southern California, the summer evening calm was shattered by the throbbing blast of outdoor speakers cranked up to maximum volume. The drum beat was relentless, while the harsh whine of electronic guitars added an eerie nerve-shattering edge to the reverberations. On and on the hard-rock played, for what seemed hours but was actually only about twenty minutes. Suddenly, a loud explosion rent the air—then total silence.

The next morning, the *Los Angeles Times* carried a one-paragraph story in its Metro section describing how an unknown assailant had blown out a $2,500.00 sound system with a single shotgun blast in the nearby bedroom community of Agoura Hills.

## Deafening Sounds

More insidiously, many huffing and puffing aerobic dancers unknowingly are losing their hearing along with their excess fat. Dr. Ray Hull, professor of communicative sciences at Wichita State University, studied music volume at fifteen health clubs in five states. "At the very first club, I knew immediately the music intensity was damaging," Hull reported. "It was so incredibly loud the women were wearing ear protectors."

In half the classes studied, the music registered an average 110 db. At that volume, a listener risks permanent hearing damage after just thirty minutes. At some clubs, the sounds raged at 120 db, equivalent to standing on the tarmac behind a Boeing 707 at full thrust just before takeoff. At that level, permanent hearing damage can hit after just 450 seconds. In 90 per cent of surveyed classes, the music was loud enough to produce permanent hearing loss after one hour—the length of a typical aerobics class.

"A big danger with loud music is that the ear anesthetizes itself," Hull noted. "After fifteen minutes of unbearably loud music, many people just adjust—without realizing the damage that is taking place."

## Music as Propaganda

Beyond loud sounds, music is used in politics and warfare to condition people. In Communist Cambodia, for example, Radio Phnom Penh devoted half its airtime to revolutionary messages sung by children's choirs after government research showed that musical propaganda made a much stronger impact on Cambodian attitudes than straight news or dramatic shows. A parallel study at American universities found that students were much more likely to believe a protest message when it was carried in song lyrics than when it was recited as poetry, narrated as prose, or read silently from a handbill.

## Musical as Valium

Most everyone alive in America today has been exposed to that soft fog of de-energized music that plays at airports, department stores, dentist offices, and factories. Industrial psychologists call it "the gentle persuader." Corporate stock market listings call it *Muzak* and it is without question the most widely applied form of tone manipulation used today.

Of *Fortune* magazine's top fifty industrial companies, forty-three of them pump the Muzak sounds throughout their work environments, along with hundreds of lesser competitors. One of the better-known holdouts was Black and Decker, one of the world's biggest toolmakers.

B and D executives were convinced they had achieved peak output at its main factory in Maryland, where three shifts of 2,700 workers ground out a steady stream of power tools and garden products. When Muzak first approached them, they said no. Muzak then offered an irresistible deal—they would provide free installation if B & D agreed to sponsor a study to measure results. No improvement, no deal and no pay.

So three separate departments totaling 1,100 workers were exposed to Muzak for a thirteen-week run, which was then compared to a benchmark period of thirteen weeks of unmasked factory noise and bustle. In every department measured, production increased—as much as 6 percent in one group and 3 percent overall. Black and Decker proceeded to sign a long-term contract without a murmur.

Playing in forty countries around the industrialized world, Muzak is just as effective in Tokyo and Munich as in Dallas or New York. A study by Japan's Nippon Electric Company found a 3.3 percent jump in switchboard assembly production after Muzak was installed. It improved Prentice-Hall's mail operations in New Jersey by 8 percent, reduced typing errors at Lever Brothers in New York by 39 percent, and raised production of California Blue Shield's computer operators by 11 percent.

## How Muzak Manipulates and Stimulates

Here's how Muzak works. During a typical day, we start out fresh and full of energy. Then we fizzle out by midmorning and pick up as the lunch break beckons. The same thing happens in the afternoon, with the low point about three o'clock. Muzak counters this cycle with fifteen-minute segments of "progressive stimulation"—subdued tone trips that trigger a mind/body lift, pump more adrenaline into our lagging bloodstreams, and so neutralize the effects of boredom and fatigue.

Muzak research shows that alternating periods of silence with the programmed sounds spurs work output even more. So in factories, Muzak plays the second and fourth quarters of each hour, with the first and third silent. In offices, the first and third quarters get Muzak with the second and fourth silent—all scientifically analyzed, tested, controlled, and applied.

Stimulating us at low points and tranquilizing us at peak hours, Muzak also programs against the days of the week. It injects turn-on sounds for Blue Mondays and mellow tones for Fridays and before holidays when our spirits soar with the beckoning free time. But squeezing the last drop of motivational blood from a worker's veins is not Muzak's only use.

Studies of shopping behavior show that after thirty minutes in a supermarket or department store, for every extra minute the shopper remains he or she will spend an extra two dollars. With Muzak, consumers dawdle an average of three minutes more inside the shopping environment. In other kinds of businesses, particularly fast food restaurants, the faster the turnover the greater the profits. So these operations use *exciting* music like soft rock or Latin salsa to stimulate quicker orders, faster chewing, and quick getaways. "Bring 'em in chow 'em down, and move 'em out," is the object here.

## Music and Movies

Arguably, the ideal environment to manipulate people through music is in a movie theater. Eddy Manson, composer and teacher of film scoring at UCLA, explains the process this way.

"We manipulate people like crazy in films, and they love it. It's a tremendous release. I can make you feel any emotion I want you to feel at any time. It's a Machiavellian power we project gut to gut."

Manson demonstrated this power before his film-scoring class at UCLA. As he played his harmonica, actor Barry Gordon walked back and forth across the front of the room.

First Manson played a slow tune in a minor key. The students described the actor's gait as "heavy," "depressed," portraying the movements of a guy whose woman had just left him. When Manson segued to a lively upbeat melody, the class saw Gordon's pacing as carefree, like someone out for a Sunday stroll in the park. Finally the music changed to an otherwordly Bartok mood. The stride was now viewed as "jittery, anxious and freaked out."

But actor Gordon, an experienced stage professional, wore earplugs that shut out all sounds. Instead he concentrated on timing his strides to be exactly the same during each sequence, mentally counting "*Left* I said then *right* she said and *left* was I to *right* the wrong." With each musical mood he appeared to portray a different character though nothing, but the *melodic mode* had changed.

In films, music is crucial to the drama. If you doubt it, the next time you watch a dramatic movie or thriller on TV, just shut off the sound and see how the emotional kick disappears. Musical shorthand sets us up for the onscreen action. For example, it can establish the film's locale—like playing a *Hora* for Israel or using tom toms to suggest an Indian camp in the Old West or harpsichords to imply an eighteenth-century setting.

To paint a scene at Big Sur, a composer may use timpani and cymbals to evoke surf and breakers while a lone flute magnifies the expanse of beach merging into a far-off horizon. The classic technique for scaring the wits out of an audience uses slow, underplayed phrases that relax tension until a shocking sight or murderous deed explodes accompanied by a tone-cluster blast.

The hit movie *Jurassic Park* utilized sound effects so vividly that terrified youngsters actually believed the huge dinosaurs were about to thunder down from the screen and munch them for lunch. Many parents reported that as the giant man-eating tyrannosaurus rex lumbered toward their screen victims, their children in the audience held their hands over their ears instead of covering their eyes to escape the unbearable strain.

## Tones as Conditioning

"Music is used everywhere to condition the human mind," Eddy Manson declares. "Notre Dame has recruited more football players by its fight song than its scholarships. TV's *Sesame Street* indoctrinates kids with socially accepted ideas mostly through its music and jingles."

While we can easily accept the way music promotes romance and sweet feelings, we don't usually think of it as an *aphrodisiac,* something that stimulates lustful feelings. But Manson is quick to remind us that record producers play heavily on that application.

"Sexy music comes out of the beat, the suggestive lyrics, and sensual singing," Manson explains. "The sensuality comes from an insistent beat that builds. That's what turns kids on today. A big motivation in record and cassette buying today is the bedroom lure, and the record companies know all about that."

Tone power—screaming, subtle, or even inaudible—is an essential element of our electronic village, playing with our emotions, selling us products, and injecting its values into our minds. Whether it's simple rock rhythms that imprint an erotic message or "pink noise" masking assembly-line sounds in factories, our behavior is affected every day at work and at play, in theaters, elevators, hospitals, funeral parlors, and at home. Many churches today offer two different kinds of Sunday worship services with two very different kinds of music—one with traditional hymns and classic choir sounds for their more conservative congregants, the other featuring drums, guitars, and a loud heavy beat for those who resonate more readily with rock.

"Hitler used Richard Wagner in a conscious scheme to condition the German masses for Nazism," Eddy Manson asserts. "Wagner was perfect for that task—apocalyptic, heroic, every man a superstar in the glorious Aryan universe. Music can poison you, lift your spirits, or make you sick without your knowing the cause. It is really a powerful drug, much more powerful than any drug used today. And much more dangerous."

"Why more dangerous?" I asked.

"Because," Manson confirmed, "nobody takes musical manipulation very seriously."

## FIGHTING BACK

An experiment at the University of California at Irvine found that listening to ten minutes of Mozart raised the I.Q.s of college students by as much as nine points. The investigation determined that classical music enhances abstract reasoning by affecting complex brain functions. As reported in the British scientific journal *Nature,* the researchers believe the complexity and harmonics of the music itself is the key.

Conversely, they conclude that more basic, repetitive rhythms, such as those found in hard and grunge rock music or in simplified new age sounds actually interfere with abstract thinking. "There is a common language the different parts of the brain use to communicate," explains Prof. Gordon Shaw, who studies brain structure and took part in the study. "Certain neurological firing patterns occur when people are involved in high levels of abstract reasoning."

In ordinary language, different kinds of music affect us differently. Instead of allowing others to lead us by the nose, as caring parents and responsible adults, we can—and *should*—harness the musical genie and make it serve a godly purpose. Four ways to do that follows:

## Begin with Classical Music

A popular computer slogan teaches, "Garbage in, garbage out." If we program dumb things into our electronic brain-machines, then dumb things are sure to come out the other end. On the other hand, if we feed it wisely, the results will be good. Solomon framed it best—"Train up a child in the way he should go, even when he is old he will not depart from it" (Prov. 22:6).

Knowing how music affects even unborn infants in the womb, common sense tells us from the time they enter the world to make sure their eargate gets the best euphonic food we can feed it. From the moment baby comes home from the hospital, choose the best kinds of music to play through your stereo.

The noted Japanese gynecologist Dr. Hajime Murooka followed up his experiments with mother Body Beat sounds described earlier with a tested program of classical music that helps newborns make the transition from the womb to the outside world. Murooka found that such selections as *Meditation on the G String* (Bach), "The Swan" from "Carnival of the Animals" (Saint-Saens), *Adante Cantabile* (Tchaikovsky), and "Panorama" from *Sleeping Beauty* (Tchaikovsky) create a peaceful, calming tone background for infants up to two years old.

After that age, playing quietly structured music by Mozart, Haydn, and Bach helps create a soothing, upbeat atmosphere in the home, just the sort of sound that stimulates the higher brain centers. In general, it is best to stay away from pounding, erratic pieces that agitate the human spirit. Babies raised around classical music will grow into children less likely to be attracted to repetitive, raucous hard-rock sounds.

## Be Observant and Involved

As our children mature, we need to keep track of the kinds of music they play and listen to. Early warnings of trouble can be spotted this way. Hidden stashes of rock records and cassettes bearing strange-sounding titles and group names should trigger our scrutiny. (For more detailed discussion of pop and rock music, see chapter 6: "Top-40 Nightmare.")

Suggest listening to the selections together. If the music proves to be angry or sexually provocative or if it contains indecent or blasphemous language or if the lyrics express anti-family or anti-social messages, you can discuss *why* the groups are offensive, the kinds of undesirable messages and ideas they express, and exactly how listening to them harms youngsters. This can be a welcome teaching opportunity, a time to help your children grow in wisdom and grace. By so doing, you will help them grow into young people who are able to make good decisions, starting with those they make about their musical choices.

## Offer Alternatives

Develop a "good list" of alternative artists to offer your children as replacements for the unacceptable choices. You might ask a youth minister for recommendations. There are also some good family-value organizations who provide guidelines and artist lists that are suitable for play by teenagers. Write or telephone:

- Focus on the Family
  Colorado Springs, CO 80995
  (601) 844-5036
  (719) 531-5181

- The American Family Association
  Correspondence Office
  Tupelo, MS 38803

- Al Menconi Ministries
  P.O. Box 5008
  San Marcos, CA 92069
  (619) 591-4696

## Turn Down the Volume

If you are not utilizing the mute button on your TV's audio system, learn to do so. Television commercials utilize high-volume, heavy rhythm backdrops for implanting their sales pitches, often accompanied by syncopated lyrics that more easily penetrate our defenses. Even when the values promoted by the advertising are not particularly offensive, the demanding tones and tempos act as an intrusive assault on your family's nervous systems. As an alternative, listen carefully to the commercials as a family and discuss with them just how the advertising tricksters work their "magic."

## Examine Yourself

Check out your own musical choices. Are they uplifting? Are you attracted by recordings that feature loud, syncopated beats? If deprived of them, do you feel uneasy or somehow "unfulfilled"? You may find that you or other adults in the family are addicted to primitive sounds. As a substitute, listen to more sophisticated artists, singers, and musicians who employ richer harmonics and more refined rhythmic backdrops.

## Examine Your Church's Music

Some churches use heavily syncopated music in their worship services, with intensive repetitions and outbursts of hand-clapping and shouting. Others use the hymnal exclusively, other have choirs singing anthems and congregational praise songs. The real question we need to answer about our worship music is this: does it make our hearts and spirit worshipful, prepared to approach God's majestic throne to praise, glorify, and exalt Him? Are our souls responding to music and words that prompt wonder, that lead us to contemplate His attributes, His sweet grace, and His presence? Are we shouting His praises and giving fervant thanks for the joy of our salvation? Or does the musical portion of our worship service merely hyperinflate our emotions, making us feel good about ourselves as we sing and listen to others perform, with little consciousness of His presence?

Gordon Boror, author of *Worship*, writes how some hymn stylists can trivialize the Scriptures. For example, he asks,

> Who on reading Psalm 18 can continue to sing "O Lordie" in a chorus of Do Lord? Football fans and opera aficionados shout about last-second winning touchdowns and great arias, and I say we have a lot more to be excited about than a whole choir of Jussi Bjoerlings and all the athletic teams ever fielded in the person of our God. Psalm 95, known as *Venite*—"I Come"—says come, but come rightly, to worship the living God. Scripture does not tell us how to sing, as far as the art is concerned, but it does tell us *how* to sing as far as the heart is concerned. We are 'to sing with the spirit and with the mind also' (1 Cor. 14:15). So singing with the spirit of the New Testament sense is singing in concert with the Holy Spirit whose task is focusing on Christ.
>
> There has long been a tendency to impose our taste and culture upon others we may be trying to affect with the Gospel. No good missionary would go to people of an unknown tongue and say in his own language, "I have great good news for you. Keep listening to me and you'll figure out what I'm saying, then you, too, will know the good news." Of course not! Marvelous work is done in the area of language study to present the Word of God in a clearly understandable context to people in their own language. But musically, we have not progressed that far. Within our culture there are numerous subcultures. Our hymnals are filled with important and relevant music for our churches, but they are composed largely of common and triple meter rhythms and melodies of past generations as in a march or waltz, with block harmonies and predictable rhythms. The youth culture is not there. We need to be sensitive to what they will hear as we attempt to reach them. Once reached, they can and should be introduced to their rich Christian heritage, and we should encourage a marriage of contemporary and traditional expression, providing they have artistic integrity.

## Evaluate According to God's Standards

Finally, ask yourself this question: do the artists and recordings you favor agree with the kind of godly values you want your own family to live by and honor? Too often, we strain to correct our children's weaknesses while we ourselves fail to note how we are attracted by similarly vulgar expressions. Apply to your own musical tastes the eternal standards proposed by the apostle Paul: "Finally, brethren, whatever is true, whatever is honorable, whatever is right, whatever is pure, whatever is lovely, whatever is of good repute, if there is any excellence and if anything worthy of praise, let your mind dwell on these things" (Phil. 4:8).

# 2

# Signs and Portents

*We are symbols, and inhabit symbols.*

Ralph Waldo Emerson

Not long ago, my wife, Juneau, and I stopped by a fast food restaurant for a burger and fries. At 12:30 in the afternoon, the place was packed with kids from the nearby high school and we had to yell at each other just to be heard over the roar. Unfortunately for us, the noise level was unable to completely mask the conversation from a neighboring table.

There, six teenagers munched burgers and simultaneously screamed a barrage of filthy epithets that would have shamed a crew of drunken sailors. We tried hard to ignore the verbal pollution but, seemingly inspired by our obvious discomfort, the assault intensified. In a frontal assault against our generational sense of modesty, the girls spewed out the dirty words even more lustily then the boys, laughing like mad as they watched nearby parental heads turn, frown, and wag disapprovingly.

After several minutes, it became clear the cursing would not stop on its own so I went over to their table. "Knock it off," I said.

The boys grew silent, turned red, and stared at the tabletop. The girls looked up at me with disbelieving shock. A moppette with curly black hair shouted an epithet, and then she laughed hysterically.

"I'll just get the manager to toss you out," I replied.

As I walked toward the front counter, the youngsters hurriedly stood and started for the door. Just before exiting, the sassy one turned back, stuck out her tongue, and put her thumbs to her ears. Signs of the times.

## How Did Dirty Words Become "Acceptable"?

Four-letter words are flying all over the place these days—on the street, at the mall, on television, in movies, in rock and rap music, in five-star hotel lobbies, and not least in the hallways of our schools. In bygone times, dirty words used to come in plain, brown wrappers to be opened only in private if at all. Today, everywhere the public congregates, you are besieged by them.

Back in mid-century, the world gasped when Clark Gable as Rhett Butler in *Gone with the Wind* told Scarlet O'Hara, "Frankly, my dear, I don't give a_____. Thirty years later, the country went ballistic when George Carlin's comedy routine featuring the "Seven Dirty Words" was banned from the airwaves by the Federal Communications Commission. Now, on the eve of the twenty-first century, epithets featuring body parts, waste products, and sex acts are so commonplace they can seem to be acceptable speech.

How in the world have things come to this pass in just one generation? Dr. Timothy Jay, psychology professor and author of *Cursing in America*, considers it a legacy of the Vietnam War era. He traces national word pollution to the in-your-face counterculture of the 1960s, seeing curse words as a relatively risk-free attack from people who believe they have been cheated by the American dream. "People who feel powerless or discriminated against use curse words to intimidate others," he explains. "Women, for instance, swear much more now, especially in the workplace. These words allow us to relieve stress and express rage without becoming physically violent."

Seen from an ethical perspective, the flood of dirty words are hallmarks of moral decay. Betty Wein of *Morality in Media* blames mass communications for the scatalogical epidemic. "The media always use the excuse that they reflect reality," she points out. "But I don't believe that. They *create* this reality. The use of four-letter words is so incredibly gratuitous. It used to be that you had to go out of your way to find filth. Now you have to go out of your way to avoid it."

## The Role of Popular Culture

Dr. Jay's research supports that view. Using as a starting point Clark Gable's single expletive of fifty-five years ago—one that cost the producer of *Gone with the Wind* a $5,000 fine for violating the film code of those years—by 1984 the Al Pacino movie *Scarface* contained a total of 299 assorted curse words, while the 1990 gangster film *Good Fellas* featured 246 usages of the worst four-letter word alone, not to speak of the hundreds of "milder" sexual and excretory terms.

Even prime-time television, once reined in by industry standards, blisters the airwaves with sounds of filth. If *L A Law* helped open the door for "adult" themes and racy TV dialogue, then *Married . . .with Children* proved how such hard-won "freedoms" could quickly translate into the rudest kind of cursing and erotic wordplay.

TV vulgarity now broadcasts regularly all but a scant few of the most extreme pornographic words. With that kind of example, one easily understands those kids at the restaurant.

Today, all modern societies are degraded on a daily basis by such gross "reflex conditioning." The Russian Nobel laureate Ivan Pavlov proved by controlled experiments how the brain of humans and animals interprets messages sent to it by the sense organs and then takes action, primarily based on optimizing pleasure and avoiding pain. Stick a frog with a pin and he jumps. Repeat it several times and before long, all it takes for the frog to take off is for the experimenter to show the pin.

Language is a "symbolic" conditioned reflex; that is, instead of pins pricking our heels, words stimulate our minds. From our first days of life as a baby, we hear sounds that accompany actions, sounds that serve as cues for baby to react. For example, as a mother breastfeeds a baby, she caresses it with a soft, gentle murmur—which sends out a message of *tenderness*. When she feels irritated, she may speak to the child harshly—communicating *impatience* or *anger*. After feeding, she will rock the baby in her arms, humming or whispering sweet endearments—*love*. In the infant mind, powerful associations begin to form.

Words such as "sweet," "lullaby," or even "shush" engender feelings of relaxation and sleep. Word associations during early-morning feedings may be less positive—like "Oh no!" or "Shut up!" or even "Stop your bawling, you little brat!"

Man is a signifying creature. It is no accident that the first word baby learns to say in all cultures and in whatever language is some form of "mama." This usually happens by the twenty-eighth week, when other polysyllables emerge along with the consonant "mmmmm." By one year, baby has a few words of speaking vocabulary and by fifteen months it babbles a mainly formless jargon, which still retains the inflections and rhythms of the family's primary language. Like a tape recorder, baby plays back what it hears. It labels things in the outside world according to messages received.

## Words Carry Emotions

Words mean things. More to the point, words carry with them feelings and emotions connected to those things. Laboratory experiments prove that certain "power words" trigger off intense emotions in human beings. The word *love*, for example, kindles warm associations and is universally favored, carrying no sense of basic conflict. But other words like *blood, pain, hate* or *death* spark different emotions. People often get verbally "blocked" or speechless when asked to say what these words bring to mind. Due to the "pleasure principle"—seek pleasure, avoid pain—whatever causes anxiety or conflict is pushed out of sight to avoid dealing with the painful emotions connected to it.

Words in and of themselves wield tremendous power to fire off emotions. In that way, words in themselves are *events*. All effective orators know and use this power to achieve their goals. A casual hearing of recorded speeches by Winston Churchill, Adolf Hitler, John F. Kennedy, or Martin Luther King Jr. gives the listener instant appreciation of how simple speech can stir feelings so powerful they will move people to join a march, go to war, write a check for charity, or murder for insults real or imagined.

In our earliest years, words are merely strings of sound which we imitate and play back. Printed words are one step removed from immediacy. As mere symbols of actual speech, they require more time to achieve that head-on-head communicative or emotional jolt.

When we first learn to read, we sound each syllable aloud as we translate the symbols—alphabet letters arranged to form words. Through repetition, the process soon becomes automatic. Over time the sounds diminish to mere "thought noise" in our mind's ear, until finally we may stifle the tone elements completely. Speed reading bypasses the "sounding" element by rapid eye scans. But by doing that, it destroys the rich associations connected with reading by sound.

Words are the building blocks of society. True civilization only became possible when human beings learned the "names" of things. In Genesis 2 we read how, even before God made a mate for Adam, He created the animals, paraded them before Adam and had Adam give them all names. In a similar way, all created things were "named" by Adam and his progeny, enabling our ancestors to discuss them, compare ideas and events, and so draw "logical" conclusions ("word" in Greek is *Logos*).

## In the Beginning Words Were Things

The earliest written words used the shape of things to show what was being represented. Tableaus found on ancient cave walls recorded battles, celebrations, and legal customs by drawings etched with sharp instruments. Even highly developed languages such as Chinese and Sanskrit still retain the direct relationship between the word and the thing it symbolized.

A biblical example is found in pre-Babylonian Hebrew. The first letter of the Hebrew alphabet is *Aleph*, written then as " Ⱥ," picturing an ox and symbolizing "strength," "first," or "leader." The next letter is *Beth*, which you may recognize in the words "Beth Lehem" (the house of bread). *Beth*, as originally written, was "_△," standing for a house and symbolizing the family living inside it. Knowing these letter pictures, we can see how the Hebrew word, *Ab*, _△Ⱥ written from right to left, pictures its own meaning. This combined word, *Aleph* ("the leader of") plus "Beth" ("the house or family") means "Father," which we know from its familiar Biblical form "Abba."

Primitive tribes in New Guinea and Equatorial Africa still use a hand language that frames the object or idea expressed. Even today, in advanced Western societies, hearing-impaired people use a sign language called "Ameslan" that clearly shows the direct link between the symbol and the reality it represents. As most of us mature, however, we tend to lose our sense of how strongly we are affected by symbols.

In everyday life, we do not usually realize that we react to symbols and shapes. Often we will express our negative reactions in a disguised or indirect way. For example, we may not criticize a margarine package design featuring a crown—instead, we grumble at its high price or greasy taste. Crossed swords on a can of asparagus may not seem openly threatening—but we may experience fear of being cut by the ragged can edge once we open it. These are examples of symbolic transference.

## How Color Talks to Us

Color is another symbol language we take for granted. Red, yellow, and green are used on traffic lights to tell us when to stop, be cautious, and go. But we are not so conscious of how various colors impact our nerves and emotions throughout the day.

A British factory owner decided to redecorate the lounge his workers used for their breaks and lunch hours. So he replaced the old traditional furniture with Scandinavian modern and painted the walls a handsome blue. Within days, employees began grousing about the stinginess of management in not heating that chilly room. No matter how many sweaters they wore, they just couldn't shake the cold, damp air in the room they had renamed the "Ice House."

Fearing a strike, the room was sealed off and redone—this time in orange and yellow. As soon as it was reopened, employees purred about the improvement. Not only was the "temperature setting" more humane, a few even complained of being too hot at times—but they would learn to dress down to accommodate the warmer conditions. In fact, the temperature had never changed. It remained at a constant 66° , controlled by the room's automatic thermostat.

Because of sensation transference, warm colors like reds and yellows actually "feel" physically hotter. Lab tests show that exposure to warm colors and bright lights raise blood pressure, increase heart rates, and even stimulate electrical currents discharged from human skin. Cool colors have an opposite effect; when used in commercial settings, they actually help reduce the landlord's air conditioning bills. Many parents have discovered how their babies cry more in yellow rooms, while computer operators find that green screens reduce eyestrain.

Commercial operations apply sensation transfers to their shopping environments in unique ways. In such stores as fast-food restaurants or discount shops where fast turnover pumps up profits, hot colors and bright lights work to "move 'em in, make 'em buy, chomp food fast, and move 'em out" for a new crop of customers. In other outlets—for example, jewelry stores or antique shops where relaxed moods and artistic attitudes work to management's advantage—low-key lighting and cool colors create that desirable mellow atmosphere.

Even police departments have applied color in the war against crime. Just recently the Florida Department of Law Enforcement advised city governments throughout the state to employ special lights to combat the growing problem of teenage "night cruising" in public places. To keep kids home at night and out of trouble, they have instructed public works officials to install low-pressure sodium street lamps because "they render caucasians' skin texture a sickly color and make acne look even more grotesque."

Beyond its neurological and psychological applications, color has always been an important part of language and symbol. Over most of the past two thousand years, Judeo-Christian, Bible-based values have exercised notable influence over Western culture. From its start in biblical Israel and Torah Scripture, color played an important role in liturgy, symbol, and metaphor. In the liturgurgical colors of the western church, the hues of the vestments vary through the ecclesiastical calendar. For example, purple or violet is the color of Advent and Lent, white is the color for Easter, and red is the hue for the feasts of the martyrs.

As applied by both the Catholic and Protestant traditions, five specific hues are universally recognized. White symbolizes light, innocence, and purity. Red symbolizes sin, fire, and blood, with its application in sacrificial expiation. Green is nature, rebirth, hope, and eternal life. Purple signifies royalty, but also repentance, affliction, and mourning. And, finally, black stands for ignorance, evil, death, grief, and the grave.

In our daily secular life, red is the color of patriotism, revolution, and passion. Being angry means "seeing red" or being in a "red rage." Yellow is the color of contempt. Cowards have a "yellow streak" down their back, while scandal-mongering tabloids specialize in "yellow journalism." Green is the color of jealousy as well as beautiful valleys in springtime. Upset stomachs turn us "green around the gills," while "green recruits" lack the competence of veteran soldiers.

Blue means depression. We suffer blue moods, oppressive "blue laws," and wail "the blues" when we feel miserable. On its up side, blue can imply wealth and status, as with "blue bloods," and we show our loyalty by being "true blue." Black is clearly the shade of negativism. Even its place in the spectrum is defined as the "absence of all color." We cast "black looks" at our enemies, "blackball" undesirables, and are persecuted by "being blackmailed" by "blackguards." Black is the color of death and mourning, and "black magic" is the supreme application of evil.

Innocent children are as "white as driven snow." Though we wave a white flag to surrender to an enemy, we are simultaneously signaling our peaceful intentions. In physics, just as black is "achromatic" or the total lack of color, white is its opposite—white light contains in itself all the possible colors of the spectrum before it splits off into individual hues. In a very real way, white is the "purest" of all pure colors.

In movies and television, one cliché that universally identifies characters is to dress them in black or white. Most westerns feature "Black Bart" types who sport black hats, black shirts, black trousers, black bandannas circling their necks, a black mustache, and rides a black horse to complete the picture. But the "good guy" is sure to ride a white horse like the proverbial "Silver." He is usually clean-shaven (if mustachioed, it is usually light tan or blond), fair skinned, and dressed in white. Before our characters speak a word, we know where they stand on the issues of good and evil.

## Why Should We Care?

Despite these long-term historical associations, we are often not aware of our real color preferences. But why should we even care? So what if we react unknowingly to words, symbols, and colors? It matters a whole lot if we want to be free of being influenced against our will. Let us look at what happened when a leather manufacturer asked a research company to test a variety of colored purses.

The researchers set up shop at a conference of women executives in a major midwest city. During a break in the proceedings, a panel of several hundred women were shown a particular purse style and then asked to name which of four colors—red, green, yellow, or blue—seemed the most suitable shade for that specific handbag. Only 25 percent chose red, 20 percent named blue, 10 percent yellow, and 4 percent selected green, with the rest expressing no preference at all.

But then the demonstrator announced the good news. All panelists were now invited to come up to the table and choose a purse, to take home free of charge as a gift for taking part in the survey. Two out of three grabbed red purses! This told the researchers that over 40 percent really did not know their own minds before they acted on a choice. As with purses, so with products and messages of all kinds. The sad truth is that anyone who knows the secrets of colors or symbols can make us react without our even knowing about it—unless we are pre-warned and pre-armed.

Having come to this point, I believe it is safe to assume that most of us now more easily understand how words have power to hurt or help, or how symbols and even color can trigger our hot buttons. But there is one sense we tend to overlook, perhaps because it is associated with an organ which is often the target of jokes and insults. I speak here of the nose. When we even stop to consider the sense of smell, we tend to ignore it or put it on the back burner. But Paul in 1 Corinthians 12:23 points out, "Those members of the body which we deem less honorable, on these we bestow more abundant honor." Such a member is, I repeat, the nose. Woody Allen built an entire comic movie around a character who tried to clone a great leader from a detached nose he left behind after an explosion.

Yet the nose, with its sense of smell, speaks a special language that indeed influences the way we think and act. Poetry abounds with rapturous praise for the scents of flowers and the Bible itself extols the prayers of the saints as "incense before Thee" (Ps. 141:2). Little research looked into the effects of scent until the British Columbia Research Council did a series of studies on the emotional impact of odors. Among their more interesting findings is that such obviously unromantic items as used cars sell more quickly and at higher prices when management sprays the interior with a "new car" scent. That finding was quickly adapted, so the next time you check out a vehicle in a used-car lot, see if you can't detect that "tanned leather, starchy new" smell when you climb behind the wheel of that clunker.

Today, the clothing industry uses a variety of perfumes to enhance exotic dresses, furs, and undergarments. Advertisers send out brochures and direct mail promotions on aromatic paper, and food manufacturers employ "scent patches" that you scratch with a pin to sample delicious smells of new culinary products.

One unusual aspect of our olfactory sense is that it develops as we mature. Children under five are usually not revolted by any smell. They are intrigued by odors that prompt adults to hold their noses or gag with disgust. But by age five, children begin to react to unpleasant smells just as adults do. What happened? That five-year plateau marks the normative start of the "latent" or quiet phase of childhood sexuality.

## How One Sense Affects Another

None of our physical senses stand alone. Laboratory tests demonstrate that when you stimulate one sense, the others are also affected. For example, if you blast the ears with the wail of recorded ambulance sirens, our eyes grow less reactive to shades of red and more sensitive to blues and greens. The scent of geranium oil creates an identical effect on color perceptions. Our eyes adapt more quickly to darkness when our taste buds are stimulated or when loud noises startle us or when we touch our flesh with ice cubes.

The human body is in fact a network of sensory cross-references communicated across our nervous systems. Though we don't usually think about such linkage, in ordinary life we use figures of speech that acknowledge them. We talk about "light tastes," "light pastries," or "light touches." Certain restaurants serve "sharp sauces," musicians play "sharp tones," and we argue using "sharp words." There are "strong or weak" odors, "dry" wines, and "hot" music. All human communication is filled with such cross-references. In fact, they constitute the very soul of poetry.

When they are artfully mixed and skillfully presented, most of us do not even notice how advertising and mass media assail our senses, play tricks with word-and-image associations, and set us up for future action—namely, to do the will of the communicator. David Ogilvy, one of the deans of American advertising, has no qualms about the manipulator's role in society when he says, "It is the professional duty of the advertising man to conceal his artifice."

## FIGHTING BACK

First meditate on the sublime wisdom contained in the Lord's admonition to ". . . know the truth and the truth shall make you free" (John 8:32). Now let's apply that to our unique and highly individualized flesh and nervous system, one that has learned to react to words, symbols, and colors.

### What Pushes Your Buttons?

List all the words you can think of that push your buttons. They won't necessarily be curse words or crude expressions. They may even be words other people would consider mild or even loving. But because of your own particular experiences, for whatever reason, you will want to make a special effort to consciously note whenever these words jump up to startle you. Knowing that consciously, instead of pushing them out of sight, takes some of their power away.

## Counter Lies with Truth

To be free from symbolic triggers and manipulators, you need to replace your irrational reactions with the truth. You will want to counter the negative responses with a positive drawn from the Word of God. For example, if the word "death" makes your heart leap, remind yourself that through Christ, you have conquered death. You have nothing to fear, because for you to live is Christ and to die is even better (see Phil. 1:21).

If somebody calls you a "loser," in your flesh you may feel depressed or discouraged. In essence, you have agreed with that false assessment of yourself and you may think, *Nothing ever works out for me*. But that is an outright lie! Things *do* work for you. Remind yourself of what you did successfully today—you got up early, put on your clothes, made breakfast for the kids, drove them to school, and so on. *Well, I don't mean the little things*, you reply. Then you need to spell out exactly what you mean. When negative or fear thoughts are triggered in you, make yourself define them. Write them down, and be specific. As you bring them to light, by the Holy Spirit's enabling grace and in time they will lose their power over you.

## Apply the Truth to Your Life

Take the same approach with any other sensitivities you discover you have. For example, if you are a sucker for the color red, check your wardrobe. If you find you have a closetful of red dresses you never wear, understand what a waste of money they represent and how they symbolize poor stewardship on your part. Once you have openly faced that truth, the next time you see a red blouse, dress, or skirt, you will be less likely to reach out and grab it.

## Accent the Positive

Use the knowledge you have gained about how certain symbols or colors project psychological reactions, and then apply them in your home or office. In rooms where you want to stay alert, awake, and active, use warm colors like shades of yellow or orange. Hues of green and blue are restful for dens or libraries. Neutral colors like beige and dark wood paneling provide easy environments for falling asleep. I have known some churches adorned with that combination, which seems hardly appropriate for a house of God. I have always been partial myself to stained glass and high ceilings, which quickly make me realize I have come to worship an awesome God.

# 3

# Sex and Other Furies

*It is with our passions as it is with fire and water; they are good servants, but bad masters.*

Sir Roger L'Estrange

Jack Haskins, former director of Ford Motor Company's advertising research, did a massive analysis of what motivated people to buy cars. What he found out applies not only to cars but to most all of our buying decisions. Haskins discovered that facts were not really needed to create ads that produced sales. What really prompted buyers to lay down their money was *emotional* response.

Every effective salesman, motivational speaker, actor, or panhandler knows the secret—if you want people to do what you want them to do, you aim not for their heads but their hearts, their *emotions*. But what exactly are "emotions"?

The word comes from the Latin *emotio* and means "movement from." *The Oxford Dictionary* defines it as "agitations of mind and feeling." In everyday life, we gauge our emotional state by asking "How do I feel?" The answer can be "sad, glad, mad, or bad." Most often, the honest response will be "I don't know" which tells us we are still in our centers of equilibrium and have not been moved or agitated away from that place of stability.

Emotions are fired off like phosphorous touched by flame, ignited by some psychological trigger. It might take a real event, like a burglar crashing through a bay window to raise neck hairs with fear. But fear can just as easily be aroused by a movie where a monster grabs the heroine as the music blares out. As viewers, we actually search for stories where we can identify with the characters and get lost in the action. That is why we experience the same feelings of grief, fear, and joy as the people on the screen.

## The "Reality" of Illusion

When researchers wire up human subjects in laboratories, they find an identical rise in blood pressure, sweating, and electrical skin-currents when people watch onscreen hostility as when they are personally enraged by some insult, real or imagined. The human nervous system does not discriminate between "real" and "simulated" emotional triggers.

Every time we react emotionally to an event, that event is imprinted in our memory bank. If we don't deal with it and discharge its energy, it lurks invisibly, waiting for instant recall at just the right time. Let's look at a typical example of such "repressed emotion." One afternoon over a cup of coffee, your good friend makes a passing comment that really irritates you. You feel that telltale surge of angry heat in your chest, but you decide to say nothing. Nonetheless, that one remark has ruined your day. The rest of the afternoon you feel like a loser. You are glum, depressed, down in the dumps. Actually, you are still angry. Unexplained despondency almost always stems from rage that has been shoved out of sight.

In spite of your effort to hide the truth from yourself, deep down you still feel victimized. Unconsciously you yearn to "even the score." That reaction simmers until the "right moment" comes along. One day when you—and he or she—least expect it, you retaliate. You find yourself insulting or provoking your friend and maybe never fully understanding why you've done it. But every emotional reaction—whether rage, fear, grief, or pity—must find expression in the outside world.

Closely tied to anger is the powerful emotion of lust. Sexual excitement, says U.C.L.A. psychiatrist Dr. Robert Stoller, is often fueled by the secret wish to hurt someone. "Hostility is what generates sexual obsessions," he explains. "Its absence for most people leads to sexual indifference and boredom. So those very qualities that should produce a feeling of love for another—good character, beauty, grace, noble or saintly traits—actually dampen a person's ability to burn with lust. They actually inhibit sexual excitement, unless they goad the partner into an attempt to sully them."

Dr. Stoller points to a range of social behaviors that illustrate this peculiar sexual rage/lust syndrome, including pornography, sexism, and the abusive words used for human sexual parts. "Humans are not a very loving species," Stoller concludes. "That is especially true when they make love."

Bolstering Stoller's findings is a major study of sexuality conducted in 1994 by the University of Chicago. In extensive interviews with 3,432 Americans, the researchers determined that in any given year, nearly half of all American men and one out of six women buy and use pornographic materials to stimulate their sex lives.

## Exploiting Sex in Advertising

Some years ago, when the producers of the movie *Lipstick* promoted the film with an ethereal close-up of star Margaux Hemingway, the audience stayed away in droves. So producer Freddie Fields ordered a new ad campaign. Under graphics detailing the latest statistics on forcible rape, Hemingway appeared in side-by-side photos, the first showing her being strangled by actor Chris Sarandon and the other with her aiming through the sight of a big shotgun.

"Women are concerned with rape," a Paramount spokesman explained. "It is what they fear, so we sell it to them. A picture of a soft, glowing face did not sell this picture, so we let everyone know it involves sex and rape and that did it." Producer Fields admitted that the new ad campaign was aimed at a "black market"—people who relate unconsciously to the hostility and revenge fantasies that stem from the vicious rape of a blonde Nordic-type woman. In the months following the refocused ad campaign, theaters showing *Lipstick* were filled with women and young people, converting a box-office dud into a big-grossing success.

Another film that exploited sexual hostility was *Taxi Driver* starring Robert DeNiro. The initial advertising showed DeNiro the loner, head bowed and hands thrust into his pockets, walking the big-city streets. Hordes of empty theater seats prompted producer Michael Phillips to run back to the drawing board. The new promotion showed DeNiro as before, hands in pockets, but now side by side with twelve-year-old Jodie Foster who played a child prostitute in the movie. Bold headline ad copy shouted: **THE GIRL IS 12! THE GUY IS A TAXI DRIVER. WHAT HAPPENS TO BOTH OF THEM**

**WILL SHOCK YOU!** The empty seats were soon crammed and a box office loser became one of the most profitable films of the decade.

"We tried to sell the film on its critical acclaim," producer Phillips explained. "When that didn't work, we aimed at a different audience, the people who go to drive-ins. I have to admit we played to the perverse side of human nature."

## Capitalizing on Rage and Disgust

As any political consultant will tell you, in the peak weeks before an election any serious challenger will charge his opponent with fraud, bribery, adultery, graft, or stealing from blind panhandlers. The juicier the scandal, the more emotion it generates and the better his chances are for replacing the incumbent on election day. If he can only make the voters angry enough, they will show up at the polls in large enough numbers to unseat the other rascal. But without that emotional fuel, he won't win.

Disgust is another strong emotion that binds the mind for future replay. Professional beggars and panhandlers often boost their earnings through injecting large doses of revulsion. Just north of fashionable Rittenhouse Square in downtown Philadelphia, a gifted practitioner of this specialized art plies his trade.

Hershy is short, middle-aged, and sharp-eyed. His stock in trade is a grizzled three-day beard, a rumpled Goodwill suit spotted with eggyolk and gravy stains, and a torn baseball cap worn with the peak high off his forehead. As testimony to his skills, his jingling moneysash bulges with cash and coins hurriedly donated by horrified passersby only too glad to pay the toll needed to be rid of his unsavory presence. What they don't know is that Hershy is in his work uniform. His apartment closet is crammed with fashionable clothes and when he goes out in the evening decked out and clean-shaven, he often spots one of his daytime clients at a restaurant or night club—none of which have ever succeeded in recognizing him as the Rittenhouse Moocher.

Anyone or anything that can trigger in us that gut reaction called "emotion" has us in its spell. The next time we run into a person, picture, sound, or symbol that recalls that response, we undergo an inner agitation. Sensed as anxiety, "nervous energy," excitement, or even physical pain, relief comes only through taking action—voting for some politician, buying a particular coffee brand, insulting or half-raping our wives, or venting verbal abuse against foreigners, ethnic groups, or welfare mothers.

Commercials and sales spiels that irritate, aggravate, or frighten us will elect candidates and sell products. But so will words that flatter us, triggering the "sweet gush" of sentiment. This inner glow, so treasured by manipulators and manipulated alike, is linked to ego stroking and identification with a person, product, or idea.

## Selling Products as "Love"

A Purina dogfood campaign boasted how their super-nutritious chow changed an apathetic pooch into an "eager eater." Two years of this "eager eater" promotion saw sales slump so badly that the panicked marketing director commissioned research to find out what went wrong. This study revealed that pet owners buy dogfood on the basis of emotion, not nutrition. The company immediately launched a new campaign with a new, simple slogan: "All you need is love—and Purina." This time, dog owners responded and sales soared.

Among the magic words of the English language, *love* enjoys a special place. *Love* to heal the wounds of marital strife, love for self, love for others, love for food, cars, flying, skiing—all express the same mushy response to romantic vulnerability.

The Greek language offers four separate words that we translate into the English catchall term "love." The first is *storge,* which is familial love, the feelings of a father for a daughter or mother for a son. The second is *phileo,* which describes the bond between close friends. Third is *agape,* the unconditional godly love that asks for and expects nothing in return. Finally, there is *eros,* which depicts sexual love and lust. Guess which one of these Greek words for "love" never appears once in the Bible?

Remember the love songs of your teenage years? Of course you do—they have been indelibly etched into your memory banks. The tempo may change from generation to generation, but the message is always the same. Such early exposures paralyze our reasoning powers and set us up for later vulnerability when the themes are repeated. Modern pied pipers play on our sentiments like master musicians pluck a finely tuned instrument. "All you need is love"—and Purina or a Cadillac or Wintergreen for President.

## How Much Fear Will Sell?

But any old emotion will do the trick, even fear. A toothpaste manufacturer studied how fear might prompt people to brush their teeth more often. So the researchers exposed people to gory, full-color photos of gum-diseased mouths, accentuated by bold scary copy, to arouse *high fear*. A *medium fear* visual displayed similar material, but in black-and-white, with less alarmist descriptive words. *A low fear* ad used words but no photos to gently remind the reader that brushing often helped fight decay and periodontal disease, while the *no fear* layout simply advised more frequent brushing without warning what might happen if people neglected to do it.

To determine the effects of such advertising, the researchers measured brushing patterns of every subject before, during, and after having viewed the test ads. In this case, the common sense expectation was overturned. To get people to brush more often—and use more paste in the process—*low fear* advertising was found to be most effective. But for motorists who as a group are generally ignorant about the workings of their cars, *high fear* sells best.

Research was used to develop a real winner in the automotive arena. No doubt you have seen this oft-repeated television commercial or one of its variations. A garage mechanic is shown working underneath a wounded car. He spots the camera, climbs out of the pit, and approaches the lens to address the viewer.

Explaining how he is replacing this car's engine at a cost of a thousand dollars, he holds up an oil filter that costs four dollars. If only the owner of this car had changed oil filters more often, he wouldn't need this new engine now.

"It's up to you," he warns. "You can pay me now—" pointing to the filter. "Or you can pay me later—" He indicates the car on the rack and shrugs. "The choice is yours." It is no great wonder why that brand of oil filter tops the competition.

## FIGHTING BACK

Dr. William Backus, pastor and Christian counselor, defines emotions as responses to our glands, muscles, smooth muscles, cardiovascular system, skin, and entire body. From a practical standpoint, we know that any emotion is simply a response plus a label—joy, sorrow, anger, fear, sexual desire, etc. Whenever our emotions are tapped, we experience a quickened heartbeat, a change in blood pressure, or we flush, blush, sweat or turn pale. All this is a reaction to something we hear, see, or feel that we consider to be real—whether it is actual or only imagined.

## Expose the Illusions

When our emotions can be easily excited by other people or by trigger words, sounds, and pictures, we are slaves to whatever outside influences push our buttons. Most of the time, these emotional goads are lying illusions, like the "great wizard of Oz" who turned out to be nothing but a sound system and a smoke maker hiding behind a dark curtain. The first step toward desensitizing ourselves and our families is to pull away the curtain and expose the illusions or "misbeliefs."

A misbelief is simply an untrue thought. But, for one reason or another, most of us over time have adopted some of these false beliefs as part of our personal identity, the batch of ideas we have about ourselves that originally came from outside ourselves. That's why certain verbal or behavioral assaults shock us, because they coincide with sensitive notions that live inside us.

Someone who spent part of his or her childhood hurt because of being overweight may, even as a skinny adult, jump every time they hear someone mention the word "fat" or "piggy." Others may react to a simple question with a feeling of rejection, telling themselves, "I deserve any bad things that come my way. I'm so worthless." Still others err the other way by *over*-evaluating themselves and stepping all over other people. Whichever way we go, we're wrong.

## Respond with the Truth

When we face a negative squarely and hit back with truth, we alter the way we feel. For the Christian who knows that God is in control of every situation and has written a good ending to every story, things will as a matter of faith turn out okay. To say otherwise is to deny the Word of God, which tells us in Romans 8:28 that "we know that God causes all things to work together for good to those who love God, to those who are called according to His purpose." The truth is that, whatever we encounter, God has a plan and will bring good into our lives.

## See Yourself from God's Perspective

The Bible tells us we are "fearfully and wonderfully made" (Ps. 139:14). Our souls feel our emotions and respond appropriately. Most often we are conditioned by our personal history to react in ways that made some sense way back when. We tend to carry with us into later life our parents' words and beliefs about us. For example, if your dad encouraged you, you are most likely to feel accepted and encourage those around you. But if he disapproved of and disheartened you constantly, then you might feel you could never succeed in anything.

If we were raised with unhealthy, ungodly notions of what sex is all about, we may easily develop oversensitivity in adult life for such "forbidden fruit." That kind of weakness results in a feeling of guilt, powerlessness and vulnerability in confronting those who use our weakness for their own selfish ends. Here is where many of us get trapped. We can make the mistake of looking back and blaming—dad or mom or whomever—for attitudes they, too, could not control. That is counterproductive, worse than a waste of time, and will only result in angry, self-pity parties that leave you feeling more bitter, frustrated, and defeated.

Instead, see yourself from God's perspective. You have great worth in His eyes, not because of what you have done but because of who lives inside you. And remember, nothing is too difficult for Him (see Jer.32:17). Even if you mistakenly feel like a failure, God loves you unconditionally. Whenever you believe false notions about yourself, you fall into Satan's trap. Satan wants to discourage you so that you are worthless in doing God's work.

## Stand on the Word

Scripture is the most powerful weapon we have for conquering negative thoughts and emotions. With the Word of God and the Holy Spirit available to lead us to all truth, whenever we don't know what is bothering us, we can ask God in prayer. James 1:5 tells us, "But if any of you lacks wisdom, let him ask of God, who gives to all men generously and without reproach, and it will be given to him." David shows us how to ask in Psalm 139:23-24—"Search me, O God, and know my heart; try me and know my anxious thoughts; and see if there be any hurtful way in me, and lead me in the everlasting way."

Nothing Satan can whisper in your ear can stand against God's Word. When you feel worthless and discouraged, claim Phillipians 4:13—"I can do all things through Him [Christ] who strengthens me." Don't get bogged down in the quagmire of negative thoughts or poor self-esteem. No one is immune to emotional upheavals or sensitivities, but you have a God who is far greater than anything we may feel. The good news is that we don't have to be perfect to enjoy His love and acceptance. God loves you just as you now are—warts, emotions, and all. And He will free your emotions to glorify Him, bring His joy into your life, and make you an emissary of hope to others. Through the power of Christ, your emotions can become your ally in living the victorious Christian life.

# 4

# The Lifestyle Trap

*With a name like yours, you might be any shape, almost.*

Lewis Carroll

Daniel Severn is forty-six.

He wears his hair full, but corporately correct. At home he frequently harangues his wife about the irrelevancy of his well-paying job and their comfortable suburban lifestyle, while seldom asking her how her day went at her law office. Their only child Jennifer is a senior at a private prep school. On weekends and special evenings the Severns really come alive when they smoke pot with friends, listen to old Stones, Beatles, and Mamas & Papas tunes on their CD player, and trade tales about how it was when they were young counter-culture rebels demonstrating for peace and love.

Daniel long ago traded in his Buick for a Ford Bronco, revels in his new Pentium PC, feels macho in his black leather jacket, and downloads counter-culture articles and porno pix from his subscription BBS. Daniel typifies a well-established social trend variously branded "the Woodstock generation," "weekend hippy," or in sociologist lexicon, the "self-realization" movement. Because of mindset and shared experiences, the Severns and their friends generally vote for Democrats or Libertarians.

They are particularly responsive to solicitations from cultural organizations, specialty publishers, makers of "pop wines" and psychedelic accessories, high-tech recording and video products, offbeat computer software, high-style foreign cars, exotic foods, and "environmentally sensitive" merchandise of any kind.

By contrast, Mr. and Mrs. Henry Carter are in their late sixties. Just one year ago, they deserted their elegant two-story home for a small condominium that features light housekeeping services, round-the-clock security guards, labor-saving built-ins, and no yard to water, weed, rake, and mow. No longer entertaining their friends with lavish parties, they declined to renew subscriptions to the *Wall Street Journal* and *Harper's Bazaar* (but not *Maturity*) and have lapsed their charge card at Saks'. Instead, they buy their clothes at discount or department stores, while Mrs. Carter frequently serves meals built around frozen entrees, boil-in-bag vegetables, and heat'n' serve rolls.

Though they eat out more often, it costs a lot less at nearby family restaurants rather than the fine dining establishments they used to frequent. With more time on her hands, Mrs. Carter has joined worthy service clubs and local charities where she now spends most of her afternoons. Still conscious of her physical appearance, she exercises regularly on a stationary bicycle and bounces to rock music with her leotard-clad TV guru of morning workouts. The Carters have begun to explore the natural beauty of America in motor trips and tours and plan to visit other parts of the world next summer.

The Carters typify a social trend called *simplification*. Though lifelong Republicans, they will vote for Democrats who promise to bolster social security and medical programs advocated by the American Association of Retired Persons. They are excellent prospects for multi-unit housing, labor-saving devices, supplementary medical life insurance, tour and travel services, convenience foods, health and vitamin products, book clubs, and mail-order catalogs. On the other hand, they pose big headaches for home builders, magazine publishers, custom tailors, electronic and computer manufacturers, and prestigious country clubs.

Now let us look at Diane Kleiner, a twenty-three-year old government records analyst. While not on the job, she wears no lipstick, perfume, or bra. She abhors eyeshadow and foundation creams and constantly lectures her parents on the evils of chemical food additives and corporate pollution of the planet. She buys "organic" foods from the health store near her job and dreams of one day living on a small farm where she can exalt in clean, fresh air away from the smog and tensions of the city.

Diana subscribes to *New Age* and *Mother Earth News*, receives all the *Strout Farm* catalogs, and has attended meetings of the National

Organization for Women (which she feels is a bit too radical). She owns a small handloom on which she weaves her own fabrics as time allows and practices needlepoint for artistic expression while watching TV. She has launched a serious exploration of yoga and is contemplating a wholly vegetarian diet.

Diane is a member of the *back to nature* mindset. She is precious to makers of vitamins and organic foods, sellers of rural real estate, and catalogs trading in handicrafts, antique replicas, camping accessories, and recreational vehicles. Cynical about politics, she nevertheless votes for female pro-choice Democrats. She is a lost cause to makers of cosmetics, frilly underclothes, processed foods, candy, upscale cars, big corporations of any kind, and the publishers of *Vogue* and *Mademoiselle*.

## Psychographic Research

These are portraits of real people, built on the findings of their psychographic or lifestyle characteristics. Psychographics comes from motivational research, which also drew recognizable pictures of typical consumers. But psychographics added a revolutionary new dimension, applying strict sampling techniques that allows marketing directors and political analysts the kind of pinpoint consumer information that enables them to influence their targets with specially designed appeals.

Listen to Russ Haley of D'Arcy Advertising on psychographics: "It's where the action is today. By knowing the psychographic profile of the consumer, we can more clearly tune in with crystal clarity on each consumer's wavelength. Psychographics give us the most definitive look at the dispositions and hangups of the consumer."

Psychographic studies project how many of each lifestyle type can be found in the general population. It can isolate where people live by zip code, what they read, and what sorts of message turn them on or off. In that sense, psychographics is very much like the composite drawings used by police agencies on their "Most Wanted" flyers and news photos. Here's how it works.

Researchers select a random sample of the general population. Then they send out skilled interviewers, usually psychology Ph.D. candidates from local colleges, to visit the target homes where they grill the residents about the products they buy, like, and use, as well as those they dislike and why. They probe for the newspapers and magazines they read, TV shows they watch, recent movies they have attended, radio programs they follow, preferred brands of cars, appliances, tools and clothing they own, real estate holdings, where they bank, who insures them for what, political leanings, religious views, whom they've voted for and why, and so on for hours on end.

Along with this mountain of facts, they ask questions about the respondent's hopes and dreams, disappointments and pet peeves, how they feel about themselves, their jobs, their families, and those around them, favorite colors, astrological signs and other clues to their personality makeup. Once the in-depth interviews are completed, both facts and psychology are fed into a computer which digests the material and prints out a "psychographic profile" like the ones you read earlier.

## How Research Pins You Down

As an example, let's look at a study by the research company Market Facts, who examined consumers of women's products. Eye-makeup users were found to be overwhelmingly young, well-educated, and living in cities. Working wives apply it much more than homemakers, and westerners use it much more than women in other parts of the land.

Heavy users of eye-makeup also buy other cosmetics more frequently, smoke more cigarettes, purchase more gasoline, and make more long-distance calls than light users or abstainers. They are regular viewers of the *Tonight Show* but never watch panel shows or sitcoms (except *Married . . . With Children*). They subscribe to fashion magazines and news weeklies but do not read the *Atlantic Monthly*, *True Confessions* or romance novels. What is immediately obvious is that users of eye makeup are not simply women who consume an isolated product but in fact are individuals involved in a whole series of behavior patterns that can be pinpointed.

Though most of the women studied were married, they were still shown to be much more intent on attracting men than single women who did not use eye makeup. Unlike non-users, they agreed with the statement "I like to feel attractive to *all* men." They are more interested in world travel, consider themselves something of a "swinger," enjoy bright splashy clothing, will swear on a Bible that "blondes have more fun," and reject the notion that "there is too much emphasis on sex today" or that "spiritual values are more important than material things." In psychographic terms, these eye-makeup ladies can be labeled "hedonists."

The same study examined another, very different consumer—frequent buyers of shortening. This woman is older than the eye-makeup group, has a larger family, and no job away from home. Mostly found outside cities, she is an avid buyer of other homey goods such as flour, sugar, mustard, ketchup, canned meats, and detergents. Not surprisingly, the shortening lady loves to bake and names her kitchen as her favorite room in the house. Though she suffers high anxiety when her house is not sparkling clean, she nonetheless rejects the idea of "taking in a maid to do housework." She also loves to knit and sew and buys the products to prove it.

Contrary to her eye-makeup sister, the shortening lady believes there is lots of love in her family. Unusually health conscious, she preaches that everyone needs to "walk, bicycle, garden, or otherwise exercise regularly—and have a medical checkup once a year." Turned off by parties, she would much rather go to a baseball game than a dance. She detests ballet and grimaces at the prospect of spending a year in Paris. Such an amalgam forms the psychographic profile of a traditional *homemaker*.

Studies of magazine subscribers found that *Playboy* people were the male counterparts to the eye-makeup ladies. Conversely, readers of *Reader's Digest* were the very models of middle-class rigidity—pro-business, anti-welfare and anti-unions. Psychographic research by the Newspaper Advertising Bureau sampled 4,000 men and women and isolated eight primary lifestyle types. Male self-images were dominated by "he-men" (19 percent), "the traditionalist" (16 percent), and "the intellectual" (14 percent). The heaviest concentrations for women included "the suburbanites" (17 percent), "the drudges" (16 percent), "the indulgers" (16 percent), "the career seekers" (13 percent), and "the puritans" (13 percent).

While all psychographic types and genders use some products equally (for example, deodorants, toilet paper, and paper towels), specialized use was discovered for items like overseas air travel (dominated by career-seeking women) and the purchase of imported wines (prevalent among intellectual men). Even when every lifestyle group uses the same product, they strongly prefer specifically different brands. That choice is invariably based on the product's "personality," defined by its packaging, brand name, and, most crucially, its advertising. The ties between human lifestyle types and product brand "personality" held true for every single commodity examined.

## So What's the Big Deal?

Why should that bother us? Where is the harm in psychographics?

Like it or not, everyone living today in modern society who is not a hermit in a faroff cave is a victim of psychographic targeting. We may resent being put in a box as a "career seeker," "homemaker," or "intellectual." So our first instinct is to deny we can be classified this way. We are "beyond" this sort of generalization, we think, and so we tend to shrug off the efforts to "pin us wriggling on the wall." But we are lying to ourselves.

There is no escaping the truth. Like it or not, we are, in fact, mixed bundles of patterns, preferences, and ideas. This is as true of secular humanists as it is of fundamental Christians or Muslims. Whatever our particular mindset and worldview, we will tend to be vulnerable when anyone who knows how to exploit our hot buttons to communicates with us. The most effective manipulators are careful watchers of social trends. Like patient fishers, they study the waters for ripples and bubbles, try new bait and lures, and measure the most optimum moment to set the hook.

Dr. Daniel Yankelovich, who headed the top-ranked psychographic research firm that still bears his name, believed that the most important skill today's executives require is the ability to steer their companies through the "treacherous waters of social change. There is a world of difference between superficial reports of fads and fashions reported by popular media and the deeper realities produced by psychographics and statistical forecasting."

Yankelovich saw experimental fads like childless marriages and communal living popular in the sixties and seventies as being merely tentative attempts at trying on a trend for size. The real meaning of these experiments, he stressed, was the revolutionary assault on sexual differences and the search for less rigid roles than the simple "male/husband/provider and its opposite female/mother/homemaker." As the current civil war of cultural values rages, his analysis proves all the more accurate.

## Setting Trends in the Electronic Village

As cable television and multi-media computer offerings speed up our exposure rate to new ideas and trends, "lifestyle" groupings become even more important as a tool to predict social behavior. The quicker flow of information has compressed the span of a "social generation" from the traditional twenty years to today's seven or eight years. College youth, once revered as the nation's pacesetters, no longer dominate the realm of social trends. While twenty years ago saw the feminist, consumer, and environmental movements launched off college campuses, today's impetus for traditional family values as well as its liberal hedonist adversaries came from the TV screens by way of the electronic church combating "adult" programming and cable-fed "premium" channels.

What makes psychographic targeting so dangerous to our democratic system is the fact that the information is fed into computers where it is then projected to cover the entire population with remarkable accuracy. Not only does it identify the various lifestyle groups in society—including such hard-to-reach elements as homeless males, prostitutes, and jailed prisoners—more importantly, it pinpoints the precise ideas and power-words that will most effectively impress each of them.

For example, while CBS' *60 Minutes* rated number one among all prime-time shows, it scored forty-sixth among Hispanic viewers. What do Hispanics watch? Fox TV's *Beverly Hills, 90210* was the most popular Latino show, while the rest of the country virtually ignores it. The same holds true for *The Simpsons,* next most watched among Latinos while for all America it was a twenty-seventh place finisher. African-Americans also display unique TV viewing habits, favoring such shows as *Living Single* (Fox, #1), *Martin* (Fox, #2), *Fresh Prince of Bel Air* (NBC, #3) and *Blossom* (NBC, #4). None of these shows score in the top twenty U.S. rankings.

In today's "narrow-casting" universe, where homes on cable and satellite systems can tune to a bewildering variety of such specialized TV channels as Court TV, The Weather Channel, Food TV, MTV, The Outdoor Life Channel, The Arts & Entertainment Channel and hundreds of other offerings, media manipulators fine-tune their messages to be "all things to all people" for the sake of influencing their behavior.

## Top of the Heap

Claritas, Inc., headquartered in Arlington, Virginia, boasts in its corporate motto that it is "The Leader in Precision Marketing." A review of its *modus operandi* only confirms its bragging rights to that title.

Every year, Claritas updates its lifestyle classifications, linking Americans to where they work, live, and play. They do this every twelve months because family "clusters" constantly shift as narrowing interests break up Americans into smaller and smaller groupings. The company's operational brochure (printed on recycled paper, naturally) describes its product in architectural terms—"Building annual demographic updates and projections is like building a cathedral: Thousands of pieces must be carefully selected and assembled into a unified whole that provides not only a strong foundation and sound structure, but also precision and elegance in its detail.

"Demographic change in the ten years between censuses can be dramatic, especially so in household income, and in small geographic areas such as zip codes, census tracts, and census blocks. Demographic characteristics change with residential and commercial development, the local economy, immigration, lifestyle trends, and many other factors." Its *PRIZM* system precisely targets and narrowly defines subgroups of Americans, underlining Claritas' claim that "PRIZM helps you send the right message to the right consumer segment." PRIZM "target analysis" provides to anyone able to afford Claritas' considerable fees answers to their most pressing Who-What-Where-and-Why questions—"*Who* are my targets? *What* are they like? *Where* can I find them? And *How* can I reach them?"

Claritas data banks break down American society into sixty-two "clusters" and fifteen "social groups," pinpointing communities, towns, and urban neighborhoods throughout the land where families are linked by social class, income, lifestyles, and belief systems, rather than crude geography. A look at a few of these groups makes the point—

According to PRIZM analysis, the nation's most affluent social group is "*S1, Elite Suburbs*. Concentrated in our major metros, with over 90 percent located within the Top 25 TV Markets. S1 Clusters share high income, education, investment, and spending levels." Within the S1 category, Claritas identifies five sub-groups, but for brevity sake, let's look at just two—top and bottom—as examples:

> *Blue Blood Estates*, Elite Super-Rich Families. These are America's wealthiest suburbs, populated by super-upper established executives, professionals and heirs to "old money," who are accustomed to privilege, and live in luxury, supported by servants. Dominant White, High Asian. One in ten residents is a multi-millionaire. College grads,

> they belong to a country club, own mutual funds $10,000+, buy car phones, watch TV, golf, and read business magazines.
>
> *Kids & Cul-de-Sacs,* Upscale Suburban Families. Characterized by married couples with children, large 4+ person families which governs all aspects of their lives and activities. One can rightly picture Cluster 5 as a noisy medley of bikes, dogs, carpools, rock music, and sports. Dominant White, High Asian. Headed by College grads, they buy trivia games, have 1st mortgage loan, own a piano, listen to soft contemporary radio, and read infant/parenting magazines.

On the middle ranges of income, let's now turn to Category T2, the "Exurban Blues." PRIZM locates these families in the "midscale, low-density towns lying at the outskirts of major metro and smaller cities." Two of these clusters are described as:

> *New Homesteaders,* Young Middle-Class Families. The only T2 Cluster showing above-average college educations, with executives and professionals in most fields of local service such as administration, communications, health and retail. Dominant White. Most are married, the young with children, the elders without, and living is homespun with crafts, camping and sports. They tend to own a powerboat, have a new car loan, drink frozen orange juice, listen to country radio and read outdoor life magazines.
>
> *Military Quarters.* GI's & Surrounding Off-Base Families. Located on and near military bases, its map skews to the nation's principal harbors and defense perimeters. The highest index for adults under 35, it is fully integrated (Mixed Ethnic Diversity), favors bars, fast cars, and action sports. These adults vote in elections, have veteran's life insurance, long-distance telephone bills $26+, listen to religious/gospel radio, and read hunting/men's magazines.

Examining all sixty-two Claritas clusters, any reader should easily find his or her home and lifestyle described. But should you still harbor the illusion that computer psychographics and the sixty-two Claritas "clusters" don't have *your* number, please read on.

## Modeling the Real World

Modern supercomputers can easily handle a billion bits of information every second, which means all sorts of cross-references and arcane data about each one of us can be—and is—processing into oblivion any quaint notions of privacy so prized by our forebears. Using a technique called "simulation," computers draw a model of the real world based on known characteristics. Programmers feed the machine bits of information that might impact human behavior.

For example, in a political campaign the consultants will enter data on ethnic trends, population shifts, public perceptions of the competing candidates, and the amount of money each one is expected to spend. Digesting each bit of data, the computer self-corrects former assumptions and reports the probabilities of success or failure based on potential moves a candidate might make. In 1980, simulation helped Ronald Reagan win the White House by precisely predicting how voters would react to the then-volatile Iranian hostage crisis. In 1992, Bill Clinton won the Presidency by correctly assessing the effects of third-party candidate Ross Perot.

In the marketing world, simulations expose electronic shoppers to electronic advertising, and lead them through electronic "virtual reality" supermarkets where they collide with audio-visual messages at a display case. In this never-never land of flashing lights and programmed responses, homemaker panels serve as willing guinea pigs. In mock-up market settings, they are bombarded by carefully worded messages, controlled environments, and sensory stimulations to see how these will affect their "free choice" among products, brand names, and package designs. Cameras and computers analyze responses in this shopper's laboratory where human pawns contribute to the growing sophistication of the manipulation game.

How does this affect you and me? By studying the real actions of real people whose psychographic details are already known, the odds for manipulative certainty becomes as sure as shooting fish in a barrel. As the use of psychographics—under whatever new name it may be disguised—gains momentum, it grows more precise, more defined, and more universal. Former head of Ogilvy & Mather Advertising, James Benson, trumpets psychographics as a global process that erases national uniqueness.

"There is more similarity between the consumer in New England and the consumer in Olde England than there is between one in New

England and another in New Orleans. Increasingly, markets are being segmented more on psychological, social and attitudinal criteria than on traditional bases of geography and demography."

Boiled down to its essentials, he means there is no longer anywhere to run.

## FIGHTING BACK

### Become Aware

All communications are aimed at affecting us one way or the other. In the case of psychographics, the communications are narrowly focused on our individual, personal choices, and worldviews. So the first thing we must do to avoid being a fish in a barrel is to *become aware* of all "targeted" messages aimed your way.

### Look Out for Scams

More to the point, look out for those who exploit those very interests that lie at the heart of who you are and what you believe. To Christians, that often means heartrending television footage of a starving African child accompanied by a narrator who appeals to our sense of faith and compassion, often citing the Lord's teachings on giving to the poor and caring for orphans. The sponsors have researched that we will respond to such a message, since we have proven as much in our responses to similar fund-raising commercials in the past.

That's not to say that the charity is not doing good work in the name of Christ. But it could be just a money-making gimmick for some unscrupulous promoter, preying on the charitable impulses of believers.

### Evaluate All Requests

So how can you know where to apply your hard-earned dollars where they will do the most good? First off, be on guard for any "simulated" charity name that mimics a well-known, respected organization. For example, if a charity carries the name *World Vista* instead of *World Vision,* that should raise the red flag. Chances are it's a phony group.

Check out any charity you are not familiar with, and take the time to update those whose reputations you know of old. Things may have changed. Write or call, and ask for a verified annual report. That should indicate how much of each charitable dollar is spent on feeding and educating that poor African orphan, how much is eaten up by staff salaries, rent, and other administrative costs, and how much is spent on fund-raising itself. If you run into any problems receiving that report or if the report they send you is vague and does not specify how the money is spent, odds are that the charity is not worth supporting. A good rule of thumb is if at least seventy cents of every dollar is not spent on starving orphans, you should find a more effective way to help those kids.

You may want to contact the Evangelical Council for Financial Accountability, which monitors this sort of information. Call the E.C.F.A. at (703) 713–1414. For secular charities, send for the publication *Wise Giving Guide,* available from the National Information Bureau, 419 Park Avenue South, New York, NY 10016. The N.I.B. evaluates most nonreligious fund-raising charities by strictly graded guidelines.

## Be a Savvy Shopper

When dealing with sales promotions, there is nothing inherently wrong with buying products through mail-order. A growing trend in television are infomercials, which are half-hour thinly disguised pitches for kitchen gadgets, cosmetics, computer devices, and other products. I have bought computer equipment and electronic supplies that way. But if you do, make sure that your purchases offer distinct advantages that outweigh the security of dealing with a local store that offers services not available from distant drop-ship houses. And do not be shy about sending back anything that doesn't measure up to the specifications. Promising something different from what is delivered is technical fraud, which the F.C.C. and Justice Department take very seriously.

## Be Yourself

Finally, remember that you are uniquely who you are. Any manipulator who pushes too finely for those psychographic "associations" will sooner or later run into connections that do not apply. Though they may define you as an "evangelical Christian traditionalist," you may not vote, think, or react in exactly the way they expect. That's because the people drawing these psychographic profiles are, by and large, *not* evangelical Christian traditionalists themselves, and it takes the One who made you to really know you.

# 5

# Pied Pipers of Kiddieville

*It would be better for him if a millstone were hung around his neck and he were thrown into the sea, than that he should cause one of these little ones to stumble.*

Luke 17:2

Rutherford, New Jersey, is a dignified town of twenty thousand souls. At 50 Park Avenue in the town's tree-lined main shopping district, *Maxine's* sells women's apparel. But in a four-room suite above the dress shop, psychologists employed by Child Research Services worked in secret. No outside sign identified its business. The front door was always kept locked. Though the lab has operated here for many years, its existence remained a mystery to its neighbors.

During test times, young children climb out of cars in early afternoon, stay a few hours, and get picked up afterward. A child recruiter who lives nearby gets most of her panel names from PTA and churches, scout troops and schools. Maintaining elaborate file cards on every child, she notes ethnic origins, family income, and social traits. When a group furnishes the children, the group keeps the fees—usually $5 per child for an hour's work, up to $50 for a full day's scrutiny. The chore of rounding up and transporting the youngsters is the responsibility of the sponsoring organization.

If the kids are recruited individually, their family gets the money. When the study requires large numbers of children, local grammar schools are happy to volunteer their students and auditoriums. Some parents are so eager to give their kids a push into "show business" that they not only hand them over free of charge but even drive them to and from the testing.

## The Child Labs

One room of the Child Research lab is equipped as a play and display center where children use experimental products or act out situations. Prodded by child psychologists, they pretend they are on a shopping tour in a simulated supermarket complete with bulging shelves of brightly packaged goods, and they demonstrate how they pester their mothers to buy products.

On the other side of two-way-mirrored wall panels, executives of the research company, the client manufacturer, and its ad agency watch and listen while hidden microphones and video recorders capture the action for later analysis. In an adjacent room, a dozen circled chairs hold children being urged to discuss their innermost feelings. Conducted by experts in dramatic improvisation, child behavior, and marketing, these sessions explore how much and what kinds of influence kids exert on family buying patterns.

Often this research involves products not normally associated with children—items like bottled water or cheese spreads or gasoline. For instance, Texaco research established that most motorists believe all gasoline brands are alike. The company surmised that child nagging power could make the big difference, so it launched a promotion giving away little fire trucks with a fuel purchase. Business improved appreciably.

Child Research Services, subsidiary of the well-known polling company Yankelovich, Skelly & White headquartered in New York City, uses special projective techniques in its lab experiments with kids. For instance, they may have children cast secret votes that are whispered to the group leader, so that one child's ideas cannot influence another's. Or the kids are instructed to express an idea in a drawing instead of straining their limited vocabularies to verbalize it. Or they are encouraged to "role-play," pretending to be their mothers, fathers, or other children. When children can hide behind the mask of another personality, researchers find they reveal more intimate information.

Some years back, Miles Laboratories approached Child Research with a problem. The company wanted to market a vitamin that would appeal to kids and was considering using a pill shaped like Batman. Child Research Services rounded up some kids and probed them on their feelings regarding a number of popular cartoon characters. Using these findings as a basis, they produced a questionnaire containing drawings of these cartoon personalities, and in more extensive tests, asked the kids to rate them for appeal.

The measuring device used in these tests was the "smiley" scale—a clever pictorial version of adult attitude ratings. This technique shows the familiar moon face with a smiling upturned mouth to indicate "I like that a lot"; a straight-lined mouth means "It's just okay"; and a down-turned frown as the child's symbol for "Forget it!" When the questionnaires were tabulated and analyzed, Child Research discovered that Fred Flintstone and friends won the popularity contest hands down. So Miles switched its cartoon allegiance for their chewable vitamins from Batman to the Flintstones—and grabbed a healthy 20 percent share of the child vitamin market.

## Research Television for Children

Similar child research takes place in laboratories all across America. The purpose is simple: to uncover kids' hidden needs—knowledge that is used to develop television programs and commercials calculated to implant values and ideas, make children grab for supermarket impulse items, or nag their mom and dad for sponsor brands. Professionals in the television industry know full well that young children are the most avid—and impressionable—of all television watchers.

Two to five year olds typically spend thirty hours a week in front of the TV set, while their six to eleven year old sisters and brothers invest twenty-seven hours. In any given week their minds are assaulted by thousands of images, ideas, and commercial messages. Do such little ones really remember what they see and hear? Absolutely! Recent studies at the University of Minnesota's Institute of Child Development prove that babies as young as eleven months can remember events and reproduce them at a later date with accuracy. In one study, children only thirteen months old could clearly recall incidents that happened eight months earlier.

That is why advertisers spend an estimated billion dollars a year to beam their communications at little people. Not only do children themselves spend $39 billion a year from their own pockets, research labs underline the powerful influence children exert on which brands of toys, candy, cereal, sneakers, and soft drinks their family buys. Less publicized is how strongly kids influence buying decisions on such adult products as vitamins, drugs, gasoline, restaurants, and hardware brands. Children are hypersensitive to TV commercials, as most parents of nagging offspring already know too well. And an entire industry of market researchers is dedicated to finding out how to make Jimmy and Jennifer dance to their sponsors' tunes.

The secrecy in the child-research arena matches the cloak-and-dagger stuff of international spying. Researchers say the concealment is needed to stay one jump ahead of their competition. But there is a far less innocent motive involved. While uncovering psychological triggers to manipulate human behavior is in itself a dubiously moral enterprise, when applied to children, it borders on the obscene.

One research executive confided, "We have two whole generations who have grown up reacting to commercials and television visuals. Add to that the tons of research done in the last four decades and you will understand why TV commercials have never been so effective. Child research is important, because if you get them young you keep them."

## In-House Testing

Some large companies like Nabisco and Coca-Cola operate their own child-testing programs. One of the more elaborate setups was used by Mattel Toys inside its Hawthorne, California, factory. On the second floor, four playrooms were set aside for kids to interact with experimental toys. Behind the mirrored wall panels, teams of researchers, toy designers, and sales executives eyeballed every move as hidden mikes and recorders chronicled the action for later replay.

The toymaker also calls on academia to aid its child marketing efforts. Faculty psychologists from the University of Southern California hone their research techniques, based on the latest theories about how children develop, learn, and take in information. These Ph.Ds measure kids' reactions to colors and shapes, experiment with proposed toy concepts, and discover which parts of any given toy really excite youngsters. The findings are then used to produce hard-hitting TV commercials designed to empty store shelves in a hurry.

Once when Mattel's ad agency filmed some test commercials, they took over a theater to see how they run. Buying big display ads in local newspapers, copywriters heralded—**"SUPER SHOW SATURDAY! CLOWNS, MAGICIANS, GAMES, GIVEAWAYS, PRIZES! LOTS OF CARTOONS, ONLY 25 CENTS!"** Studies show that middle-class children react alike to toys and dolls and are also the best customers for these products. So the monthly test theater travels from one neighborhood to another, minimizing repeaters and avoiding upscale areas like Beverly Hills or depressed sections like East L.A.

The newspaper ads normally draw a crowd of about eight hundred children, mostly six to eleven years old. A magician walks onstage, tells a few jokes, gives out door prizes, and asks the kids to fill out a questionnaire. Specially designed for youngsters who do not read well, the format contains mostly photos of toys—trucks and cars for boys, dolls for girls, with four pictures per page. One photo may show an experimental Mattel product, while the other three are successful toys already being marketed by competitors.

"Which toy do you like best on page one?" the magician asks. The children mark their preferences with an X. "How about page two?" After the four-page survey, houselights dim and the show begins—a near-perfect replica of Saturday-morning children's television. First the kids see two minutes of commercials, followed by ten minutes of cartoons. Finally they get the main attraction, usually starring dolphins or other friendly creatures. When the program ends, a clown bounds onstage with some "bad news."

It seems the first questionnaires have been "lost" by the magicians or "ruined" by another clown who spilled grape soda all over them. To qualify for the special drawing, the kids will need to fill out the questionnaire again. By comparing results of the first set of questionnaires to the second, along with "control" commercials of known selling power, Mattel marketers determine which of the new commercials are the strongest child persuaders.

## Kid to Kid

More recently, a one-stop research firm called "Kid2Kid" was formed to develop new child products, marketing concepts, package designs and slogans. Using focus groups with a new twist, they hire other children to run the sessions. When a toy marketer wanted to find out if a line extension of its best-selling toy would be a winner, Kid2Kid designers developed a character they felt would fill the bill.

Then they scheduled a focus group discussion, led by a youth leader just a year or two older than the rest.

The presenter was wired to adult researchers hidden behind two-way glass, who prompted him through his earpiece with their own questions and probes. The children then wrote stories and drew pictures to express their feelings about proposed concepts. As members of the group read their stories, the youth moderator asked them questions, prompted through the ear piece from the hidden adult researchers.

According to a Kid2Kid executive, using young people as moderators really makes the difference between "truly insightful information" and useless trivia. "The minute an adult walks in, the kids tend to turn into angels," explained company head Whiton Paine. "And angels are not people who buy. It's the little devil within the kid that goes for most of the purchases."

Noted pediatrician Dr. Lendon Smith, who has authored highly regarded books on parenting, objects to such child research. "It's a dirty trick to research them this way," he noted. "Young people should not be turned into whiners for advertised products. Kids can't stand the pressure. They think that anything adults do is okay. That's why they're so vulnerable. For kids under ten, there is no sharp line between fantasy and reality."

## The Loss of Innocence

The most damaging aspect of the electronic communications age has been its distortion of the normal growth process. Before radio and television, information came through the written word. And up to a certain age children could not read. Even when they grew older, they still could not understand much of what they saw in adult literature. So these differences in literacy and comprehension not only protected the childhood state but also guaranteed its innocence.

Now radio and television have corrupted the childhood phase. Since kids don't have to "learn" anything to watch television, even preschool children can understand—if only at a naive level—adult situations on the screen. Where a young child might pick up a paperback romance and turn to an erotic passage, he or she could still not understand what was going on and soon lost interest. But when that same scene is played out on a TV screen, the action becomes obvious even to a young mind. What is true for sex is also true for other moral questions such as truth-telling, manners, and violent behavior. As a result, the innocence of children is no longer protected.

One result is that our children are *physically* growing up sooner. The age of a girl's first period, called *menarche,* has been getting lower and lower. From 14.8 years in 1895, the age has fallen to 12.5 years in 1988. And government statisticians predict that the numbers for 1995 will push the average even lower. This may very likely be a significant factor in the growing incidence of teenage sex and pregnancy. Many of today's ten-and eleven-year-old girls are at the same point as a 16-year-old girl in 1800.

There is a direct tie between how mature a girl looks and how people treat her. Researchers find that girls who develop early are at a higher risk for sexual abuse. They get more pressure from adults to act more maturely than their years and are, in effect, robbed of their full childhood years. Even the timetable for teen addictive risks from drugs, smoking, and drinking has fallen dramatically.

## Weakening Young Brains

More directly, there is evidence proving that TV watching actually changes the shape and functioning of children's brains. Educational psychologist Jane M. Healy notes that flashing television images produces shorter attention spans, diminished perseverance, and degraded verbal ability. Citing research showing how watching television alters brain waves—the longer people watch, the stronger become their alpha waves associated with sleep and trances, and the weaker their beta waves indicating conscious, rational thought—Healy points out that growing young brains are physically shaped by such repeated experiences.

"By age three to five, the height of the brain's critical period for cognitive and language development, the average child watches television about 28 hours a week. Television keeps our kids' brains unnaturally alerted—but at a responding level rather than a thinking level. That builds up the brain structures that reinforce the activity being practiced. As a result, teachers find that if something doesn't have an easy solution, students are reluctant to try it. Their social skills are impaired, and they don't have the stick-to-itiveness to work with other kids. Thought-out language is weakened, which is why they use phrases like 'Like, you know,' which are fillers for words that just aren't there."

Supporting evidence from Israel reveals that this "diminished capacity" trend is international in scope. Dr. Raphael Schneller, head of Bar-Ilan University's Educational Communications School, studied one thousand youths and five hundred adults during that nation's television strike in the 1980s. His findings parallel similar research in Great Britain and Scandinavia. "The growing addiction to television has serious implications on our youth's health, education, social development, and culture," Dr. Schneller observed. "They are cut off from reality; everything is imaginary. They don't meet real-life characters and cannot hold a normal conversation, as they have grown used to hearing—not listening or talking, but hearing. The longest conversation with their friends might be 'pass the peanuts.' Their attention spans are reduced to the ten to fifteen minute span between commercials."

## Beware the Cartoon Creatures!

*Well, we think, there are always the cartoons. Those are harmless enough.* Not true! From The Flintstones to G.I. Joe and the Addams Family, animated creatures more easily break through a child's defenses by obsessing attention and sparking the flow of adrenaline to implant ideas and trigger aggressive impulses. By using animated images that are clearly imaginative rather than photographically realistic, the mind relaxes and ethical judgments are set aside as we give ourselves over to the action, dialogue and humor. That's why television is such a powerful medium for selling things to kids.

Such animated characters as the Muppets, Big Bird, and more recently Barney the Purple Dinosaur create an ongoing love affair with their adoring young fans. Crooning a theme song that preaches, "I love you; You love me; We're a happy family," Barney and his gang of kid-pleasing recordings and videos seem the perfect babysitter for the nation's progeny. But nothing is as innocent as it appears. Unlike Mickey Mouse, Goofy, and Daffy Duck of earlier generations, Barney is a sugar-coated propagandist in the evolution/creationism wars. Teaching that the "prehistoric" creatures died millions of years ago, killed by lava from erupting volcanoes, the alternative view of extinction during the worldwide Noahic flood is effectively denied.

Shows like *The Simpsons* present parents as buffoons not worthy of respect. Other shows like *Beavis and Butthead* encourage children to disdain and sass their parents and other adults.

Another grim social consequence is a more violent society. Over the past few years, the top-rated TV shows for preschool children include the long-running *Teenage Mutant Ninja Turtles* and the more recent *Mighty Morphin Power Rangers*. Both shows feature wildly furious fighting scenes, with devastating punches and headkicks as a repeating theme week after week. Not only do children quickly grow addicted to the adrenaline rush triggered by the onscreen violence, but it also dominates their fantasy life as a way of dealing with conflict, at home or outside.

It should come as no surprise that toys and games based on Teenage Mutant Ninja Turtles or Power Rangers top the best-seller lists. Where Ninja Turtle action figures sold half a billion dollars worth in 1994, in little more than a year the Power Rangers share of market jumped from 4 percent in 1993 to 40 percent in 1994, with sales of $1 billion. A special *Mighty Morphin Power Rangers* show toured the country in 1994-95, with ticket sales of over $2 million at the Universal Amphitheater in Los Angeles alone. Billed "a rock 'n' roll theater for pre-teens and teens," the extravaganza—co-sponsored by 7-Up, Nabisco and Toys R Us—played at scores of arenas and theaters throughout North America.

Equally unsurprising, chilling reports from American daycare centers detail how three year olds cart their *Power Ranger* lunch pails and knapsacks to the facility and get together at free time. Comparing their *Ranger* paraphernalia, amid riotous laughter they start trading vicious karate chops and spin kicks, often resulting in injuries. Experts agree that when kids view such TV violence on a regular basis, they will act out the television mayhem in real life. "Research shows that heavy doses of that kind of cartoon behavior increases the risk of kids being involved in violence," notes Del Elliott, director of the University of Colorado's Center for the Study and Prevention of Violence. "But if the kids are in a good social environment, the effect is short-term. The more serious problems are with kids who are not being supervised and are watching this alone at home."

## Trying to Stem the Tide

One North American nation has already stepped in to remedy the problem. In 1994, the Canadian Broadcast Standards Council ruled that the violence in *Power Rangers* was too great for children to bear.

So the show's Canadian distributors—CanWest Global—agreed to cut all the kicking and hitting segments. The net result? There was no drop in viewing, and the show still ranks as the number one Canadian children's show without the graphic brutality. Meanwhile, more than seven million American kids continue to absorb the full load of *Power Ranger* savagery every weekday afternoon.

Industry apologists argue that cartoon violence acts as a healthy discharge for juvenile aggression. They claim that once the show is over, kids don't carry any of the brutality away into everyday life. Is this in any way true? In a letter survey conducted by the Los Angeles *Daily News* in 1995, children answered the neutral question: "What do you think about the *Power Rangers*?" Their answers speak for themselves:

> "I like the *Power Rangers* because they have karate moves."
>
> *Hugo Salazar, age 11*

> "I don't like the *Power Rangers* because the show is too vilent [sic]! I hate the *Power Rangers* show because it is too much hitting."
>
> *Alisha Thompson, age 8*

> "I dislike *Power Rangers* because it makes little kids think that they can do things that they really can't and they get hurt."
>
> *Dominique Mowry, age 11*

> "What is great about them is their karate."
>
> *Raquel Saenz, age 10*

> "I do not like the *Power Rangers* because there is too much fighting. My little cousin is afraid of them."
>
> *Rahul Mohan, age 9*

> "I dislike them because my brothers and sisters act like their [sic] *Power Rangers*. So they drive me crazy. Sometimes they hit me when they are playing."
>
> *Mayra Ahumada, age 12*

"I don't like *Power Rangers* because blood does not come out of them when they get hurt."

*Jonathan Suarez, age 8*

"I don't like the *Power Rangers* because I saw on the News that little girls were playing Power Rangers. One of them went in the kitchen and got a knife to pretend that it is a sword. The girl that had the knife killed the other girl."

*Crystal Holguin, age 9*

"I dislike the *Power Rangers* because my cousin used to be so sweet and nice but every sense [sic] he started watching the Power Rangers he has been so mean. So now everytime I go to his house he is always fighting with someone."

*Angela Anaya, age 10*

"I don't like the *Power Rangers*. You see it gives young children like me the thought that going out and hurting someone is okay."

*Ryan Yerton, age 9*

## Reaping the Whirlwind

It is hardly coincidental that with such shows glamorizing combat, childhood violence now rivals the three r's as the top concern in the nation's public schools. Today, the epidemic of shootings, stabbings, and assaults has spread from inner city districts to the wealthier suburbs and small towns. Where in more innocent times it was mid-and post-teen brutality that captured public attention, today's carnage often involves pre-teen youngsters.

In Chicago, two boys—ten and eleven years old—dangled a five year old out of a fourteenth floor window, fought off a rescue effort by the boy's eight-year-old brother, and dropped the child to his death—all because he refused to steal candy for them. In the San Fernando Valley, two girls—one eleven and the other fifteen—repeatedly stabbed to death a sixty-two-year old librarian while their sixteen-year-old sister pumped up the stereo volume to drown out the dying women's screams.

In Redlands, California, a thirteen-year-old student at a Catholic middle school faced with disciplinary action shot the principal with a sawed-off shotgun, then went out to the parking lot, and committed suicide with a blast to his own head. In Columbus, Georgia, seven students were arrested on charges of attempting to murder their teacher, by poisoning, stair-tripping, and shooting her with a concealed pistol. Their ages? Twelve and thirteen. And by no means is the child-killer phenomena confined to the United States. In England, a pair of nine year olds beat a five year old boy to unconsciousness and then crushed his head with a boulder to make sure he was dead. In Oslo, Norway, a five year old girl was battered to death by three boys—ages five and six.

Whether these outbreaks involving child murderers can be tied directly to previously ingested media violence may be argued. But one fact is beyond dispute—at no time in the 220-plus year history of the United States has the incidence of juvenile murders been so high. Since 1986, the number of youngsters treated for knife and gunshot wounds at the Children's National Medical Center rose *1740 percent*—over seventeen fold! During the same period, the number of juvenile girls arrested increased an average of 57 percent each year. While other factors may also play a role in this foreboding trend, responsible observers are in full agreement about this one fact—namely, that television directed at children is a major factor in this crazed new world of juvenile barbarism.

## FIGHTING BACK

What can we do to control the flood of media poison aimed at our kids? The focus must target not only the superfluous violence but the equally harmful ideas and values that undermine parental authority and religious faith.

### Start with Yourself

"But prove yourselves doers of the word, and not merely hearers who delude themselves." (James 1:22)

Children are inveterate imitators. We have already seen how they copy what they see and hear from mass communications. But an even more powerful influence can impact our kids than either mass media or school—we, their parents. So the first place to start is with ourselves.

How well do we control our own environmental influences?

- Do you listen to music that is calming and uplifting, or do you fill your home with raucous primitive sounds?
- Do you model the sort of lifestyle you wish your children to follow by your own choice of television viewing?
- Make a list of the television programs the family head(s) watch. It may take a bit of effort but the benefits are huge. Reviewing that list will soon tell you what sorts of unspoken messages you are sending your kids
- Do the same for the radio programs you listen to—music, talk, news or whatever.
- Finally, code those shows and programs for value content. *"G"* for good, positive Biblical values; *"N"* for neutral; and *"P"* for poor. Determine immediately to cut out all the P-rated shows and *do it*.
- Tell your children what you are doing and why. Explain to them how what you—and they—watch and hear has a good or bad effect on the way you live your lives. Give them examples, as how Power Rangers excite kids to kick and punch each other.
- And continue to monitor all your own N-rated fare, as well as the G category shows, to see whether any of these need to be recoded. Vigilance is the price free people must pay for liberty.

## Supervise Your Children

Monitor and control your children's media influences.

- A new mechanical television monitor called Time Slot allows parents to limit the number of hours their children can watch the tube. The child receives a magnetic "credit card" that they pass through a slot to "buy" TV time. Parents can program the device to lock out late-hour programs and shows containing violence and sex. Selling for about $150, Time Slot promises to change child attitudes and improve school grades. However, this is not the way to truly confront the problem. The truth is that Time Slot is just one more way parents can avoid responsibility and let technology "solve the problem"—a sure formula for failure.

- The more effective—and long-lasting—approach is to simply take the bull by the horns. If your children waste after-school hours watching television or listening to rock radio or CDs, discuss with them why it hurts them and then tell them about the new house rules you are establishing. Once they walk through the front doors after school, they enter an environment of more structured time. That might boil down to ninety minutes of homework, rewarded by an hour of playtime. After dinner, sixty minutes of book reading earns an equal amount of "selective" television viewing or music appreciation.

- During summer vacation when there is no homework, weekdays still call for a similar structure. For example, dedicate their mornings—9 A.M. to noon—to reading books, writing stories or book reports, practicing piano, trumpet or violin, and doing artwork. After lunch comes time for their friends and free play.

- Will the kids yell, pout and mutter over such "structured time"? You bet they will! But hang tough, and before too long your children will begin to appreciate the structure, particularly when their grades improve and they experience the benefits of calmer, more disciplined spirits.

- How much television should you allow your children to watch? Most child-development experts agree that *what* a kid watches is less harmful to healthy maturation than *how long* he or she watches. The reason is that during a child's formative years—birth through age six—his skills develop through practicing them. In other words, the more a child uses his or her imagination, language, and problem-solving abilities, the more those faculties grow. Considering that the typical child stares at 5,000 hours of flickering electronic images before he ever enters the first grade, the developmental damage is self-evident.

- A good rule of thumb is not to allow your child to view more than a few hours *per week* until such time as he or she has learned to read with proficiency. At that point—generally by the third grade—you can increase the television ration to five hours a week, but no more.

- Which programs are reasonably wholesome and appropriate for your kids to watch? According to Hollywood sound editor Harry Cheney, even the Saturday morning "KidVid" ghetto contains some decent shows. These include ABC's *Winnie the Pooh*, which offers gentle lessons in human relationships; *Bugs Bunny and Tweety*, many of whose episodes were produced years ago but which retain their innocence, freshness, and good humor; *Land of the Lost* contains a "magical" element, but does stress the traditional values of a family working together for survival; ABC's *Weekend Special* has episodes that present good substance but others, like a Halloween special, that promotes ghosts and occult themes; CBS's *Garfield and Friends* displays the same dry humor as the print cartoon, with occasional take-offs on classic fairy tales like *Jack and The Beanstalk*; *Mother Goose and Grimm* is mildly funny, with inoffensive self-esteem messages embedded in the storylines. The Cable channel Nickelodeon has inventive programming but often irreverent material, which means parents need to carefully monitor each show for suitability. And a Burbank firm has recently launched the "Children's Cable Network," devoted to nonviolent programming for preschool children. It will air such 1970s and 1980s series as *Dusty's Treehouse* and *New Zoo Revue*.

- Be your own programmer. Use your VCR to record the very best shows broadcast during the week. For example, try some of the older comedy classics in re-run, such as *Leave It to Beaver* or *I Love Lucy*. Or tape some fine old Disney movies, such as *Snow White*, *Fantasia*, or *Cinderella*. You can also rent pre-recorded videos from outlets like Blockbuster, and let your kids enjoy such Disney hits as *The Shaggy Dog* or *Flubber*. Or you can try the local Christian bookstore for such Biblically-oriented offerings like *Secret Adventures*, *Christy*, *Adventures in Odyssey*, *The Greatest Adventure* and *Adventures of Woof*. As an antidote to the basic computer principle, "Garbage in, garbage out," feed your youngsters' mind the choice cuts of TV and KidVid fare.

- When birthdays and gift-giving holidays arrive, buy smart instead of macho. Lots of new learning toys challenge young imaginations to build, solve, and hone their developing skills. The nationwide chain Toys R Us inaugurated special sections called "Books R Us," while the Target chain doubled its shelf space for construction toys and increased by 40 percent its displays of electronic learning aids, citing a mushrooming interest in child "gifts for the mind." So at the very next gift occasion, simply bypass the *Mighty Morphin Power Rangers* and try these mind-nourishing toys for your youngsters.

# 6

# Mind Control in the Living Room

*You foolish Galatians, Who has bewitched you?*

Galatians 3:1

A group of people sit in a darkened room, held in rapt silence. Assuming slumped postures, their eyes glaze over as they stare at the front of the room where a steady flash of lights plays off the walls and ceiling as a harpsichord softly tinkles a Mozart-like etude.

Cartoon fantasies in soft pastels drift across the screen synchronized to the music . . . plump propeller-driven aircraft swoop past sand castles and fairy landscapes . . . gigantic flowers stretch animated petals up to lolling roseate clouds while teddy bears frolic and tin soldiers march toward lush candy forests . . . nothing short of a childhood dreamland in thirty magical seconds. Then a hushed male voice speaks in angelic tones: "This Christmas dream has been brought to you by Bank Americard. Bank Americard—an easy way to help make dreams come true."

The fantasy images linger a few more precious seconds and then fade out into a promo for the upcoming movie of the week. The spell is shattered and the family breaks into frantic conversation covering schoolwork, office politics, last-minute shopping needs, and an upcoming party in overlapping bursts that sounds like the babble of a mad mob, even though only five people share the room. Totally oblivious to their shared experience, the Richards family—along with fifty million other American households—has just been subjected to a full-blown hypnotic interlude, complete with a post-hypnotic suggestion to "spend, buy . . . with Bank Americard."

## Hypnosis!

The word itself conjures up images of a sinister practitioner with piercing eyes and a dangling watch or sparkling crystal that charm the victim into a state of helpless trance. Such a highly imaginative—and fictitious—image comes from many popular movies and novels. But the truth is far more subtle and dangerous. Literally dozens of techniques invoke the hypnotic state—including soothing or syncopated music, low-key lighting, metronomes or other rhythms set at precise intervals, flashing lights or pulsing strobes, words repeated over and over in a hushed tone, swirling circular images that fixate the human eye—sound familiar?

They should. Every day of your wakeful life, you and I and every other typical person in modern society are bombarded by nearly all of these varied hypnotic-induction techniques via our radio and television sets, home computers, at movie theaters, markets, shops and restaurants, elevators, airports, doctors' offices, and even from the mouths of our own families, friends, work associates, and strangers at our doorsteps.

Boiled down to its essentials, the hypnotic state is really just a series of conditioned reactions. As we have seen, even in the womb, we responded to the sounds, sights, and other sensory stimuli around us. From infancy on, we take our cues from the authority figures around us. Our suggestible attitude is the sum total of all those early impressions, and when we are exposed to hypnotic triggers, the brain's higher cortical centers governing thought and reason are temporarily paralyzed. At those moments, we surrender our own will and yield it to others.

Strange things happen at such times—mostly bad, occasionally good. Dr. H. I. Kupper was treating a twenty-four-year-old man who had suffered from periodic seizures for six years. E.E.G. (electroencephalograph) tests showed irregular patterns characteristic of epilepsy. Under hypnosis, Dr. Kupper "regressed" his patient in time. In regression the practitioner "suggests" to the patient that he is living at an earlier time in his life. When he reached the man's twelfth birthday, suddenly the E.E.G. tracings became normal! Significantly, they remained normal as the patient was brought forward in time until he came to his eighteenth year, when he had suffered his first epileptic attack—and the design showed disturbance again. At no time during the hypnotic session had Dr. Kupper ever mentioned that the patient's E.E.G. was under scrutiny. Evidently, the body and nervous system remembers its own behavior across historical time.

## Supernormal Memory

Another peculiarity of someone in a hypnotic state is the ability to recall the most obscure details he or she cannot normally remember. A researcher for the National Institute of Mental Health, Dr. G. Scott Moss, tested a student's ability to recall, after one quick glimpse, what sort of clothing another student at the back of the classroom wore. In his normal state, the student couldn't even remember the colors of the apparel. Using automatic writing, which involves writing longhand in a pad without consciously thinking about it, the student came up with a sketchy if imperfect description. But when waking hypnosis was employed, strongly suggesting he *would* recall details, the student drew a remarkably accurate description of his classmate's clothes. However, there was one obviously glaring error.

The student insisted that his associate was wearing a white shirt with a dark stripe, even though it was clearly evident to everyone else that the shirt was pure white. Despite repeated urging that he would recall the pattern *more accurately*, the student insisted on his recollection of the dark stripe. It was not until the experiment was concluded and the class dismissed that the contradiction was resolved. When the young man whose clothes were the subject of scrutiny came up to the podium to ask a question, at face-to-face range Dr. Moss saw that his white shirt had once had a dark stripe that repeated washings had faded to a subtle shadow!

## Acting Against Our Best Interests

Words all by themselves are keys that trigger suggestibility, causing people to act in ways often at odds with their own best interests. The dean of American conditioning research, Dr. Abraham Salter, defined hypnosis as a state of vulnerability where words or other sense stimulators fire off a set of connected automatic reactions. The word "sleep," for example, is a commonly used tool for inducing a hypnotic trance, as in, "You are feeling sleepy, your head feels heavy, your eyelids are drooping, you are going to . . . sleep . . . sleep . . . sleep . . ." Ever since childhood, we have been trained to associate those same feelings of drowsiness, heavy heads, and *surrender of consciousness* to the sleeping condition. That is why it works so well on us.

But the word "sleep" itself is not half so crucial in inducing hypnosis as is the willingness of the subject to surrender his or her will to the operator. To demonstrate that fact, Dr. Moss substituted a nonsense word— "phozz"—for sleep during his classroom induction experiments. The results were exactly the same as if he had used "sleep" instead. Belief in "word magic" is so powerful that several of his medical students came up to him after class, notebooks open, to ask Professor Moss for the exact spelling of the word "phozz!"

## Waking Hypnosis

Waking hypnosis will produce all the effects commonly achieved through hypnotic trance—anesthesia from pain, muscular rigidity, and even control of heartbeat and blood pressure. These have all been obtained in normally awake people after mere suggestions from a "believable" operator. What kinds of people make the best subjects? Anyone who is predisposed to accept the operator's words as true and believable "statements of fact." From then on, they will "conceive and perceive" reality exactly as the operator defines it.

A study by the University of California tested the effects of various techniques on arm strength. First, the participants pulled a lever under normal conditions to set their measure of strength normality. Then, three "aids" were introduced. The first involved firing a starter's pistol to signal the moment when the lever should be pulled. The second aid was the use of grunts and karate shouts to accompany lever pulls, while the third was a simple waking suggestion that the subjects' strength would increase. Tests found all three methods significantly improved performance. The track pistol triggered an average 10 percent gain, grunts and shouts raised the level 15 percent, while the waking suggestion registered an average strength gain of 30 percent. Interestingly, when the same test was applied to professional weight lifters, the effective strength pull was *not affected* by the three techniques described.

Waking suggestions will produce blisters, cold sores, and digestive upsets. Medical students classically experience "intern's syndrome," where they suffer many of the disease symptoms associated with the particular pathology they happen to be studying at the time. Most of us recall incidents when we read about or watched films depicting illnesses or operations and afterwards were tormented by compulsive fears that we ourselves might have that disease. Watching a television show dramatizing heart disease or cancer, we soon feel strange little chest pains or imagine lumps on our lungs or bowels.

Three clinicians named Corn-Belcher, Welch, and Fisichelli report a polygraph experiment where they strapped electrodes to a study group. Once the lab was darkened, words were projected on to a screen, followed by a "reinforcement"—the actual thing the word symbolized. For example, the word "music" was immediately followed by playing a recorded symphony, "light" was succeeded by a brilliant flash, "clock" by tick-tock sounds, and so on. After ten such sequences, the word "electric shock" flashed on the screen but was not reinforced in any way. Nevertheless, three out of four subjects registered a polygraph reading far greater than to any of the previous words. To these people, the word *was* the thing.

As a group, children are more suggestible than adults. Starting from infancy, hypnotic vulnerability increases with age until it peaks between eight to twelve years, and then declines into adolescence. A sixteen year old is in fact no more susceptible than his parents, and often less so. Vulnerability is directly related to developing personality traits, inevitably tied to a person's parents and other authority figures.

## Who Is Vulnerable?

Some years back, the Rochester (N.Y.) Mental Health Center noted a marked increase in the number of two year olds brought to the clinic by parents. Most all displayed similar symptoms—constant babbling, a compulsion to recite numbers and letters, constant movement, and a tendency to cry hysterically when touched. All of these disturbed children were found to be either outright fans or secret viewers of PBS's *Sesame Street*. Parents admitted to using the show as a baby-sitting aid and/or an educational device. Later analysis of *Sesame Street*'s production techniques found a stress on repetitive words, phrases, and visual symbols; sensory shocks via sudden escalations of sound or light intensities; quick transitions to hold attention, and dominating sight and sound explosions. In effect, *Sesame Street* was found to be a highly effective hypnosis-inducing vehicle!

In adults, hypnotic vulnerability is a fairly fixed trait rooted in patterns formed by early childhood. Both genders are equally susceptible, but there is a connection between vulnerability and social conformity. Numerous studies, including those by Barber and by Wilcox and Faw, show a strong relationship between easily hypnotized persons and such character traits as outgoing personality, sociability, and emotional stability. Vulnerable people see the world in much more positive terms that those who are resistant. In fact, the most predictive identifier for hypnotizable people was their *regular attendance at church*. For such people, the old adage—"The serious Christian doesn't check his brains at the church door"—doesn't seem to apply.

## Three Factors for Hypnosis

Three factors are always present during hypnosis—relaxation, the focusing of attention, and the presence of an operator to execute suggestions. Hypnotized people will never admit that the things they do are the result of suggestions. They will invent the most far-fetched explanations to explain foolish actions, all to protect their precious self-image as a reasonable, self-directed being. The most effective suggestions are those that hide the fact the impulse was implanted by someone else. Ideally, the victim should feel that the idea has originated inside himself for his own self-interests. That is the task of artful persuasion of any kind, whether it be waking salesmanship, advertising, propaganda or unabashed hypnosis—namely, to make the subject believe the whole thing was his or her own idea.

You do not even have to be paying attention to the message for the implant to take effect. In fact, it is often more potent when your attention is diverted, as in conversations with family or friends. That is when the message sidesteps the consciousness threshold so it will feel as if it truly came from your own intellect and will. In such cases you will have no conscious recollection of ever having seen or heard the communication. It is only when you reach the "arena of action"—a market, drug store, or polling place—that you reach for a product or vote for some politician who has been subliminally sold while you were not paying attention.

Does this sound spooky and hardly credible? Then I suggest you try the "pantry test." Simply check your home medicine cabinet or kitchen cupboards for products with "name brands," those who invest heavily in costly television commercials. Then ask yourself why you paid more for items whose generic versions are available for half or a third the price of the advertised brands. You will usually find that the answers you come up with are precisely the same marketing arguments made by the commercials.

Sometimes when the idea implant is painful or abhorrent—such as disease, death, or taxes—or when the communicator has limited funds and needs to make his hypnotic point in a hurry, then the shock technique may come into play. This frontal assault on the nervous system is best illustrated in suspense movies when shifting shadows hint of hidden danger and mellow violins suddenly veer into eerie crescendos while an oboe starts to softly moan until, very suddenly—the *monster appears*! Cymbals crash and lights flare while our hearts and nerves leap in tempo—at that point we're ready to accept anything. Even the most absurd and thoughtless story line holds our numbed attention as we stay fixed in this highly suggestible state.

## Television—The Electronic Valium

Some commercials pull out all the stops, tossing a whole fistful of induction routines at us, including repetition, drum beats or other syncopated sounds, shock effects, hypnotic suggestion, and implantation. Some years ago a popular breath mint crammed all these techniques into a thirty-second spot with such extraordinary skill that even today it stands as a model of how advertisers can quickly—and forcefully—shove their message into the consumer's skull.

ONSCREEN: A young man rides on a big-city transit bus, seated between a matronly woman and a middle-aged man who is reading a newspaper. As the woman stares uninvitingly straight ahead, the young man wears a smug smile as if holding back an unshared secret.

A metronome ticks steadily while a booming male voice chants in rhythm with the beat—"Tick, Tack! Tick, Tack!" The cadence grows increasingly louder, more irrepressible—"TICK, TACK! TICK, TACK! TICK, TACK!"

The young man's grin beams broader, more ecstatic—"TICK, TACK! TICK, TACK!" Suddenly from out of nowhere there is a ear-splitting shout—"YAAHOOOOOOOOOOOOOOOOOHHHH!!!"

A pregnant instant of shocked reaction. The young man smiles contentedly, even as the man frowns, angrily rattles his newspaper, and continues to read while the woman wags her head disapprovingly. As the bus rolls merrily on, a chorus of female angelic voices sings—"There's a bright explosion of mint in your mouth! A clean fresh explosion of mint."

This thirty-second spot first played in the 1970s on prime-time network programs to introduce a new breath freshener imported from Italy. Just two months after the commercials began playing, Tic Tac became the top-selling impulse buy at supermarket and drugstore chains all over America. It was no accident that much of its initial business came from little children's hands that reached into the display racks for a quick grab on the way past the cash registers.

Not long ago, some Memphis psychologists wired up thirty-one children, sat them down in front of a TV set, and turned on *The Wonder Years*. In a matter of seconds, their vital signs began to degenerate. Heartbeats and metabolic rates plunged to even lower readings than during rest periods. The flicker of television images, transmitted at 30 per second, is three times more than the conscious mind can process. Registering *sub*consciously, they fester until the child can relieve the pressure by acting out the images.

The longer they watched TV, the greater the youngsters *alpha* brain waves (associated with trance)—and the *weaker* their beta waves (indicating rational thought).

Soon they were transfixed, changed into miniature couch potatoes. In a few short minutes, they had become transformed into prototypical children of the electronic generation.

## FIGHTING BACK

Professional hypnotists know that, for suggestions to take effect, the subjects, namely you and your family, need to like the person doing the suggesting. Drs. Howard D. Tawney and Ben Benson point out emphatically (in their book *Hypnosis and You*): "If your subject does not like you or mistrusts you, your attempt to hypnotize him will end in failure because of unconscious resistance. The prestige factor heightens the power of suggestion" That is why the most successful spokespeople on television commercials are popular well-known personalities or, if unknown, then likable motherly, fatherly, or grandmotherly actors.

## Be Alert

Both professional hypnotists and the Bible agree that the best weapon against being lulled and vulnerable to outside influences—as in a "hypnoid" state—is to be alert and watchful. Jesus teaches us that as we await His return," be on the alert—for you do not know when the master of the house is coming, whether in the evening, at midnight, at cockcrowing, or in the morning—lest he come suddenly and find you asleep. And what I say to you, I say to all, 'Be on the alert!'" (Mark 13:35–37).

The apostle Paul likewise tells us that, as the time of world testing approaches, we need to be wide awake and ready: "for you are all sons of light and sons of day. . . so then let us not sleep as others do, but let us be alert and sober." (1 Thess. 5:5–6).

The master hypnotist, however, sees your alert, watchful mind as an insurmountable shield. Drs. Tawney and Benson tells their students, "In preparing the subject for hypnosis, tell him to keep his mind *passive*. In no manner should he *try to analyze* the various things that go on. The power of suggestion lies in its appeal to our emotions, not our intellects. If we were to *evaluate* a suggestion, we would *destroy much of its power*. Analysis by the subject *destroys its hypnotic effect*" (emphasis added).

## Evaluate and Discuss

The antidote to unwittingly absorbing someone else's ideas from an electronic source is simply to *evaluate and discuss* it. Instead of trying to hide from commercial messages or mute out the sound, pay conscious attention to it. Make it a family practice to analyze the commercial. Talk about the way it uses believable spokespeople or key power words and images, background music, or jingles to charm, lull, and implant the sales pitch. Before long, that analytic attitude will become a habit and our watchfulness strengthened.

## Know the Word

Many cults and religious groups use self-hypnosis and autosuggestion as standard practices. It is an established fact that suggestion is at the heart of such groups as Christian Science, Science of Mind, "Divine Science," and other mental "sciences." Some professing "Christian" organizations claim to be Bible-based but in practice rely on a charismatic figure who controls his flock through an unhealthy "prestige" he applies to condemn independent thought among the "faithful." Recent examples include David Koresh's Branch Davidians, Garner Ted Armstrong's Wide World Church of God, and other sects that focus on a central personality and not the authority of God's Word and His Holy Spirit.

When it comes to new age and eastern religions, their entire foundation is based on autosuggestion and self-hypnosis. Yogis such as the Maharishi Mahesh Yogi (TM or Transcendental Meditation) teach *monoideism*, which means to concentrate strictly on one idea or one thought. TM assigns to each new "devotee" a single name of a Hindu god which he is to repeat over and over again each time he meditates. Other sects repeat a phrase or gaze hypnotically at a concentric design or simply go into a hypnotic state by folding their hands and staring at their thumbs.

All of these techniques create *disassociation* (where the personality "splits off" from the outside world). This is a very dangerous state, since the person becomes very vulnerable to dark spiritual influences from the demonic realms.

PART 2

# Manipulation in Action

# 7

# Television—The Phantom Reality

*History is now shaped by television.*

Lech Walesa,
Polish Solidarity leader

Fifty years ago, British prime minister Sir Winston Churchill described an ominous "Iron Curtain" of communism that had fallen across continental Europe. Today, while that iron curtain has lost its former power, another even more destructive force threatens the planet—not with intercontinental ballistic missiles but through ongoing sensory assaults on every human nervous system, heart, and spirit on earth. I call this worldwide blight the "Media Jungle."

## Creating Contempt for History

If communications serve as the neural pathways of society, then the leap from print to radio was the shift that triggered the electronic revolution. Over three generations—from the radio generation born during the 1930s to the post-1945 baby boomers raised by television and *their* children who came of age playing computer games—we have experienced monumental changes in the way we receive information and perceive the world around us. This biosphere of electronic "reality" has gradually but relentlessly conditioned us to place great value on *immediacy* while instilling indifference if not outright contempt for *historical perspective.*

Now, over the past fifty years, this age's most powerful medium—television—has increasingly transformed those born to it and raised by it. To a large extent, this metamorphosis has sprung from the very nature of the medium itself. Unlike real life, where contacts between flesh-and-blood beings are usually halting, repetitive, sometimes boring, and occasionally irrational, television transmissions flow rapidly from one moment to another. Painstakingly edited to compress time, television shows present viewers with images that smoothly form, move, speak, and vanish with the speed of light, only to be displaced by new, equally fleeting images that do the same thing.

Over time, we have been programmed to react to a two-dimensioned television universe that dissolves the difference between illusion and reality. One effect of this change has been to numb our minds to long-term causes and effects, belief in absolute truth, and the inevitable consequences of violating time-proven realities. That is why those of us who receive our primary sights, sounds, and operative facts of life through our television screens tend to identify past events not as prologue to future effects but as mere antiquated, irrelevant rubbish. History thus becomes reduced to powdered wigs, costumed fops, stilted speech, and unreal motives.

## TV's War Against Traditional Values

Losing our sense of history sense is just part of the TV quagmire. While early TV programs served to reinforce traditional family life and values, today's television subverts or openly repudiates those same principles. In their book *Prime Time,* sociologists Richter, Richter, and Rothman aptly define our present dilemma. "Television," they write, "once served as an agent of social control. But it has now become an agent of social change. It now fosters suspicions of traditional mores and institutions . . . and is apt to cast a jaundiced eye on the very standards the medium embraced so enthusiastically a mere generation ago."

How does this play out in everyday life? Let us look first at the much-discussed issue of "sexual harassment." Researchers at the University of Dayton studied sexual behavior on prime-time comedy programs broadcast by the four networks—ABC, NBC, CBS, and Fox—and found that two of every five encounters involved sexual harassment. While 40 percent of the accosted women did *not* welcome the approach, 36 percent *did*, and 24 percent displayed no visible reaction. Popular shows like *Roseanne*, *Murphy Brown*, and *Married . . . With Children* constantly portray sexual remarks, leers, and gestures, along with invasive touching and grabbing, as nothing more than harmless humor, thereby establishing it as acceptable behavior. So the basic message telecast is clear: "Boys will be boys, and most girls really *like* it!"

The second shoe drops with another study on sexual harassment in public schools. Conducted by Louis Harris and Associates among 1,600 students in eighth through eleventh grades, the investigators found that *four of every five* pupils report being sexually harassed during the school day. "America's schools are filled with hostile hallways where students are daily targets of sexual harassment," a study spokesperson concludes. "Our children learn at a very early age that sexual harassment is just an everyday part of life."

Tie that assertion to recent news items. In New York City, twenty boys ages twelve to seventeen years old link arms around a lone girl at a public swimming pool. Playing a "game" called *Whirlpool*, they chanted "Oops, there it is!" while pushing her under, ripping off her swimsuit and grabbing her chest and private parts. In Fort Worth, Texas, six boys ages twelve to fourteen held down a thirteen-year-old girl while another boy sexually assaulted her on a crowded school bus as other students laughed and cheered him on. In Lakewood, California, nine suburban high-school students molested and raped girls in a competition to accumulate "points" for sexual conquests.

A survey of New York youngsters by the *New York Times* underscored the coarse, vulgar world inhabited by today's teenagers. Romance has disappeared, replaced by casual sex and filthy language. From vulgarity to sexual harassment and fornication—willing or forced—today's adults and youth alike receive much of their inspiration from the never-never land of television's ratings-driven "morality." From morning gabfests to afternoon soap operas to prime-time sitcoms and dramas, sex runs like a glossy glue that attracts viewers and binds it all together.

## Prime Time Filth

A brief survey of today's soap-opera heroines illustrates the trend. Ashley claims an abortion drove her insane; Maria thinks she miscarried while horseback riding; Vivian filched another woman's eggs to have her lover's baby; Adam has three children by three different mothers with another on the way by wife number four; and Michelle keeps a jar of condoms on her coffee table for everyday use.

Where ten years ago one had to pay for premium cable channels to receive "Blue TV," today's airwaves are filled with freely distributed network raunch, available to anyone with a TV set and a rooftop aerial. Any time of the day or night, channel surfers of any age can encounter grappling, groping human bodies or some talk-show panel featuring sexual athletes, freaks, or "experts." The trick these days is to find a drama or discussion show that does *not* degrade and exploit our procreative impulse.

Morning talkfests like *Rolanda, Jerry Springer, Richard Bey,* and *Leeza* give way to the noontime soap operas. The afternoon talk shows like *Donahue, Geraldo,* and *Oprah* segue into drive-time news shows followed by evening prime time sitcoms and dramas. Throughout the day Americans everywhere are deluged by a flood of programming depicting recreational adultery, perversion, teenage sex, child molesters, gender-change freaks, and degenerate exposes veiled by a overlay of hypocritical "objectivity" to lend this filth an aura of respectability.

## The Ratings Game

It is virtually impossible to really understand why networks and television producers so eagerly embrace this garbage until we look at the ratings game that rules the industry. Since advertising pays all the bills on television, advertisers who buy time on any TV show naturally want to know how many people—prospective customers—will be exposed to their commercials. The more people, the more products they will sell. So the entire industry has anointed one judge to count viewers' noses—the A.C. Nielsen Co. headquartered in Northbrook, Illinois.

Ratings act as judge and jury for all network and local-station shows, deciding which ones stay on the air and which are canceled. Ratings are typically based on a secret sample of approximately 1,500 homes, chosen from "random locations" from a Census Bureau list. Nielsen field reps then drive to the designated neighborhoods and try to persuade families to join their ratings panel. To help convince them, they offer prospects $50 to sign a contract, $50 for each of the five years they stay on the panel, and half of all TV-set repair costs during that period.

Once a family says yes, the hardware moves in. The house gets an audiometer wired from a closet or basement to every TV set in the house. The meter records when the sets are on or off and which channels are being viewed. Special telephone lines feed the meter to Nielsen's Florida center, where all TV watching is tabulated twice a day by company computers. The family gets regularly mailed literature, chatty newsletters, and periodic calls from the field rep. The home has become a "Nielsen family."

During any biweekly rating period, not all Nielsen families are counted. Some have agreed to allow the hardware into their homes but have not yet been visited by a rep and wired up. Others are lost because of malfunctions in the telephone lines or the meters. So, on any typical day, the Nielsen ratings report viewing information from about 1,200 homes. A ratings number is the percentage of those 1,200 homes tuned to the same show.

For example, if a top-rated show like *Roseanne* scores a "13 rating" for the week, that means that 13 percent of the sample homes had tuned in *Roseanne* for at least six minutes—about 156 sets throughout the entire U.S.A.! Nielsen then assumes the same proportion of all American TV households—some 93 million—are watching *Roseanne* and so reports in its rating books that an estimated 12 million homes are tuned in. Nielsen sells its ratings service to TV networks, program producers, ad agencies, and advertisers. All of them pay fees based on a portion of their total business. A top-ten ad agency may pay $500,000 a year for the Nielsen service. Networks pay more; other users less. In return for their money, subscribers get a series of reports filled with rows of numbers—Nielsen estimates of TV-show popularity.

The public sees the tip of the ratings iceberg in newspaper stories explaining how ABC is beating NBC and CBS 20.1 to 19.6 to 18.3 or through banner headlines in the entertainment section exclaiming "Seinfield Tops Again!" Behind the scenes where the money changes hands, the game of who pays how much for what is based strictly on the Nielsen numbers. Networks and local stations base their charges for commercial time on the ratings. A commercial minute on a top-rated show like *Seinfield*, for instance, costs an advertiser $500,000 compared to a charge of $60,000 or less for shows scoring low in the ratings.

That is why new shows die so quickly—often within six weeks—and old shows with respectable numbers hang on so long. Observes a media buyer from a top-ten ad agency, "Agencies are forced to live and die with the Nielsen numbers. There is no appeals court." Former NBC-TV president Grant Tinker summed up the feelings of many insiders when he said, "I've spent 40 years of my life in television. And all those years I've been vitally affected by the Nielsen ratings. Quality shows go down the tube because Nielsen says nobody is watching. I hate to think I've been living a lie all these years."

The sad truth is that Tinker and the others have been "living a lie" when it comes to the ratings. Let's start with what statisticians call "sampling error." Whenever you set up a panel of 1,200 homes to represent 93 million, sampling error says that a ratings of 13 points could actually be 2.5 points *higher* or 2.5 points lower. That means that *Roseanne* might really score as low as 10.5, which would drop the show from sixth place down to fifteenth place. The even more serious problem with the Nielsen ratings, however, is the question of which kinds of homes get wired for viewing.

About half of all families asked say no. Two classes of Americans are much more prone to be suspicious of anyone putting recording machines in their homes, namely higher- and lower-income families. Another factor is liberalism versus conservatism, where liberals tend to be more agreeable to experiments of this kind while conservatives are not. Those who do sign on are mostly the more susceptible middle-class families. When the field reps interview prospective families, they will bypass homes where TV viewing time is minimal. So what the ratings really reflect is a highly selective panel of television addicts, mostly responding to shows that appeal to the emotions—in short, sex, fear, and bawdy humor. And so, an axiom of the industry is that if you want to attract high ratings, you need to inject sensationalism, gossip, blood, and money into your programs.

## Our Children Are Watching

For the rare reader who has somehow avoided running into this circus of television carnality, a brief survey of soap-opera storylines will show how the formula works. To quote excerpts from newspaper summaries covering the major soaps for a typical week, consider the following:

- *All My Children:* "Julia, fearful she will get pregnant or contract AIDS, is terrified when Louie insists on unprotected sex. Noah learns of an impending drug bust and rushes to tell Louie. Noah arrives in time to stop Louie from forcing himself on Julia. When Julia tells Noah she can't be a hooker, he says she doesn't have to work the streets and can stay with him as long as she wants."

- *Another World:* "Ian tells Josie he supports her plan to be a model. Josie stops Ian just as they are about to make love, revealing she has tested positive for a sexually transmitted disease and must wait for her latest test results. Donna is thrilled when she learns that what she thought was early menopause is actually a hormone imbalance."

- *As The World Turns*: "Tom is furious when he learns that Barbara told Margo he and Dawn had an affair."

- *The Bold and the Beautiful:* "Karen told Macy she is in love. While Karen waited for Connor, he was making love to Brooke, who said she wanted a relationship with him. The next morning, Karen was crushed when she went to Brooke's pad and saw Connor, who had just stepped out of the shower."

- *Days of Our Lives:* "Billie planned to seduce Bo. After Alan threatened Alice, she lied on the witness stand that he was a gentleman after their one date. The judge threw out Sami's rape charges against Alan after his lawyer forced Carrie to testify Sami has a history of telling lies."

- *Guiding Light:* "Matt later accused Vanessa of being ashamed of their Summit Lake romance. Alan heard Vanessa ask Matt to return her key chain. As the contractor, Dylan assigned Matt to a remodeling job at Vanesa's home. After looking at Cutler's mug books, Tangie and Alan-Michael learned Harry attacked her on the beach."

Even though prime-time sex-drenched sitcoms like *Married . . . With Children* is scheduled at 9:00 P.M. in most markets, reruns air during "kid-prime" hours in the mid or late afternoons. So it should come as no surprise to learn that young children tune in these shows by the millions every weekday. The A.C. Nielsen Co. reports that not only are *Married . . . With Children* reruns the most popular afternoon/evening show among kids ages twelve to seventeen, but it also ranks tenth among toddlers and youngsters ages two to eleven.

## Long-Lasting Harm

Should any reader be naive enough to suppose that viewing such raunch has no long-lasting harmful effects, the U.S. Center for Disease Control discloses that better than one out of *every five* Americans is currently infected with a sexually transmitted disease. The Center estimates *56 million* people are afflicted with such pestilences as hepatitis B, chlamydia, HIV and gonorrhea. Some 31 million Americans—one in eight—carry the genital herpes virus, an incurable infection that can break out at any time. It keeps getting worse. Currently about 12 million new infections occur every year, and two thirds of the victims are *under 25* years of age and *one fourth* are *teenagers.*

A quick look at a few charts will complete this mini-tour of television sexuality—

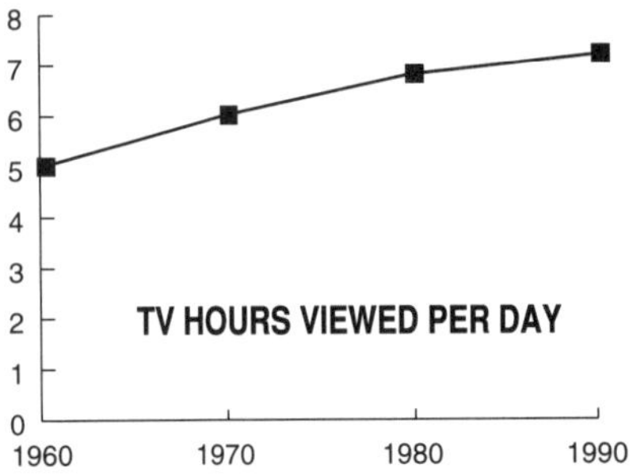


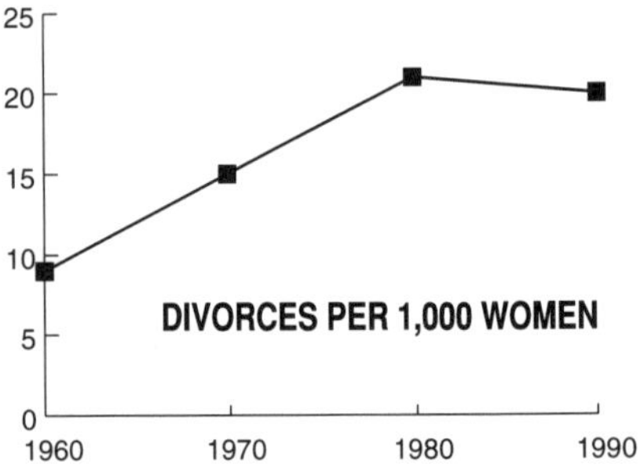


No cause-and-effect relationship can be *absolutely* proven between the 40 percent increase in TV watching, the proliferation of dramatized sexual promiscuity on television, and the 265 percent jump in the divorce rate over the past thirty-five years. Still it takes an ostrich with head buried in sand not to see a connection between TV's relentless "liberalization" of sexual content from 1970 onward and today's popular acceptance of casual sex, "swinging," and adultery in American society.

Finally, two other end-of-century trends confirm our thesis. First, the U.S. Census Bureau indicates that 1993's median age for first marriages hit its oldest level ever at 24.5 years for women and 26.5

years for men. "More and more couples are choosing to live together first," says marriage therapist Thomas Seibt, in explaining this drift to later marriages. Second, another government report reveals that half a million U.S. teenagers have babies each year, the highest adolescent birth rate in the *entire developed world*. Is television solely and exclusively to blame? The answer must be no. But if the question is changed to "Does TV play a role in the carnal decay afflicting America?" the answer is clearly yes.

Researchers from *Children Now,* a national advocacy group, interviewed 750 youngsters ages ten to sixteen and asked them how, if at all, television influenced the way they lived. The results were surprising. More than two out of three admit they are strongly affected by what they see on television. Though 77 percent complained there was too much sex before marriage portrayed, two out of three admitted that TV and movies influence "their peers" to have sex too young. Another two out of three said TV encouraged youngsters to disrespect their parents. A separate independent study at the University of Illinois found that television molded a child's character more than any other societal influence—including their own families!

## The Case for Violence

While apologists for the television establishment may deny its influence on *sexual* behavior, when it comes to television *violence*, the facts are not even arguable. A study by the American Psychological Association estimates that before he or she ever leaves elementary school, the typical child will have viewed 8,000 TV murders and 100,000 violent acts. By the time he or she graduates high school, that number has more than doubled.

Television spokesman George Vradenberg, vice-president of Fox Inc., offers the chicken-or-the-egg argument. "We aren't really certain whether some people who see violence tend to become violent, or whether violent people just like to watch programs with violence," he says. Hog wash, counters Leonard Erons, one of three authors of the A.P.A. research. "The scientific debate is over."

Eron has researched TV violence for more than thirty-five years, tracking a study group of the same 875 males and females from age eight to thirty. His analysis clearly established that those boys and girls who watched more violent television as children were much more likely to commit serious crimes and to use violence when disciplining their own children. "What one learns about life from the television screen will be transmitted to the next generation, as well," Eron concludes.

The Center for Media and Public Affairs recently monitored a typical June day's worth of programs to check for violent acts. The stations monitored included network fare on ABC, CBS, NBC, and Fox; PBS offerings; independent station WDCA in Washington, DC; and cable stations WTBS, USA, HBO, and MTV. After eliminating all acts of unintended or accidental savagery, violent sports encounters, or brutality by animals on nature shows, over an eighteen-hour period the Center counted 2,000 intentional, scripted, and real-life violent acts. Even more alarming, the majority of this mayhem appeared during children's programs, with cartoons registering twenty-five violent acts per hour.

Underscoring the international aspects of this phenomenon, another study published in the *Journal of the American Medical Association* concluded that the introduction of television into the U.S., Canada, and South Africa almost exactly paralleled the increased murder rate in all three nations. From 1945 to 1970, the murder rates rose 92 percent and 93 percent respectively in the U.S. and Canada. In both countries, ownership of TV sets increased at almost the exact same proportions as the homicide rate.

To factor out the volatile racial climate in South Africa, the study focused strictly on the murder rate for whites. The analysis found a gradual decline in the murder rate from 1945 to 1970, which stabilized until 1975, the year television was first introduced into that nation. Thereafter the murder rate exploded, rising 130 percent by 1983. In an incendiary footnote, the editors of the *Journal of the American Medical Association* estimated that up to half of all homicides are inspired or influenced by television. Underlining that point, a French mother sued Television Francaise because her son was killed by a homemade bomb he made after a recipe aired on the American TV series *MacGyver.*

## Blood on the Streets

On the street, youthful carnage is epidemic. In California, homicide is the second leading cause of death for youngsters thirteen to nineteen years old. Nationwide, the Center for Disease Control reports that the homicide rate for teenage boys ages fifteen to nineteen almost *tripled* between 1985 and 1991. Arrests for crimes of violence by children under eighteen has almost doubled between 1970 and 1992.

Youths are arrested for violent crimes at earlier ages. In 1982, 390 youths ages thirteen to fifteen were arrested for murder. By 1992, this figure had jumped to 740. Teenagers are 2.5 times more likely to be victims of violence than those over age twenty. Three million thefts and acts of violence now take place at our nation's schools each year. One in five students carry weapons to school, while metal detectors and body searches are as common as fire drills and recesses. In a nationwide survey of 65,000 teenage schoolkids, two out of five say they "do not feel safe in their school."

## Carnage Becomes Casual

The almost casual way youngsters use violence today to settle disputes or take someone else's possessions is frightening. In Los Angeles, a teenager shot a cheerleader for her portable radio. In Oakland, a teenage boy stabbed another boy when he refused to pay back a twenty-five-cent debt. In Monrovia, a twelve-year-old boy killed a store owner over a bicycle. A fourteen-year-old Venice boy pushed an elderly woman out of the moving car he was trying to steal. A thirteen-year-old student at a parochial school in Riverside shot the principal and then himself.

In Harlem, Georgia, a ninth-grader killed one boy and wounded another in the school corridor. At an Atlanta high school, a fifteen-year-old was shot to death in the lunchroom by a boy with whom he had differences. In Dallas, another fifteen-year-old was fatally shot in the hallway by a fellow student. In Dartsmouth, Massachussetts, a ninth-grade boy was stabbed to death in his classroom by three other boys who laughed and traded high-fives after the attack. In Portsmouth, New Hampshire, a sixteen-year-old boy was convicted for raping and repeatedly stabbing a twenty-eight-year old woman who miraculously survived the attack.

And it's not just the children of the poor who commit mayhem. At a prep school in New Hampshire, two students, ages fourteen and fifteen, bashed a sixteen-year-old acquaintance over the head with an aluminum baseball bat, severely injuring him. "We're seeing an epidemic of youth violence," observes Sgt. Paul Famulari of the Portsmouth Police Department. "Kids now deal with any dispute by using weapons."

## The Television Industry Agrees—Almost

Even people in the television industry itself now concede—albeit grudgingly—that there is a causal relationship between TV violence and the acting out of aggressive feelings by children. A survey of television executives, writers, actors and directors by *U.S. News & World Report* found that three in five—63 percent—of the Hollywood elite say the industry glorifies violence. The majority even admit they have avoided watching a program because of its violent content. But when it comes to cutting down on the savagery, Hollywood's ideas on how to improve things amount to pasting a bandage on an arterial wound.

While the four networks have established onscreen "parental advisory warnings," industry spokesmen admit that only one prime-time program—ABC's *NYPD Blue*—had been judged violent enough to merit such a warning notice. No cartoons or sports shows were so labeled, and cable networks and independent stations are totally outside the coverage. In actual practice, these voluntary "violence warnings" now apply almost exclusively to TV movies and miniseries.

Venerable Hollywood producer Aaron Spelling, commenting "There's too much of this going on in society," offered a sop in the form of a *Beverly Hills 90210* episode that had one character buy a gun with near-fatal results. Naturally, he made the pistol the villain rather than violence per se. Another producer, Arnold Shapiro, produced a CBS *Schoolbreak Special* called *Kids Killing Kids* that featured four unconnected short dramas all ending in violence. But once the Congressional hearings ended, media concern abated and with the pressure eased, it was back to showbiz as usual.

Other efforts to quell television savagery have been well-intended but ultimately useless. For example, researchers from Harvard University launched an anti-violence campaign named "Squash It," featuring lead television characters who say "Squash it!" while walking away from potentially violent confrontations. Another Harvard-led commission recommended school programs to teach students how to manage anger, negotiate conflicts and adopt another child's perspective as an antidote to television incitements. Mainline church groups have launched a Christian Peacemaker Corps, challenging recruits with the motto "Are you willing to lay down your life for peace?" Sending "peace foot soldiers" to inner-city streets, they are trained to "treat every human being like they are a child of God." Sounds noble, but after six years of operation, the Corps has proven highly ineffective—not to say dangerous—against long knives, semi-automatic weapons, and the contemptuous barbarians who carry them.

Even as American society feels helpless against terror on the streets, the people see through the subterfuge and directly connect the carnage to the profusion of violence on television. According to a *Los Angeles Times* poll, four out of five Americans are convinced that television entertainment programs directly affect the level of violence in society. That same majority supports government intervention in the form of guidelines to restrict the mayhem on TV.

Overseas, violence on television is far more restricted than in the United States. Great Britain, Germany, Sweden, and Australia openly banish violent programming during key parts of the day, use strict rating systems to warn viewers, and impose tough penalties on those who violate government standards. While foreign rating boards are composed of social scientists and child development experts, the American board—the MPAA—only requires its board members be parents. In fact, the MPAA panel consists of people connected to the television industry, a case of the fox guarding the hen house.

## TV's Assault Against Christian Values and Truth

But as harmful as television's embrace of carnality and carnage may be, the deeper philosophical level from which it operates explains why it has been so destructive to modern society. It is television's *life values*—the ideas the medium chooses to emphasize and extol at the expense of Judeo-Christian principles—that have spearheaded the decline of western culture.

Peggy Wehmeyer, an evangelical Christian who works for ABC Television, reported, "The elite in this country—the courts, education, media, the arts—tend to view people who take their faith very seriously . . . with a smug, arrogant attitude." Harvard law professor Alan Dershowitz told a National Public Radio audience that Harvard Law School would never hire an evangelical Christian, since they would fail to pass the "acceptable ideology" test applied to all applicants.

Irving Kristol, prominent Jewish writer and conservative chronicler of the "culture wars" between leftist secularists and Judeo-Christian traditionalists, has emphatically declared victory for the left. "Those wars are over," he observes. "The Left has won. The Left today completely dominates the educational establishment, the entertainment industry, the universities, and the media. There is no point in trying to inject 'family values' into these institutions. They will debase and corrupt the very ideal while pretending to celebrate it."

Do those views paint a true picture of today's moral landscape? Sadly enough, they do. Three of four Americans today do not believe in absolute truth. More shockingly, nearly two of three professing born-again Christians reject the idea of absolute truth. To understand how this happened, we must consider the most basic battleground of all—the traditional family. For thousands of years the western world has held the biblical model as its highest ideal—a man and woman leave their parents, join together as "one flesh," honor their parents, raise children according to dictates of Scripture, reject divorce except in cases of adultery, and hold fast to the moral absolutes defined by the revealed Word of God.

Then, with the advent of television came a gradual erosion of historical perspectives and Bible-based morality. By 1962, the erosion began to show itself at all levels of society. The next year the Supreme Court, ruling on a suit brought by atheist Madalyn Murray O'Hair, effectively banned moral instructions and all activities based on religious teachings from public schools and by extension from all public institutions.

From that time on, the decline was dramatic. On the premise that ten pictures are worth 10,000 words, the following series of graphs speak for themselves and vividly illustrate the way the media jungle has impacted the decline and fall of the U.S.

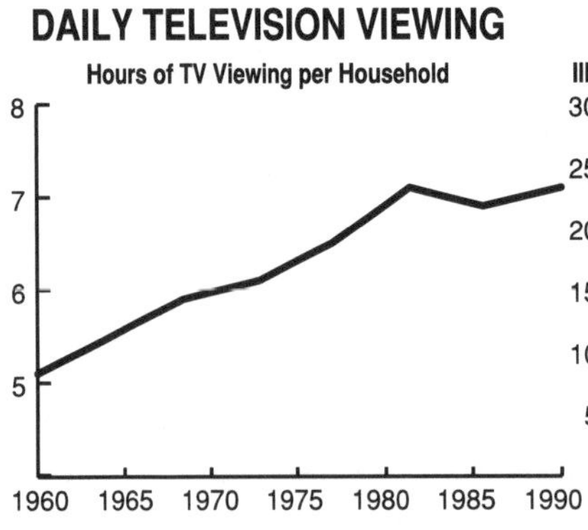


Source: Nielsen Television Research

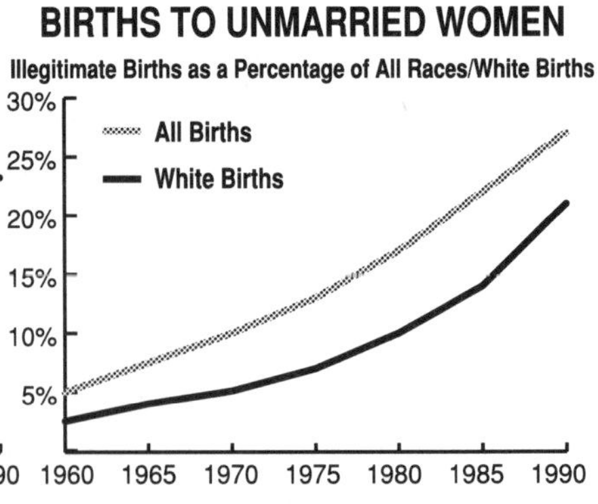


Source: National Center for Health Statistics

## MARRIAGE AND DIVORCE RATES

**Marriages per 1,000 Unmarried Women** | **Divorces per 1,000 Married Women**

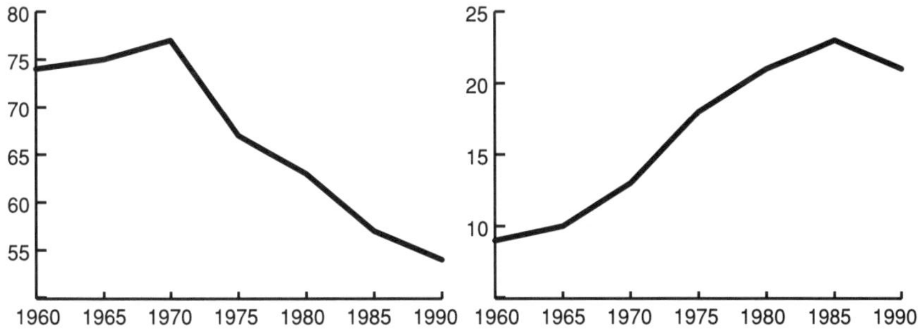


Source: National Center for Health Statistics

## SINGLE PARENT FAMILIES

**Percent of All Families with Children**

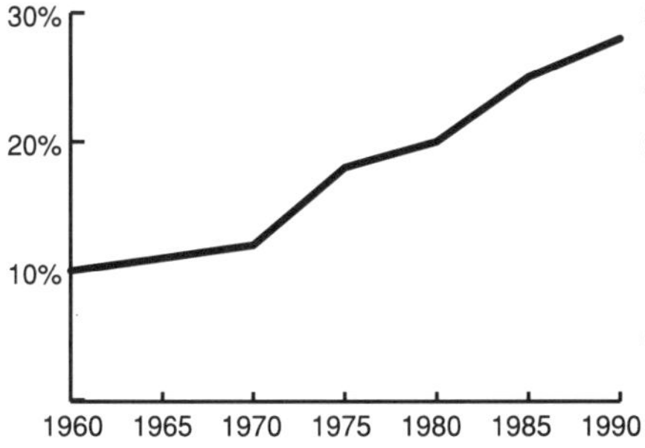


Source: US Bureau of the Census

## CHILD ABUSE

**Millions of Cases Reported**

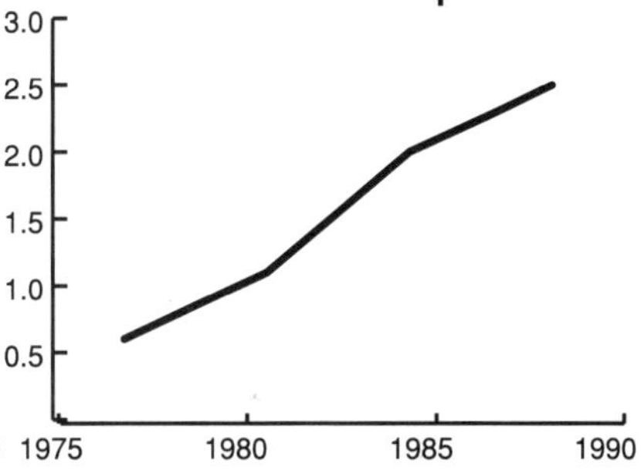


Source American Humane Association; National Committee for the Prevention of Child Abuse

## NUMBER OF CRIMES COMMITTED

**Millions of Violent Crimes** | **Millions of Total Crimes**

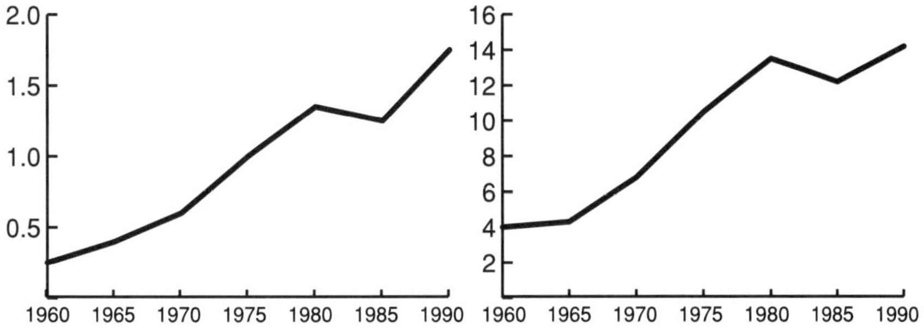


Source: FBI

**JUVENILE VIOLENT CRIME ARREST RATES**

**Violent Crime per 100,000**

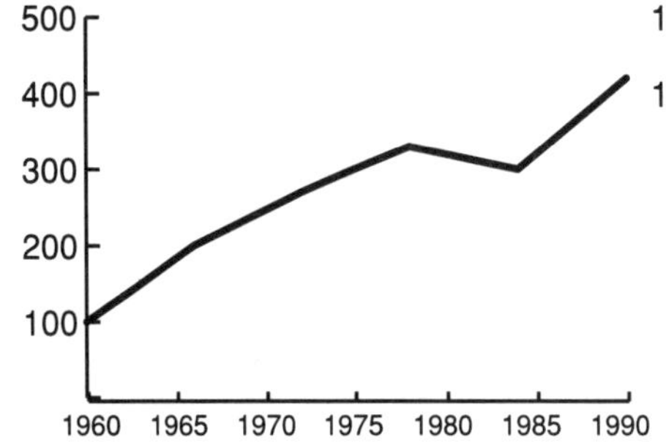


Source: FBI

**TEEN SUICIDE RATE**

**Suicides per 100,000 15-24 Year Olds**

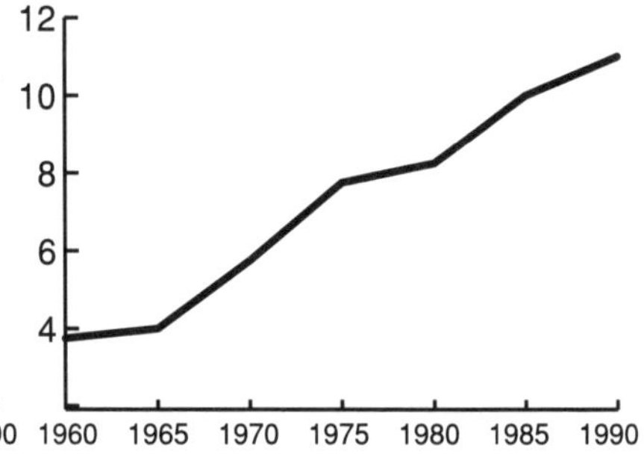


Source: National Center for Health Statistics

**SAT SCORES**

**SAT Combined Scores**

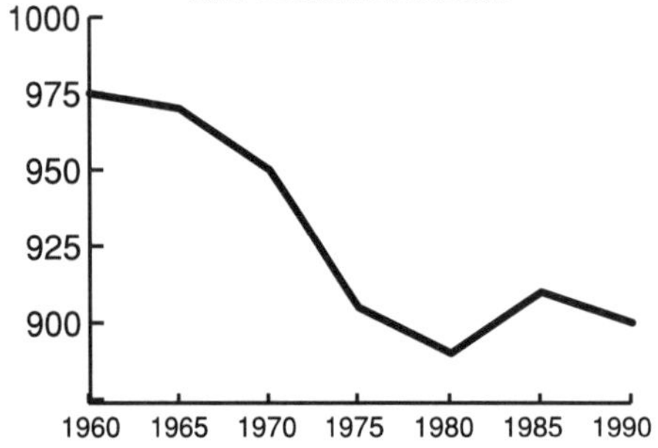


Source: The College Board

## Lying and Love as a Lifestyle

A recent survey by the Josephson Institute of Ethics found that lying, cheating, and stealing are now "an acceptable norm among high school and college students." Three out of five high schoolers and a third of all college students admit they cheated on an exam the past year, a third of the preppers and 16 percent of the collegians report stealing something during that same period, while 16 percent of the high school kids and 32 percent of the college students confessed to lying on a resume or job application.

People have always lied, but in the era of the electronic village, young and old alike see and hear the rich and famous lie in full TV color. From George ("read my lips") Bush to Richard ("I'm not a crook") Nixon, the Menendez brothers ("someone's killed our parents!"), and Susan Smith ("a man stole my children"), the nation has seen lying elevated to a tactical communications tool. Jack Benny remained a perpetual thirty-nine-year-old, actor David Leisure as "Joe Isuzu" made the line "he's lying" a potent sales tool for Isuzu cars, *Saturday Night Live* featured a pathological liar named Tommy Flanagan, and Olympic skater Tonya Harding's tearful denial of her plot to cripple arch competitor Nancy Kerrigan is a vivid memory.

Whether treated as comedy, drama, or political tragedy—and even when their lies were exposed—only one of these widely publicized liars went to jail (Susan Smith) and one (Tonya Harding) was rewarded with fame and accompanying wealth as she went on public appearance tours. The unstated social message is that lying pays off.

Numerous studies of the Hollywood elite reveal that they share a predominant worldview—one that evolved out of the 1960s "love generation." This mindset favors "alternative" lifestyles and advocates recreational drug use, sexual experimentation, nontraditional "families" that live together without legal or social sanction, and affirmative action for women, blacks, and other ethnic minorities. It champions homosexual and lesbian causes, bends over backwards for anything carrying the "environmental" label, and grows misty-eyed over third-world and socialist peoples "victimized" by "western imperialism" around the world.

On the negative side, most television movers and shakers detest all things military, America's European heritage, and Bible-based morality. They bear particular animosity for evangelical Christians and their "narrow" beliefs. Under the protective mantle of *entertainment*, they use dramatic, comic, documentary, and musical formats to popularize their ideas, values, and philosophy. As a result, today's television programming offers a relentlessly "politically correct" vision of America—a view that constantly tears down the middle-class, family-centered motifs of earlier generations.

## The Death of Family Viewing

The best example of this revolutionary change is the so-called "family viewing hour," the 8:00–9:00 P.M. period when the entire family supposedly gathers before the TV set and watches network shows that reflect idealism, innocence, and uplifting themes. But in the

1990s, the 8:00 o'clock hour has turned into a quagmire, as networks "liberalized" their guidelines and broadened their definitions of what constitutes "appropriate" early-evening fare.

"There is no 'family hour' anymore," laments Joah Ganz Cooney, founder of Children's Television Workshop. "The standards have fallen. I suspect it has to do with what has happened to the family in general. Family life has simply disintegrated along with the proliferation of media, and the lowest common denominator is finally prevailing."

Once upon a time, mom, dad, grandma, and the kids would circle the TV set after dinner and the network shows spoke to them. *The Waltons, The Brady Bunch, The Flying Nun, The Partridge Family, The Odd Couple, Happy Days, That Girl,* and *Little House on the Prairie* spun wholesome, clean-funny, uplifting yarns that primed the children for a sweet night's sleep. Even into the 1980s, the family hour was characterized by such comparatively noncontroversial programs as *Webster, The Facts of Life, The Cosby Show, Highway to Heaven, Full House,* and *Murder, She Wrote.* Then came the revolution.

## The New "Family Hours"

Parents sitting down with their kids to watch today's 8:00–9:00 P.M. shows find themselves hit by a bucket of sludge. NBC's *The Nanny,* for example, features a character who often makes racy sexual jokes. Fox's *Get Smart* episodes on Sunday evening features its lead characters doing slapstick stunts about copulation. The same network follows up on Mondays with *Melrose Place,* a soap opera about young men and women perpetually lusting after one another. On Thursdays, they run *Martin,* where the title character is constantly enmeshed in some kind of sexually provocative situation.

"All bets are off," notes Grant Tinker, former head of NBC. "The networks can do pretty much what they want. And that is even more true of cable. They seem to care very little about what kind of material is seen by the family."

The industry unashamedly confirms Tinker's view. Peter Jacobson, producer of CBS's *The Nanny,* insists that a show needs to be "hip and sexy" these days or it will fail. "You've got to be able to compete with the New Order or get left in the dust," he points out. "There's always room elsewhere for children's programming. It's up to the parents to judge what's appropriate. I believe it's okay to run anything on television any time. Freedom of choice is what made this country, and if you don't like it, you can change the channel."

Ed Hynes, director of the nonprofit group Morality In Media, feels we've reached the end of the road. "The death of family viewing on television is inevitable in a medium so dedicated to gratuitous sex, nudity, and foul language," he says. "Kids are being bombarded with smut, and not only in the evening. You see people grabbing their crotches and mooning one another during the daytime shows, too."

## Television and Christianity

When it comes to religion generally—and the Christian faith particularly—television is, in the words of former FCC Chairman Newton Minnow, a "veritable wasteland." At a time when four of five Americans profess belief in Jesus Christ and 100 million claim a "born-again" experience, and Bible churches experience dramatic growth, the world of television largely ignores or belittles the Christian faith.

A recent study conducted by researchers from Duke University Medical School, Northwestern University Medical Center, and the University of Dayton examined a random sample of one hundred network TV episodes. Out of 1,462 characters, only 82—or 5.6 percent—had an identifiable religious affiliation. Five of those eighty-two were members of religious cults while none were identified as being observant Jews. If few characters were notably religious, almost none were shown praying, attending church, or enjoying a group Bible study or other religious experience. The research report concludes, "The exploration of religion and spirituality in the lives of fictional characters is nearly invisible on network television."

A 1994 Media Research analysis studied 1,700 hours of prime-time programming and found religion alluded to only 253 times. That works out to only one mention of faith for every seven hours of prime-time programming. And when religion is referenced, it is usually demeaned, as when characters in NBC's *Cafe Americain* joked about having sex in a confessional booth or when an actor portraying a Protestant minister on CBS' *Picket Fences* quipped that the Vatican opposes contraception because a population explosion will enable Rome to dominate the world. Thomas Johnson, the study's co-author, observes, "We have a cultural disconnect between mainstream America and the creed of the Hollywood community."

The networks do occasionally throw a bone to Christian America—as in a Fox movie about the role of faith in former New York Jet linebacker Dennis Byrd's recovery from paralysis, or the later miniseries *Christy*. But William Fore, author of *Television and Religion*, thinks the small increase in shows showing faith as part of life is more an attempt to mollify the outrage of viewers and possible government regulators than an idealistic desire to fairly portray the role of religion in society.

## FIGHTING BACK

### Get Involved

We can try to change the television industry's way of doing business. Christian organizations have launched a frontal assault on the television industry itself, sponsoring periodic letter-writing and petition campaigns aimed at television network executives and corporate sponsors of objectionable programs. One has even instituted a nationwide boycott of sponsors' products to pressure them to withdraw their advertising from programs "which attack our values, our children, and our families." If you feel this is an effective tactic and wish to get involved, you may contact them directly as follows:

- American Family Association
  107 Parkgate, P.O. Drawer 2440
  Tupelo, Mississippi 38803

- Phyllis Schlafly
  Box 618
  Alton, Illinois 62002

### Recognize the Addiction

There is also the personal approach. Although we cannot guarantee what anyone else does, we can take full responsibility for what *we ourselves* choose to do. On that premise, then, we need to understand that television watching is an *addictive habit*. Reams of research conclusively show that TV viewing contains all the defining characteristics of *any* addiction, even including drug addiction. These include a mind-numbing effect that allows one to escape the stress of everyday realities, a powerful compulsion to repeat the experience, and telltale withdrawal symptoms encountered when one attempts to eliminate the addiction from one's life.

Bio-chemistry reveals just how we form our habits and addictions. Our nerve cells contain fibers for sending *out* messages (*axons)*, and other fibers for receiving *incoming* messages (*dendrites*). When we use axons frequently, they form little bumps called "boutons." The more boutons a nerve cell has, the easier it is to send out messages. Habits are simply actions we repeat over and over again that build boutons on our nerve cells, which makes it easier and easier to repeat that same action. Even when they are no longer used, boutons do not disappear. Because the old pathways are still there, we always risk the chance of falling back into an undesirable habit, just like an alcoholic who "falls off the wagon."

## Form New Habits

So how do we break free? We build new habits and responses that are stronger than the old ones. Before too long, more boutons will grow on the new pathway than the old one, and the "path" will grow deeper. Then it actually becomes easier to travel that new route and a new, more desirable habit is established.

Most people find it takes about three weeks to form one new habit. Applied to television, we can substitute other, more uplifting activities in place of just staring like dummies at the tube. For example, we can choose to lead a family devotional time. Or we can read classic stories to our younger children. Or we can all gather around the piano for singalongs, or play Pictograms. Or we can institute a family reading and study time after dinner so the kids can do their homework and we can start some of those fine books we've always meant to read but somehow have gathered dust on our bookshelves.

## Banish TV

Once we have weaned ourselves and the family from the habitual TV "fix," we can go one of two ways. The first is the more drastic decision to banish television from your house. Families that have taken this step recorded their family's reactions in daily logs. A common response was a feeling of aimlessness experienced most strongly the first week of the blackout. "We kind of hung around, not knowing what to do with ourselves . . . ." "Sometimes I'd just go and look at the [TV] set, even though it was off . . . ." During this initial withdrawal period, many reported feeling "disoriented" or "weird."

Then the substitute activities kicked in. The "no TV" families found themselves enjoying the following benefits:

- more interaction between children and adults;
- greater feeling of closeness as a family;
- children more eager to participate in household chores;
- more peaceful home atmosphere;
- more outdoor play and sports activities;
- children playing together more;
- longer meal times with more discussion;
- more reading by everyone;
- earlier bedtime and rising hours;
- improved relations between parents and other adults in family.

There were some negatives, too. Cold-turkey families report missing the fine, uplifting programs such as *Masterpiece Theater,* the Disney Channel, the Family Channel, or *The 700 Club.* Another minus was the fact that parents had lost one of their most effective disciplinary tools, namely the threat to withhold television viewing as punishment for bad behavior. Over time, however, most families who "go black" eventually opt to turn the set back on again, though this time with much more awareness of their viewing choices and time spent before the tube.

## Use Grace Control

Which brings us to a second alternative, what I would call "grace control." The overriding principle here is to use television instead of letting it use you. That is the standard we have set for our own home, and you may find it will work for you, too.

It requires that you set up new house rules and strictly observe them. From now on, you and you alone will be responsible for ensuring that your family will watch only those shows that are good, uplifting, useful, and appropriate for building up and upholding your family's Christian standards. (see Phil. 4:8)

That necessitates that you take total charge and become your own programmers. It does take some work and planning, but the benefits far outweigh the efforts. Each family's preferences will be unique, so I won't presume to specify what you should include in your viewing schedule. But whatever your family's choices, they need to be *limited as to time* and *fully supervised.*

An adult should sit with the kids during their viewing times to help them understand any complicated ideas, show them how commercials use tricks to excite them to want things that may be of poor quality or not good for them, and teach them that hitting, punching, and kicking is a bad way to solve problems and only makes things worse.

If at times that's not feasible, the very least you should require is that the children report on what they have viewed. Ask them to tell you why they thought they learned something new, or how to be a better person or in some other way benefited from their TV experience.

As for prime-time viewing, it's best not to watch as a family until you feel secure that you won't be "surprised" during "family" shows by unexpected allusions to sex, drugs, or other undesirable subjects. You can get some help from a guide called *Parents' Guide to Prime Time* published by the Media Research Center in Virginia. The booklet reviews all major programs from the four networks (ABC, NBC, CBS, and FOX) from 8:00–11:00 P.M. daily. The guide costs $7.95 and can be ordered from the Center by calling 800-672-1423.

# 8

# All the News that's Fit to View

*Pilate asked, "What is truth?"*

Luke 18:38

"It must be true, because I saw it on the news!"

We have all heard that argument time and time again from our well-meaning but ill-informed family and friends. If a "news" story came out of the well-paid mouths of Dan Rather, Tom Brokaw, or Peter Jennings, by definition it had to have been double-checked, verified, and written in stone. This belief is widely held by a large number of Americans. At the very least, the great majority are convinced that these bigger-than-life anchor stars are sincere, experienced journalists who give the people all the news that's fit to air, and that they present such news as fairly and in as much detail as time restraints allow.

That, my friends, is why so many of us carry around a notion of reality—the "truth of life"—that is as illusionary as Disneyland. The truth is that the "news" we see telecast each evening is an artfully crafted porridge of selective facts, half-facts, and lies, all skewed to serve a particular worldview and the very narrow interests that pay for it all.

## Media Manipulation Game

Anyone who relies on television news to draw his or her sense of what is going on in their community, the nation, and around the world is at best ignorant and at worst a fellow player in the media's manipulation game. Over time, and not very much of it, the words and images conveyed by television newscasts model to us what is and is not important enough to be considered "news" and tell us how we should feel about the information they deliver to us, if we want to be "decent and well-informed Americans."

In their landmark study *The Media Elite*, authors Lichter, Rothman & Lichter researched the worldviews of working newsroom reporters. The results surprised no one inside the business when it found a consistent pattern of beliefs. For example, half these opinion-makers embrace the notion that government should guarantee everyone's jobs. Half blame society for its alienated citizens; two thirds insist that government should reduce the income gap between rich and poor; 80 percent demand strong affirmative action for blacks; 97 percent say government must not place any restrictions on sex; 90 percent champion abortion; the majority think adultery is fine and only one in four feels that homosexuality is wrong.

Co-author S. Robert Lichter offers this sobering conclusion: "If there is one thing that has changed American politics in the 20th century, it is the media. Politicians no longer fear the publishers of newspapers; they fear the network anchors and the investigative reporters. They have become the arbiters of political life, the interpreters rather than mere reporters of news. They don't simply tell you what is happening in the world; they tell you what you should think about it."

## Politically Correct News

"Political correctness" is the phrase used to describe "what we should think about what we hear." Veteran reporter Robert Novak, host of CNN's *The Capital Gang*, notes that journalists today express their opinions in presenting the news, the most extreme example being network television, where media operatives decide whether a news report will be covered at all and what "slant" shall be used to present it. Novak noted a series of "liberal axioms" held almost universally by the national media, some of which follow:

- The rich—defined as including middle-class Americans—are getting richer and the poor are getting poorer.
- Americans are undertaxed, so the government should raise rates, especially for those who earn more, save more, and invest more.

- There is a nationwide health crisis, and only the government can solve it by establishing universal coverage for health insurance.
- The "religious right"—a term that lumps together ordinary believers with a few extremists—is a serious menace to American society.
- Being pro-choice is not enough, there should be absolutely no interference with the reproductive rights of women.
- To support school choice, through vouchers or credits, is to support the destruction of all public education.
- It is far better for the armed forces of the United States to be under multinational command than for them to be controlled by our own military commanders.
- Conservatism is a narrow, selfish philosophy; liberalism is more broad, far-seeing, unprejudiced, and compassionate.

When it comes to religion, television network news shows have virtually blacked out its coverage of American faith. In a nation where most people regularly attend religious services and believe in God, the Media Research Center reports that "religion and religious issues are hardly ever mentioned, much less covered on network television morning and evening news and magazine shows. Analyzing 18,000 nightly news shows in 1993 by ABC, CBS, NBC, CNN, and PBS, the Center found only 212 stories—just over one percent—that dealt with religious content. Of these, only 134 were taped segments featuring a reporter; the rest were brief anchor reads. And even of those religion stories that did make the news, the majority (60 percent) were confined to Pope John Paul II's visit to the United States.

"Stories on hot-button issues such as abortion and homosexuality are never done from a religious viewpoint," the study noted. "Religious figures are regularly portrayed as reactionary roadblocks while their positive influences are rarely covered. News shows portray them as 'cold, intolerant and oppressive.'" Repeating the study in 1994 found that news coverage of religion, characterized as "meager" the year before, had actually decreased even more. "Network news continues to operate on the false and ignorant premise that good news is no news, even if it affects the overwhelming majority of Americans in a positive way," the report concluded.

## Why Christians Are Feared

So why should we be surprised when the Gallup poll reveals that Americans consider people who hold strong evangelical Christian convictions as threatening and anathema? Gallup's field interviewers asked people all across America to rate those whom they would like to have as neighbors. Near the bottom of popularity, well behind Catholics, Jews, blacks, Koreans, Hispanics, Vietnamese, Russians, and unmarried couples, came the Protestant "religious fundamentalists." Only members of outright religious cults were found to be more despised.

So what are their motives? Is there a global conspiracy behind it all, pulling the strings of mass communications? A number of theories currently make the rounds, claiming to know and expose the powers that rule the airwaves. The most persistent one links international banking with groups like the Council on Foreign Relations, the Bilateral Commission, the Bilderbergers, and the Group of Eight—all conspiring to unify the world under one monetary system, one satellite-linked communications umbrella, one political order, and one great ecumenical religion.

Let me here relate a bit of my own experience. For many years I worked for *TV Guide*, covering the television industry. During that time, editors suggested certain "slants" for the stories I reported. They might, for example, ask for a personality profile, with the added urging to "really get that swine!" Other times, without any explanation that made sense, completed assignments were "spiked"—set aside and never published—even though the research had been solid and the story itself compelling. In all my time there, no one ever sat down with me and explained precisely how I should think or write about the subjects I covered. There was, however, an unspoken set of assumptions that were never articulated. In practice, a new writer starting with the *Guide* went one of two ways—either he or she *intuited* what was "acceptable," and thereby survived, or he or she just "didn't get it" and was quickly off the scene.

That, I believe, is how the entire system operates. Everyone involved goes along to get along, and if you are too "dumb" to know how to play the game—a game whose rules are unwritten but tacitly understood—you do not get to play. It is possible that at the highest levels, conscious collusion does take place, but I could not testify to that directly. So, on the premise that anyone but an eyewitness is a false witness, I will say nothing more on the conspiracy theories except this one thing. If you live your life tied down by conspiracy theories, you end up depressed and unable to make any difference in a troubled world that needs all the help it can get.

## Ratings Rule the News

Drawing on my direct experience working in and covering television as a reporter, I can testify on those aspects of television news I can document and prove. Earlier in this book, I described the powerful role played by the Nielsen ratings in deciding what gets on the air and stays there. I also showed how powerful emotions like sex, terror, and sensationalized gossip pushed up the ratings numbers and so made more money for the networks and local broadcasters.

The same principles apply to television news. In some ways, the TV news "business" is even more vulnerable to ratings pressures, since news is the "public service" anchor around which the rest of the entertainment programs swirl. While the network news telecasts are measured daily and reported every two weeks, local news shows measure viewing every three months in quarterly "sweeps." And you can always tell when a sweeps period is coming up.

On-air teasers show snatches of film footage and promise to outrage or shock you when you turn on the five, six, or eleven o'clock news later that day. While film segments show a bearded hulk shrouded in shadow, huge graphics scream "BEHIND THE SCENES WITH THE MANSON GANG!" Or you may see a side view of a topless young woman with a tag reading "THE HORRIBLE REALITY OF BREAST CANCER." Or during a late afternoon talk show, the newsroom breaks in with a shot of a field reporter shown peering at three motionless bodies lying side by side in the morgue: "These are the latest victims of the westside slasher. Latest developments just ahead on the six o'clock news!"

The first commandment of television "journalism" teaches that good news is boring. Most viewers, particularly the middle-American Nielsen viewers, get hooked on the juicy sex-violence-scandal stories. And, frankly, so do most of the rest of us, even God-fearing church-going Christians. Sensationalism has become so pervasive that it is sometimes hard to tell the difference in content between the news half-hours and their spinoffs, the television tabloid shows like *Inside Edition, Hard Copy,* and *20/20*. The news has become a virtual national gallery of depravity.

Who can forget 1995's real-life soap-opera obsession, the televised O. J. Simpson double-murder trial? Or 1994's fascination with Heidi Fleiss, the "Madam to the Stars"? Or the mutilation ordeal of Lorena and John Wayne Bobbitt? Readers can undoubtedly recall their own examples of overblown, overcovered, and oversensationalized "news" stories in their own television market area. The fact is that Americans have an inordinate fascination for famous personalities, particularly when they fall from grace. This feeding frenzy for juicy gossip is a trait long recognized by foreign observers. Over 150 years ago, French politician and social commentator Alexis de Tocqueville, after an extended visit to the U.S., wrote, "Americans are uncommonly drawn to gossip, most likely to prove to themselves that prominent men are no better than themselves."

## The News Anchor Cult

Sometimes overlooked in this cult of personality are the bigger-than-life network news anchors, those "talking heads" we turn to before dinner to find out what in the world has been going on while we were at work. Over the years most of us choose favorites among them, whether it be Tom Brokaw, Dan Rather, Peter Jennings, Bernard Shaw, or Robert McNeill/Tom Lehrer. But even if we, the news consumers, may not be consciously aware of how strongly our personality choices impact our network perceptions and preferences, the network bosses know down to the last rating decimal place how vitally their on-camera "news readers" affect the ratings numbers of their enterprises.

Anyone who doubts the huge impact of these anchor personalities on overall network success need only look at their multi-million dollar annual salaries to settle the issue. As an example, Diane Sawyer signed a $7 million contract with ABC to do weekly news-magazine segments. Each of the afore-mentioned anchor stars have multi-million dollar annual salaries, infinitely greater than the top journalists working for daily newspapers who feel fortunate when they break the $75,000-a-year level.

With the fate of their entire networks hanging in the balance, corporate brass is not content to trust their own judgment when it comes to hiring and firing news anchors or changing the style of their news shows. Just as Lever Brothers tests its detergents, networks run periodic tests on their news personalities, both those working as network anchors or fill-ins and any up-and-coming talent appearing at local TV stations.

In recent years, networks have turned to ever more exotic techniques to gain the upper hand in their newscaster ratings wars. One such test is called "G.S.R." for galvanic skin response. It's not new, having been used for years as part of the standard polygraph, or lie-detector, test. What GSR does is measure emotional responses. When we are stirred up, our hearts beat faster, we breathe more heavily, and we perspire. GSR is an automatic reaction, no more controllable than a sneeze or eyeblink. And it's easy to measure, because dry skin is a poor conductor of electricity but sweaty flesh gets those electrons racing. By measuring how much current flows from our bodies, researchers can tell how turned on we are by whatever we are looking at or listening to. What it does not measure is which emotion is causing the reaction, since to a GSR machine, fear, love, hate, envy, and desire all look the same—a rising peak on a basically flat trace line.

But in the TV-ratings derby, identifying the emotion really does not matter. One emotion works pretty much as well as another in keeping viewers hooked and coming back for more, resulting in big ratings numbers. Emotion is one way network executives can red-flag newcomers who possess "presence" or star quality. In practice, the researchers round up a hundred typical viewers who are paid $35 apiece to attend a special screening at a hotel. Once seated, the volunteers are fitted with electric sensors attached to their fingers—two metal plates bound to the pads of their index and ring fingers of the same hand. Once the audience has been wired, the houselights dim and the show starts with recent videotapes of newscasters. During each segment, GSR meters trace the skin currents; after each segment, the houselights go on and participants are provided with questionnaires.

These forms ask participants to assess these personalities. Are they friendly, cold, warm, or distant? Too aggressive, not aggressive enough, or just right? Are they shifty or believable? Attractive, plain, dull, or enthusiastic? Good diction, syntax, and vocabulary? Do they remind you of anyone you know? Then on to the next tape and the next newscaster. At the conclusion of the session, the researchers collect the questionnaires, tabulate them, run them through a computer, relate the GSR reactions to the questionnaires, and issue a report with conclusions and recommendations.

Directions might include such advice as "Fire her!" or "Team him with a less aggressive woman, preferably young, blonde and Nordic," or "This guy needs to relax. Teach him to adopt a chatty approach with his co-anchors, weathermen, and sportscasters." Occasionally the executives may call in a team of psychologists who go on weekend "retreats" with the news people and subject them to "relationary workouts." In this form of group encounter, the consultants goad their subjects to spill their emotional guts, purge innermost secrets, work through animosities and learn "teamwork and mutual support" techniques. The hope is that this exercise will produce "harmonious on-air interaction" that will make viewers feel more comfortable, more secure, and therefore more likely to grow channel-loyal.

## The Art of Lying

But such new age hi-jinks are relatively innocuous when compared to the more basic defects of the news business. To put it straight and simple, the national TV news purveyors—those who collect, choose, write, and read news in front of the cameras—are willing players in the game of lying practiced by news reporters and news makers. Paul H. Weaver, a Harvard Ph. D. in political science and former editor at *Fortune* magazine and public affairs editor for Ford Motor Company, outlines the way the American "newsbiz" operates in his book *News and the Culture of Lying: How Journalism Really Works.*

Weaver describes the process like this: "Most things covered by the media as news events are, in fact, conceived, scripted, and performed by the newsmakers with the knowledge of the news reporters. The media are not the fly on the wall they pretend to be. They don't look down on things in the real world and cover them without influencing them. Because of their concept of news, the news media cue and give a script for the newsmakers to follow. The two have a tight little relationship in which they share a secret and that secret is that what they project to the public as real events and news is actually a fabrication, a performance, a fiction."

## Creating a News "Crisis"

In the major media, particularly the television networks, news is defined as a story of "crisis—crisis and emergency response." That is the kind of event that gets coverage and that is how newsmakers—

politicians, corporate chiefs, special interests and advocates of any kind—must package their objectives if they want to get coverage. When President Clinton came to present his health care program, he did not address some of the problems associated with our medical coverage as it now exists but instead he announced that we have a "crisis," with all the urgency he might have used for revealing an atomic attack or a 10-point Richter scale earthquake.

All journalism schools teach aspiring reporters that this "crisis" format and their rules about "objective reporting" is the right way to present the news. When reporters get into the newsrooms, they learn that's what gets them rewarded in their careers and praised by their bosses. So they believe they are doing the news "professionally." Add to this the fact that the "new guard" TV field people are "vid-kids" who are much more interested in filming, editing, and graphics than they are with such niceties as "the truth." But there is a growing sense of uneasiness between what TV reporters show and tell the public and what they really know is the "reality of the story."

News magazines like *60 Minutes* or *Prime Time Live* are notorious for their on-camera exposes, where hustlers and flim-flam artists are exposed for all the world to see. But the "truth of the story" is almost never told. For example, *Prime Time Live* assigned reporters Chris Wallace (son of Mike) and a young staffer named Julie to do a story on sex discrimination. So they visited a car lot and a golf course, where hidden cameras captured their quest for unequal treatment. At the car dealer, Chris gets a test drive and a lower price than Julie, who isn't even allowed to take the car off the lot. At the golf course, he gets a 9:35 morning tee time while Julie has to wait until 11:40.

Then Chris moves in for a close-up kill. Confronting the offender with proof of unequal treatment, the startled salesman offered a lame excuse. "Prices can be different from one hour to the next," he mumbled. The report concluded with an implied conclusion that this sort of gender bias is widespread and rampant. But when *Prime Time* itself was later confronted, they admitted that their hidden cameras had uncovered such discrimination in less than 10 percent of the episodes they had filmed. By not reporting on the "rest of the story," they left the viewer with a false notion of the truth.

## The Nagging Truth

Dr. Weaver notes, "All journalists have a nagging sense that the story they've narrated on TV does not fully reflect their experience of the story. The sense that they're not telling it all is because they know they're leaving out the process, the interactions, the offstage interaction between journalist and newsmaker that's really the story behind the public story they then produce and put out on the air. In that sense, they know they're lying.

"Another problem is that the public conception of the way a news organization works is misguided. Most people speak of journalism as the product of the working journalist, and they leave out the most important fact that the working journalist has a boss. He's carefully supervised, edited, controlled, rewritten, and managed from hour to hour and day to day. Nothing gets broadcast on a news program that several editors haven't scrutinized and validated. So the key figure to understand in a news organization isn't the reporter; it's the boss—the big editor and his lieutenants, the sub-editors."

No events better illustrate the way today's newsmakers control the mass communication process than the way President Clinton bypassed the national media by staging carefully crafted electronic events. Using a band of young techno-addicts, the Clinton White House represented a new wave of manipulating voter sentiment—the Digital Democrats versus the old Analog Republicans. Bypassing the old media, they exploited new, safer ways of getting political propaganda to the people by using CNN's *Larry King Show*, televised satellite speeches, and "town hall meetings" that featured staged "spontaneous" questions and comments from the audience.

For example, when CNN hosted a NAFTA debate between Vice President Al Gore and Ross Perot over *Larry King Live*, of the 2.2 million telephone callers who tried to get on the air with their opinions, only eight succeeded. And all eight were later exposed as CNN employees, carefully scripted to convey a wave of "popular support" for the controversial measure—which was later passed by both houses of the Congress and signed into law by the President.

## Deception Is the Rule, Not the Exception

Deception is a prevailing aspect of TV news coverage. On its most basic level, weathercasters who point to giant screens alive with maps, moving fronts, and whooshing jet streams, are actually standing in front a blank wall. The spectacular images are inserted electronically before the program is sent out to your TV set. News reporters are often shown wearing journalist raincoats, standing in front of the White House or Supreme Court or other recognizable governmental buildings. In fact, many times they put on their coats in the studio and have the engineers plug in the Capitol background during the editing. At the 1992 Democratic Convention, remote-controlled cameras led viewers to believe ABC's Peter Jennings was reporting from a box high above the floor when in fact he was buried in a studio under the stands.

But creating illusions for the sake of "immediacy" is the least harmful aspect of televised subterfuge. The real harm is done by their ongoing "exposés" in the name of protecting the public. Recently the networks launched a crusade against the American automobile industry, using faked footage and staged crashes to falsely indict major manufacturers. *Dateline NBC* rigged a General Motors truck to explode by placing incendiary devices inside the vehicle and presented it as a bona fide structural defect self-destructing. *NBC Nightly News* showed footage of hundreds of dead fish from Clearwater National Forest in Idaho, reporting how clear-cutting practices by the timber industry had contaminated the streams and killed the fish. In fact, those fish were not from Clearwater and they were not even dead, merely stunned beforehand by forestry rangers so they could count them and check their health—which was excellent, thank you.

Not to pick on NBC, CBS' *60 Minutes* ran a feature about the Audi 5000, the car that supposedly launched into sudden acceleration even while the driver's foot was down on the brake. Presenter Ed Bradley invited viewers to "watch the pedal go down by itself." What Bradley never told his audience was that a technician had drilled a hole in the car's transmission and pumped compressed air into it. The tank of air, with its attached hose, sat on the front passenger seat of the doctored vehicle so the driver could trigger the event while the cameras ignored the tank and focused on the gas pedal.

With the auto industry open game, ABC televised its own phony assault against Ford Motor Co. on *20/20*. The Ford Pinto had been criticized because of its supposed tendency to catch fire when hit from behind. The show stressed the point that not just Pintos but many other Ford cars were rolling fire traps. The program's shocking episode showed a Ford sedan being rear-ended at 55 mph and immediately bursting into flames. Of course, the presenters never told the viewers that the car was wired with incendiary bombs set to go off at the slightest impact.

Not to leave the super-elite Public Broadcast System out of the swindle game, the network recently ran a documentary called "The Liberators," dramatizing how black American soldiers in World War II liberated the Dachau and Buchenwald Nazi death camps. Nominated for an Academy Award, the PBS executives did not see fit to pull it for consideration even after Holocaust survivors denied being rescued by "all-black liberators" and after members of the black regiment that supposedly freed the starving Jews admitted their outfit had never been near either one of the camps.

## Lying in the Name of "The Cause"

Beyond factual misrepresentations, television news often lies to further its own "politically correct" views. When the "World Population Conference" was held in Cairo in late 1994, the network news reported that "World population is exploding! This represents an unprecedented threat to the planet." Solutions proposed by newscasters included crisis birth control and abortion, and they named fundamentalist Christians, Catholics, and Moslems as those getting in the way. The real story, reported by the *Wall Street Journal* and *U.S. News & World Report*, stated that world population growth has been matched by food production, that population growth historically follows economic development, and that voluntary use of contraceptives has been a failure wherever tried.

Such "cry wolf" stories are standard operating procedure for network news departments. Other examples include the Alar pesticide scare of the early nineties. The ubiquitous Ed Bradley announced on *Sixty Minutes* a few years ago, "The most potent cancer-causing agent in our food supply is a substance sprayed on apples to keep them on the trees longer and make them look better." That statement launched a nationwide panic, with major media reporting that as little as a few bites of Alar-treated apples could cause instant death. Sales of apples plummeted, forcing farmers to dump their crops and costing the apple industry over $100 million in losses. Two years later, a panel of international scientists analyzed test results and concluded that Alar was perfectly safe to eat as a trace residue in food. But the harm had been done, and Uniroyal—Alar's manufacturer—pulled its product from the market. To this day, Americans still believe that Alar is a deadly poison.

## The Most Terrified Society

Today, the wealthiest, longest-lived, best protected society in the world is also the world's most terrified. Life expectancy in the United States is 75.5 years, up 13 years since 1940 and over double what it was in 1900. Since 1970, the infant death rate has been cut in half, heart-disease deaths have dropped 27 percent and stroke deaths are down 44 percent. Polio and smallpox, which not too many years ago decimated children, today are virtually unknown. Yet psychiatrists and psychologists are enjoying booming business, precisely because we are arguably the most frightened, anxious society in history.

Why? Because thc news media, with television leading the way, are in the "outrage business." They constantly warn us about benzene in Perrier water, Alar in apples, and asbestos in our schoolhouses. They inform us that popcorn, margarine, red meat, ethnic foods, and the air we breathe all contribute to heart failure and cancer. Aluminum and zinc cause Alzheimer's disease; alcohol and caffeine poison our blood vessels; cellular phones, Dioxin, high-power lines, computer monitors, aerosols poking holes in the ozone layer all pose risks—nothing seems safe and healthy any more. Environmental reporter David Ropiek admits that TV reporters "are seduced into playing up what is dramatic. They say that everything you eat will kill you, every breath will poison you. That profoundly colors the public psyche. We start living like Chicken Little's being told the sky is falling."

A 1992 study by researchers Robert Lichter, Stanley Rothman, and Mark Mills analyzed 1,147 stories on cancer and found that major broadcast media focused on manufactured carcinogens that scientists generally deemed "low risk" while almost totally ignoring the natural occurring carcinogens they universally found to be "high risk." For example, one cup of coffee contains ten grams of natural cancer-causing agents—the amount the average American consumes in pesticide residues in an *entire year*. According to biochemist Bruce Ames at the University of California at Berkeley, the average American ingests 10,000 times more natural pesticides than manufactured pesticide residues every single day.

A flagrantly false perception has been drawn of the AIDS threat. The past few years, hundreds of TV newscasts have drummed into our collective heads that whereas AIDS began in the homosexual community, it has now become a major heterosexual threat, infecting married couples and dating partners alike. The truth is totally opposed to that claim. The latest series of annual statistics from the Centers for Disease Control clearly reveal the lie—only 6 percent of all U. S. AIDS cases involve heterosexual contact, and this figure has remained stable over a five-year period. AIDS today, as before, remains overwhelmingly a homosexual disease, followed by bisexuals and intravenous drug users.

## Viewers Are Fed Up

In issue after issue, television news presents a false picture of reality. The only hopeful note comes from disillusioned viewers, who more and more appear to be getting the message that something truly stinks in the "news biz." Following the 1992 mid-term elections when Americans elected a Republican House for the first time in fifty years, exit polls conducted for the Times Mirror organization found that three out of five voters gave the news media a grade of "C" ("fair") or lower for its election coverage. Only 38 percent said the media merited an "A" or "B" for "good" or "excellent" coverage.

A later 1993 nationwide survey by the *Los Angeles Times* revealed a long-time trend to Americans losing confidence in news media generally, and in television news in particular. Overwhelming, people named "truth," "honesty," and "accuracy" as the most important qualities required of those dispensing the news (87 percent out of 100 percent). But when asked whether the incident of NBC's staging the truck explosion cited earlier in this chapter was commonplace or uncommon, 56 percent replied "common" and only 36 percent said "uncommon." In 1985 28 percent believed network TV news did a "very good job" in terms of impartiality, eight years later that figure had slumped to 21 percent. Two out of three felt that news media gave more coverage to stories that support their viewpoint and three out of five believed the news media has "too much influence over what happens today."

Unfortunately, vocal criticism has not materially changed the way we Americans inform ourselves. In the same study where they had previously chastised newspapers and television as losing "fairness and impartiality" in their reporting, with seeming perversity almost three out of four still name "network television news" as the place where they get their "best information about current events these days." Half depend on daily newspapers, even though they acknowledge them as biased, while only one in ten or less named alternative media like news magazines, talk shows, and radio news shows. The net result is a society where most people sense they are being misinformed but have no alternative plan to remedy their programmed ignorance.

## FIGHTING BACK

In the final analysis, you, and I and everyone else in this nation has to bear responsibility for the way we process information. Whether you learn something from your husband or wife, your children or their teachers, your favorite uncle or your next-door neighbor—or the television network news department—it is up to you to consider it, dismiss it, perhaps believe it, and ultimately base your life decisions on it. Information is power, and for that very reason, it is vital that you and your family monitor and evaluate the reliability of every "fact" you permit to be fed into your minds.

So the real question remains: how can we best do this?

### Stop Watching Television News

Some people have taken the self-censoring route. They simply do not watch the network evening news and choose one of two alternatives. The most extreme is to decide that since you cannot do anything about the ethnic strife in Eastern Europe or the latest machination by the Federal Reserve Board, you would do better to replace the daily evening network "news fix" and the local newscasts with other family activities.

For example, you may want to use that hour for a Bible study using a good devotional or perhaps spend the after-dinner time to share the day's happenings, discuss them in terms of Biblical principles, and pray for one another's concerns.

Or you might want to watch some good videos together, either for simple enjoyment and relaxation or to organize a discussion around their themes and stories. Perhaps you may want to listen to good music or play some table games like Pictionary or Scrabble. Those families who have adopted this sort of "news blackout" report that they experience a decrease in anxiety over world affairs and feel less fear about the possibilities of being mugged, murdered, or attacked while shopping or driving home from work.

## Watch with a Jaundiced Eye

In the heyday of the old Soviet Union, there was a popular saying about their network news media called *Pravda* (Russian for "the truth"), "There is no *pravda* in *Pravda*." I do not think that we can apply that *total* principle to NBC, CBS, ABC, and CNN—yet. But if you really hope to develop a serious measure of reality in the information conveyed by the network news telecasts, you must view and listen through the lens of *real politik*—the actual way things work and not the illusion we are being fed.

*Beware of the anchor's "lead-in."* When viewing a news story, take particular notice of the "lead-in," the one-or two-sentence introduction used by the news anchor to "tell you what you are about to see." This is invariably where the bias or "slant" is injected, an editorial comment under the guise of straight reporting. For example, the lead-in to a story about an abortion protest might be—"Today in St. Louis, Bible-carrying protesters sparked a near-riot outside a clinic where a doctor was shot last month."

Watch to see whether the following film footage matches the news anchor's description. Most always, you will be shown a scene where a dozen pro-life people are harangued by whistle-blowing, chanting, sign-carrying lesbians, homosexuals, and pro-abortion zealots. Based on the actual presentation, any "near-riot" condition would apply more fittingly to those supporting abortion rights and not the "Bible-carrying protesters," only one of whom may be shown in the report. In today's tele-news, the term "Bible carrying" is a perjorative shorthand tag for "evangelical Christians." Incidentally, in most instances, these kinds of intercept protests are organized and attended by members of "Operation Rescue," a predominately Catholic group.

*Never take a news report at face value.* As you view, always ask yourself what is the "intentionality" behind this story? Because newscasters are constantly involved in a game of creating fabrications that support their view of the event or crisis, you must develop a state of mind that asks, "What message does the news reporters wish me to take away from this story? Why has the news editor chosen this particular event to highlight, and how does that advance his personal or corporate agenda? And what are the actual, incontrovertible facts of this story, divorced from the slant and editorializing?"

In effect, you adopt a practice of "deconstructing" the news as you watch it. You get rid of the pieces and comments that are stage management and manipulation, while hanging onto the core of the story that represents the facts of the matter. A good example was the Clinton health-care proposal in 1994. Behind all the hysteria of "crisis" and the "rush to quick passage" of Clinton's plan, which was essentially centralized socialized medicine, there were some valid facts and discussions we needed to hear, such as which Americans were not covered by any insurance, possible solutions, and cost factors.

There is always room for improvement in our society, and there are problems that we, as citizens, need to know about, think about and come to reasoned-out decisions about. The problem stems from the fact that the sources providing us the information on which we base our decisions deliver false perceptions, false scenarios of cause-and-effect, and even false "facts" that we carry about in our minds. Particularly widespread is their use of selective quotes to condemn a public figure ("Read my lips" for President/candidate George Bush), or showing a hand-picked spokesperson to represent a total religious group (a mainline minister who "speaks for the evangelical church.")

## Find Alternative News Sources

Once it was possible for the television networks, their affiliates, and the major newspapers—the "media gatekeepers"—to absolutely control the flow of information to the American people. But the 1990s are characterized by a host of rival information sources—cable systems with "narrow-casted" specialized programming, home-satellite dishes with hundreds of channels, computer bulletin boards and Internet forums, and "talk radio" as a purveyor of alternative news views and reports.

Most areas can receive *The 700 Club*, which starts each weekday show with a news roundup and news features of interest to Christian families. *The 700 Club* can be found on cable systems on The Family Channel. Homes not wired for cable can find *The 700 Club* carried by the Trinity Broadcasting Network and other independent Christian broadcasters.

Other Christian television shows that present news of interest from a Biblical and prophetic perspective include *Prophesy in the News* (found on Family Net Satellite Network), *Peter LaLonde* (Trinity Broadcasting), and *Jack Van Impe* (Trinity Broadcasting).

Christian radio stations can be found in most major cities and suburbs, on radio carrier channels over cable systems, on audio carriers via satellite, and on shortwave channels. Talk show hosts on these stations frequently review news of interest to Christians and book guests who report on issues often "spiked" by the major secular media. In Los Angeles, *Duffy Live from L.A.* presents a lively three hours daily that does a good job in covering politics, international affairs, and Christian-interest news.

Naturally, even when getting our information from Christian sources, we need to make sure we do not check our brains while watching or listening. There will be some doctrinal differences and biblical perspectives we may take issue with, but at least you can feel reasonably confident about their motives.

Surprisingly, secular radio today offers a number of syndicated talk shows that look at the news from a conservative or even Judeo-Christian perspective. Among those I have found useful as news sources are *The Ollie North Show* and the *Rush Limbaugh Show* (both radio and television). Be wary of becoming just another "dittohead," however. Evaluate everything you see and hear. Ultimately, you are responsible for determining what actually is "the truth, the real truth and nothing but the truth, so help you God!"

Another secular source I have found extremely useful for understanding geo-political events unfolding in the Middle East is the international edition of *The Jerusalem Post* (this world-renowned newspaper offers a free three-issue sample subscription on request to Jerusalem Post Subscriptions, P O Box 1981, Danbury, CT 06813-9825).

Finally, a variety of newspapers, magazines, and newsletters serve to keep us apprised of the full facts of many stories. Often, they serve as clearinghouses, having scoured both American and international wire services and overseas sources. Among these are *The Christian Report, The Washington Times* (secular), *The Prophetic Observer* newsletter, *Prophesy in the News* magazine, and *Midnight Call* magazine.

I would also include *Moody, Focus on the Family* magazine and Christian Broadcasting Network's *Fact* sheets. Sadly, there is one long-time Christian resource I have found notably uneven and sometimes less than courageous in its coverage of evangelical Christian happenings, namely *Christianity Today*. In recent years this magazine seems to have sacrificed the unleavened Biblical approach to reporting for a more mushy ecumenical umbrella that in many instances waters down or even distorts journalistic realities in order not to offend its broad constituencies.

# 9

# The Top-40 Nightmare

*The man that hath no music in himself, Nor is not mov'd with concord of sweet sounds, Is fit for treasons, stratagems and spoils.*

William Shakespeare

An old adage says, "Sing me the songs of a generation and I'll tell you the soul of their times."

All of us can recall some pop tunes from our own youth, "the soul of our times" that helped form our values. For those who entered adolescence in the aftermath of World War II, naive exuberance characterized much of the popular music. The medium was radio, mostly late-night radio. Almost every city had its own equivalent of a "dawn patrol," where DJs punctuated their record plays with intimate late-night requests. "This next tune is for Lorrie from Joe, who understands and wants you back, Lorrie, it's the Mills Brothers singing *I Guess I'll Get the Papers and Go Home*."

Over the years and generations, some things never change. One is the sleeping habits of youngsters entering puberty. As their hormones kick in, teenagers tend to stay up late and linger later in bed the next morning. Research conducted at Brown University finds that this late-to-bed late-to-rise syndrome is not just ornery rebellion but actually caused by a special teenage biological clock.

Another thing has not changed, as well. Teenagers moon over romantic love tunes. Circa 1950, the songs we hummed and danced to included *The Things We Did Last Summer, Nature Boy,* and *You Ain't Nuthin' but a Hound Dog.*

The lyrics of one typical love song makes the point sharply— "Unforgettable" by Irving Gordon (© 1951).

> Unforgettable in every way,
> And forevermore that's how you'll stay,
> That's why, darling, it's incredible,
> That someone so unforgettable,
> Thinks that I am unforgettable, too.

Now leap ahead a generation to those who entered puberty during the apocalyptic, psychedelic sixties. Where earlier composers came mostly from Broadway traditions and were trained by show-tune forms, by the 1960s most top-40 tunes flowed from writers either members of or linked to rock groups. Indisputably, the most popular of all the sixties pop groups were the Beatles, whose *Sgt. Pepper's Lonely Hearts Club Band* remains one of the best-selling albums of all time.

While the forties and fifties reflected youthful innocence and optimism, the sixties mood shifted to questioning cynicism. A cut from the *Revolver* LP presents a perfect icon of those years— "Eleanor Rigby" by John Lennon and Paul McCartney (© 1966 Northern Songs Ltd).

> Father McKenzie, writing the words of a sermon
> that no one will hear, . . .
> Eleanor Rigby, died in the church and was
> buried along with her name,
> Nobody came.
> Father McKenzie, wiping the dirt from his
> hands
> As he walks from the grave,
> No one was saved. . . .
> Aaaaah, all the lonely people.

## Today's Harvest of Rebellion

If the forties and fifties were naive, and the sixties and seventies cynical, the eighties and nineties marked the harvest of rebellion, anarchy, and despair. Is that too strong a characterization? You be the judge.

When it comes to today's teenage music, "angry rock" is king. From "punk" to "heavy metal," the melodies are minimal, the electronics harsh, the rhythms incessant and relentless, and the lyrics—those that describe interactions between the sexes and not just killing cops or rebelling against society—focus heavily on raw sex, rape, pain and death.

Even as the sixties sounds were transplanted from England via the Beatles and Rolling Stones, so the eighties mode came to America in the form of a British punk rock group, the Sex Pistols featuring Johnny Rotten and Sid Vicious. The group was thrown together as a cynical ripoff of a rage-and-anarchy trend by rock promoter Malcolm McLaren. Hyping the band as "bigger than the Beatles," McLaren brought them to the U.S. to the enthusiastic hoopla of the mass media, taking back $100 million after a whirlwind tour.

In a striking parable for the punk rock genre, Sid Vicious set up housekeeping with a young American heroin addict who followed him over to England. Before long, Vicious got hooked, too—juggling concerts, partying, and groupie raves, he was racing down a classic dead-end road. One foggy morning he woke up, turned over, and found his girlfriend with a knife sticking out of her stomach. She was stone-cold dead. Arrested for killing her, he got out on bail. A few weeks later, Vicious overdosed with heroin and died in that same bed, purer poetic justice than any of the stupid lyrics he screamed while onstage.

## The MTV Phenomenon

While the juveniles of the fifties listened to their music mostly on car radios, the sixties and seventies kids added cassette players into the mix. When it came to young sounds, though, television was still a virtually unused vehicle. It was not until the early 1980s, with the advent of the cable industry, that a whole new element entered the picture—Music Television (MTV), the phenomenon that revolutionized the music industry. Today, that is where rock music is headquartered. FM radio has today been relegated into either a nostalgia ghetto for their baby-boomer parents or a teenage brothel of sex-chatter rock-talk personalities like Howard Stern, "Dr. Drew," "Poorman," and "The Greaseman."

But the real teenage action takes place on MTV. There, for twenty-four hours each and every day, kids get their libidos inflamed, imaginations stoked with psychedelic-style fantasies, covetousness fired up by luscious commercials, hedonism applauded by pleasure-worshiping values, and rebel natures nourished by anti-social propaganda. MTV advertises itself as "not a TV channel, but a cultural force. MTV has affected the way an entire generation thinks, talks, and buys." A typical day's programs follows.

| | |
|---|---|
| *Morning* | |
| 7:00–7:30 | *The Grind*—a 1990s version of the old *American Bandstand* with the costumes showing lots more skin and the dancing inspired by gyrating girly bars. |
| 7:30–8:00 | *Most Wanted Jams*—videos (discussion to follow) |
| 8:00–9:00 | *MTV's Rude Awakening*—comedy videos (?) |
| 9:00–10:00 | *MTV's Blocks*—segments |
| 10:00–Noon | *MTV's Jams*—videos |
| *Afternoon* | |
| Noon–4:00 | *Music Videos*—videos |
| 4:00–4:30 | *The Grind*—same format as the morning show |
| 4:30–5:00 | *Sand Blast*—physical "challenge" show, featuring bikini or wetsuit clad youngsters running, swimming, climbing, etc., in water, on sand, and over physical barriers. |
| 5:00–5:30 | *The Real World*—dramatizations |
| *Evening* | |
| 5:30–6:30 | *Most Wanted Jams*—videos and interviews with singers, musicians, and rock bizz personalities |
| 6:30–7:00 | *Lip Service*—a team of young men competing against a team of young women in "lip synching" a video, grinding in dance, and "body mechanics" as they mimic the rock group performing the tune played. |
| 7:00–8:00 | *My So-Called Life*—drama set among schoolkids, subtly supporting rebellion, |

| | |
|---|---|
| | sassing bickering parents, and glamorizing a partying, rock-grinding lifestyle. |
| alt. 7:00–7:30 | *Sand Blast*—same as afternoon entry |
| 7:30–8:00 | *Special*—best videos of the nineties or a fashion show for teens or other special events |
| 8:00–10:00 | *Prime Time*—top-40 videos, featuring artists like Madonna, Elton John, The Cranberries, etc. Themes are totally secular ("I Believe in Love," "Suicidal Tendencies," "Ode to My Family—Does anyone care?", "Words—Let's get unconscious, honey!"). Lots of sexual and drug innuendo, bodies writhing, grinding, self-pity, rebellion, cynicism, and despair. |
| *Late Night* | |
| 10:00–10:30 | *Oddities*—The Maxx, a "spacey" cartoon fantasy. |
| 10:30–11:00 | *The State*—a "topical" comedy troupe with "teen-correct" sexual attitudes, self-centered values, and hedonistic themes. |
| 11:00–Midnight | *Beavis and Butthead*—see separate discussion later in this chapter. |
| Midnight–1:30 | *Alternative Nation*—New Age, "Grunge" videos and interviews |
| 1:30–2:30 | *MTV Dreamtime*—sick, nightmare videos |
| 2:30–7:30 | *Repeats*—replays of *Dreamtime, The Grind, Rude Awakening, & Most Wanted Jams* |

The dominant sell on MTV is sex, sex, sex, with all of the shows feeding one way or another into a teenager's most powerful drive. Most videos feature fast cuts that show lots of skin just short of nudity, with cleavage, self-stroking of bellies and thighs, and couples clutching suggestively a constant repeating element.

A strong African-American presence dominates these videos, where young black men appear as symbols of virility and base sexuality. Most of the white men shown are guitar-playing musicians or wimpy-looking party dates. The overall effect is racist and primitive, powerfully reinforcing the stereotype of the black male stud. It is curious that, as far as the author knows, none of the black service organizations have stepped forward to protest this kind of destructive stereotyping.

## Beware Beavis and Butthead

While the $5 billion music industry bankrolls MTV, which hawks their videos shamelessly day and night, a sprinkling of entertainment tries to keep the kids amused and tuned in. So if rock music is the MTV message—and it is—then its prophets and social commentators are *Beavis and Butthead*. Most adults have heard of this teenage odd couple, but few in fact, have taken time to sit down and catch their act.

Cartoon characters both, Beavis is a dumb blonde while Butthead has dark hair and wears braces on his teeth. Beyond those innocuous touches, these two spinoffs of *The Simpsons* say and do things that sane youngsters never (or should never) even think. They steal cars, fondle themselves, torture pets, encourage pyromania by loving "to burn stuff," and make idiotic comments on the dumb, often outrageous videos that are MTV's stock-in-trade. Throughout their dialogues, rife with identifying a variety of things that "suck," they emit their trademark cackle, "huh-huh, huh-huh, huh-huh."

Beyond engaging in all kinds of rude, lewd, and crude acts, they model a philosophy of life that can best be described as "in-your-face anarchy." In one segment a farmer hires Beavis and Butthead to paint his house. The moment he leaves, they scrap over the paint thinner, sniff themselves into a stupor, and proceed to give the farmer a paint job that is every homeowners nightmare. In another episode, they go to a rifle range where they accidentally shoot down an airplane. When they have a hard time opening the burning plane's door, they shrug and leave the women and children inside to be incinerated.

When a five-year-old Ohio boy set his bed on fire with a cigarette lighter after watching Beavis and Butthead talk about burning things and praising fire as "cool," he did not know he would be burning his two-year-old sister to death. A few months earlier, in Sidney, Australia, the B & B boys were credited with inspiring three girls to torch a neighboring apartment house, destroying the homes and possessions of twelve families.

Beavis and Butthead merchandise, from T-shirts to posters, pins, ragdolls, CDs and denim jackets, accounts for an estimated $100 million in annual sales. And the B & B act is now international, with MTV Asia (in Mandarin and English) beamed into India and the Philippines, MTV Australia, and other MTV versions in Germany and England, and MTV Latino going throughout Central and South America.

Even with the late evening play time, young kids find a way to watch. Los Angeles psychologist Renee Fraser found trouble in her home with her seven-year-old daughter, who she found walking around babbling "huh-huh huh-huh" and chanting the name "Butthead." Says Fraser, "When kids see cartoon characters express cynical attitudes like Beavis and Butthead do, they think it gives them the right to speak the same negativity." Christian parents who believe their children are exempt from the MTV infestation need to wake up. According to recent audience studies by the Barna Research Group, Christian youngsters were *more* likely (42 percent) to have watched MTV during the past week than nonbelieving families (33 percent).

## The Religion of Rock 'n' Roll

Rock music is the MTV catalyst, and teens are the target. Lest we tend to downplay its influence, the truth is that both young fans and the performers they idolize regard their rock 'n' roll music as a sacred expression. Rocker Terence Trent D'Arby articulates this view: "Rock 'n' roll is like a religion to me. Any decent rock star has a Messiah complex. Part of you believes music can change things, inspire people—and that is what ultimately drives you."

The problem is that much of what "inspires" young fans is rebellious, sacrilegious, and perverse. For example, the group Nine Inch Nails in its composition "Heresy" preaches, "Your God is dead/ And no one cares/ If there is a hell/ I'll see you there." Another called Deicide boasts that its purpose is to show kids that Christianity is useless: one member has had an upside-down cross branded into his forehead to show Lucifer he is serious. Danzig's lead singer, Glenn Danzig, crows how their music is not designed to make anyone feel good. "Basically," he says, "I just hate the world." The ensemble Cannibal Corpse sings, "I wrapped my hands around her neck; squeezing out her breath, eyes rolled back in her head, clawing at my skin; I know now it's not my fault; she was asking for it." Pantera brags in one song, "I'm helping to legalize drugs on your street and I'm making a fortune."

While most young people will vehemently deny being affected by such offerings, more and more violent incidents have been directly tied to hard rock and rap. A nineteen-year old told police he killed a state trooper under the spell of cop-killing lyrics from rapper Tupac Shakur's album *2Pacalypse Now*. Two seventeen-year olds admitted they killed a Milwaukee policeman because they were "geeked up" to stalk the officer by Tupac Shakur's angry cop-hating rap lyrics in his album *'N Gatz We Truss*. Another youth confessed that he stabbed his father to death inspired by lyrics from the rock group Metallica.

A seventeen-year old shot his father dead while "The End" by The Doors blasted out his stereo. A thirteen-year-old boy brought two loaded guns and a machete to school, planning to take his classmates hostage as depicted in the video "Jeremy" by his favorite grunge band Pearl Jam—that very video won MTV's "Best Rock Video of the Year" in 1993. Another teenager and two friends listened to rapper Snoop Doggy Dogg, then went over to his grandparents house, and stabbed them dead. The rapper Snoop Doggy Dogg—aka Calvin Broadus—was arrested himself for murdering someone in 1995.

## Rap, the Sounds of Destruction

Few "musical" expressions are more patently destructive than rap music. While the rap category accounts for about 8 percent of all music sales, it is actually a misnomer to call it "music." For anyone who has not heard it, rap is more accurately described as a relentlessly rhythmic word-chant flow. Listeners experience some of the same hypnotic excitement usually associated with Hindu or Buddhist chanting, with the added element of inflammatory lyrics that glamorize rape, brutality, filthy speech, knives, guns, and killing.

Popular rappers like Ice-T, Vanilla Ice, Domino, Snoop Doggy Dogg, Warren G. & Nate Dogg, Mista Grimm, Tupac Shakur, Naughty by Nature, LL Cool J, Dr. Dre, N.W.A., and Eazy-E are idolized by their (usually) teenage fans. Almost all rappers are African-Americans, who grew up in predominately black southern California communities like Compton, Watts, and Long Beach. Their angry, radically subversive compositions have been exploited by a Westwood-based rap publisher called Death Row, formerly part of the giant Time Warner media complex. In the 1993-94 period, the label grossed $90 million from tapes, CDs, and merchandise sales. The bottom line with this "music" is the bottom line—despite the costs to American society in rap-inspired assaults against life, liberty, and property, rap music makes lots of money.

Of all the entertainment giants jumping on to the rap bandwagon, Walt Disney Records would seem the most unlikely. But in the fall of 1994, the producer of *Aladdin, Cinderella* and *The Lion King* soundtracks issued its first all-rap album "Mickey Unrapped," featuring

Mickey, Minnie, Goofy *et al* in rap-counterpoint with a popular rap duo called *Tag Team*. Disney executive Mark Jaffe explained why the child-oriented company has now moved into rap, "There are more rap albums purchased in suburban America than urban America. Rap has taken over the American popular psyche like no other [music trend] since disco."

By writing Mickey special lines like "I'm so cool, my ice cream never melts" into rap parodies titled "Ice Ice Mickey," "What a Mouse," "You Can't Botch This," "Ducks in the Hood" and "Whoomp! (There It Went)," in tandem with the original group *Tag Team* whose "Whoomp! (There It Is)" was a monster hit seller in 1993, Disney intended to transform a violent, lecherous musical form into something innocent.

Jaffe stressed that the album aimed "to provide a positive lyrical approach, and we were very conscious of how we chose our lyrics and the context in which they were sung." Even so, in Mickey's version of "Whoomp! (There It Went)" Disney included the phrase "get busy" which most parents would overlook as meaning "be industrious" but as a street term familiar to most young people, it has a lascivious "wink-wink" sexual connotation. In the words of Jesus, "No one puts a patch of unshrunk cloth on an old garment, for the patch pulls away from the garment and a worse tear results" (Matt. 9:16). Patching a filthy rap garment with innocent lyrics only serves to spread the appeal of the indecent rap message.

## Christian Pop Music

A similar dilemma crops up with much of so-called "Christian" pop music. For many years now, rock and pop musicians have crossed over from the secular field—often after "born-again" experiences—to launch "Christian musical ministries." Known as "contemporary Christian music"—C.C.M.—the genre took root during the 1970s "Jesus Movement" when young musicians got saved and began using folk and rock tunes to express their newfound faith. Playing in church basements and coffee shops, they sang in order to witness and preach.

From those early years, a wide range of styles has evolved. Today, those expressions include Las Vegas saloon-style pop to soft and driving rock and now rap, all transformed into "Christian" music by merely exchanging worldly lyrics with Christian ones. Christian rock groups like Stryper favor an onstage dress style that mimics hard-rock weirdos, play overloud, use frenetic rhythms, and wail "Christian" lyrics that are as hard to make out as those of most secular groups.

There are Christian versions of "grunge rock," featuring blues-chording guitars and wailing vocals, with groups like poo old lu, the Prayer Chain, and Curious Fools. "Hip-hop" bands, like 2 Live Crew, blending rhythm-and-blues instrumentation with rap lyrics, have their Christian counterparts in such groups as Preachus, Gospel Gangstas and T-Bone. Even "heavy metal," the wailing "music" of anger and anarchy with its guitar distortions and overpowering beat (Led Zeppelin, Black Sabbath, Van Halen and AC/DC) has its Christian mirror-image in groups like Guardian, Bride and Whitecross. The sound is similar, but the difference between sacred and profane is mostly the words, with Christian groups mimicking the costuming and performance style of the secular.

Be not deceived, Christian music is a huge moneymaker, pulling in over $1 billion a year. Mainstream outlets such as Tower Records and K-Mart report a 40 percent jump in Christian music sales in the most recent reporting year. Even *Billboard,* the secular music industry's bible, now publishes monthly charts of new Christian albums. When pressed, top Christian artists admit that CCM is first-and-foremost a business.

P.K. Mitchell, of Neon Cross, explained it this way, "There is a place where business starts and ministry stops. It's not always true that Christian bands play a gig just to minister. Business is business and Christians can do business with one another, but there is no such thing as Christian business. It would be disastrous for a record label to be run like a church if you want to make money. The grunge style is the style of the '90s and I hope more Christian bands who are up to date with the music of today would provide something kids could really get interested in."

## The Latest Trend

A brand new group called Malicide exemplifies that latest trend. Drummer Brant Diboe defines their approach to "Christian rock" in this way: "Our major influences have been Black Sabbath, Metallica, and Megadeth. We kind of sound like Vengeance Rising." One song they single out as special to them is called "Skydiving

Without a Parachute," which they describe as "an allegory about man falling away from God and God waiting up in heaven for you to come home."

Remember Alice Cooper? Well, s/he now claims to be "born again" and has recorded a first Christian album called *The Last Temptation*. The lyrics from one track, which Alice sings to a loud and heavy beat, is titled "Cleansed By Fire" and reads, "What about truth/ What about life/ What about glory/ What about Christ/ What about peace/ What about love/ What about faith in God above . . . / You lose and I win/ You couldn't suck me in/ It's over, you have no power/ You're lost and I'm found/ And I'm heaven bound/ Go back to where you belong/ To where you fell/ Go to hell!"

Finally, the newest secular craze to invade the Christian teenage scene are "raves." Raves came out of the colleges, where computer bulletin boards announced impromptu parties held in garages, lofts, and warehouses. There hundreds of youngsters gathered to flashing lights, thick smoke, designer drugs, and ear-splitting, pulsating music and danced frenziedly until the wee hours of the morning. It did not take long before a Christian record producer in Chatsworth, California, formed a company called N Soul Records solely to make and market "sanctified dance music" suitable for Christian raves. One of his releases, "Nitro Praise," spent twenty-six weeks on *Billboard*'s top-50 list and another—World Wide Message Tribe's "Dance Planet"--hit number one on the contemporary Christian music charts in the fall of 1994.

Today, late-night raves featuring the same flashing lights, smoke, and frenzy found at secular raves are organized by church groups as evangelistic tools. A recent rave held at Azusa Pacific University, a conservative Christian school in southern California, drew over 1,300 enthusiastic, bare-midriffed teenagers who danced past midnight. Sponsored by Calvary Chapel of Diamond Bar, a representative of the church strongly defended their advocating raves. "We want kids, who are so influenced by music, to see that Christianity is not square."

An Episcopalian priest named Matthew Fox launched a high-tech, high-decibel "rave Mass" in the basement of San Francisco's Grace Cathedral. Fox came up with the idea after visiting a band of young Anglicans in England where "rave in the nave" showcases loud music, women dancing in bikinis, and video monitors flashing arguably religious messages such as "Eat God." Says Fox of his offbeat worship style, "This kind of rave Mass is a very friendly experience for a generation raised on television."

## Evaluating Contemporary Christian Music

Clearly, when it comes down to a Christian evaluation of secular hard rock, heavy metal, grunge, rap, and raves, the problem is black and white. Considering the fact that this music is predominately dissonant, the rhythms primitive, and the lyrics fleshly and often anti-Christian, we should fervently pray that our kids find more uplifting, God-honoring music to enjoy. However, when the music styles and rhythms remain unchanged but only the lyrics are adapted to reflect Judeo-Christian values, we have a real problem. Seeking wise counsel, one recalls Genesis 27:22. "The voice is the voice of Jacob, but the hands are the hands of Esau." To paraphrase, "The beat and the fury are the sounds of rock, but the words are the words of the Bible."

In past decades, contemporary Christian music *did not* imitate the popular secular sounds of their era. For example, Negro spirituals were *not* jellyroll blues with biblical words nor was gospel music just country-western fitted out with born-again lyrics. But the times they have a'changed, to paraphrase Bob Dylan. So we come to the crucial bottom line. How can well-intended Christian parents steer their preteen and adolescent children through the raging storms of rock and rap—and not lose their kids in the process?

## FIGHTING BACK

### Part of Identity

*Music is part of your child's identity.* When thinking about how best to "train up your child," we often want to jump right in and lay down the law. By assuming the role of police officer, though, we can many times trigger resentment which fosters future rebellion. If we want to have a helpful impact on our children's musical tastes and choices, we need to remember one overriding principle—any person's choice of music styles and favorite artists are not only matters of choice but are, in fact, part and parcel of a person's *identity*. That means that whenever we criticize our youngster's rock idols, we attack them.

## Preferences Grow Slowly

*Musical preferences grow gradually.* If we are honest with ourselves, most of us can think back to a time when the kinds of music we danced to or snapped our fingers to are light years removed from the sort of music we appreciate today. Musical maturity, like physical maturity and mental maturity, does not happen all at once but is part of a natural growth process.

Earlier in this book we saw how children today first learned about music from television, plus any other auditory input they received at home. Later, when they go to school and become socialized, they listen to the kinds of music their friends favor, talk about, and believe speaks to their "inner self." Their choice is clear: if they want to belong, they need to conform. So record by record, cut by cut, over time they acquire a taste for those sounds. It has become part of who they are. They gravitate to music that speaks to their situation—their feelings of powerlessness, hidden hurts and sensitivities. For most kids today, that means they connect with rock, grunge, rap, and the rest. Usually, by the time we see the danger and want to do something about it, their identification with their music has been set.

## Look Before You Leap

Long before you initiate any discussions with your children, check out their cassette and CD titles. Make a list of them, particularly noting multiple albums by a single group or artist, which indicates their favorites. Then take the trouble to do some research. Ask the clerk at the record shop about the groups or artists your children prefer. Often the record companies will publish brochures that describe the material these groups specialize in. Read the liner notes on the tapes and CDs, and finally listen to them yourself.

## Tell-Tale Traces

Al Menconi, who specializes in ministering to young people caught up in the harmful aspects of rock and heavy-metal music, advises parents to look for clues in the kinds of albums your children buy. In his book *Today's Music: A Window to Your Child's Soul,* Menconi sets out the following personality traits associated with various rock-music forms.

*Dark Music.* Gloomy and morbid point of view that attracts more introverted, passive youngsters. Called variously "new wave," "alternative" or "new rock," the music is somber and the lyrics focus on broken hearts, betrayal, and everything wrong in everyday life. The musicians stress that the world is doomed, not worth saving and the best thing to do is sit passively waiting for the end. Though the eschatology may indeed be true, the emphasis on pessimism feeds into the darker moods of adolescents.

*Hard Rock and Heavy Metal.* Featuring driving energy and bizarre, colorful costumes and imagery, this music offers teens the promise of mental escape from the harsher aspects of growing up. The message here is that life is just one big party and the love of your life is just about to make his or her appearance. Escapist by its very form, "party metal" devotees criticize everything and everyone—except themselves.

*Black Metal.* Kids drawn to these sounds are likewise trying to escape their realities and responsibilities, but instead of partying, they are looking for personal power. They entertain revenge and punishment fantasies. Often black magic is preached by these groups with its promise of achieving great things, being protected against harm, overcoming rivals, and injuring one's enemies. Young fans have usually been deeply hurt and disappointed by those near and dear, and now seek to get back what they feel has been robbed from their souls.

*Rap Music.* Rap projects much the same message as heavy metal—rage, revenge fantasies, power, pain, and death. There is an overpowering "macho" element, with street-wise bravado and brutal sexuality. While some rappers reject drugs, they will glamorize violence, gangs, and a contempt for society. This "talk music" boosts a teenager's feelings of insecurity and poor self-esteem and makes them feel good about their "toughness." Kids with a predilection for gangs are drawn to rap.

*Pop and Dance.* This ballad soft-rock expression is strongly sexual (seen in the records and videos of Madonna, Paula Abdul, etc.). The appeal here is to young girls who feel unattractive and look to "sexiness" as a shortcut to popularity. By imitating the sexy women they see on videos, television, and movies, they hope to find the boys of their dreams.

## Deal with the Problem

First, we need to pray. James 1:5 promises, "If any of you lacks wisdom, let him ask of God, who gives to all men [and women] generously and without reproach, and it will be given to him [and her]." Lord knows we need wisdom above all else when intervening in our child's private life (and you can be sure he or she regards her music collection as *very* private).

Next, based on the insights we garnered researching our youngsters' music preferences, we need to try to build them up in their areas of insecurity. For example, is he alone too much? Then try to involve him in family activities and church youth groups. Does she dress extravagantly and mimic high-style rockers or party punkers? She needs to know you are there for her no matter what. Is he seething with anger, cynical and back-biting? Go with him to a ball game, have a coke afterwards, and talk about some of the traumatic events of his life—perhaps a divorce, death of a family member or some other triggering episode. If you can get him to talk about these things, much of the poisonous energy can be discharged.

## Watch and Listen Together

When you've established a real bond of friendship-love (not merely parental oversight), mention some little-known trivia about a favorite group or artist. Let her know you're not as square as she thought, and by saying something positive—not merely railing against his choice of "satanic" or "filthy" music—you will open a door to gaining his confidence and trust.

Then suggest watching one of his favorite shows (*Prime Time* on MTV, or VH-1) or listening to a treasured CD *together*. Often just sharing the experience together fosters bonding and your presence may enable her to gain enough objectivity to hear and see some of the more objectionable elements herself, without your even articulating any criticism. She may feel embarrassed by the lyrical content or visual immodesty, and so be less accepting of what she has long taken for granted.

Determine whether the Christian video network "Z Music Television" is available via local over-air broadcast stations or your local cable-television provider. If so, you may want to invite your children to try it as a contemporary Christian music alternative to MTV. While some of the musical styles offered on Z-TV resemble

MTV—from pop to rock to rap and heavy metal sounds—the lyrics are life-affirming and biblical. Some of the featured artists include Amy Grant, Petra, Michael W. Smith, Gary Chapman and DC Talk.

## Apply Loving Censorship

Go over each child's music collection and videos. When you encounter some obviously objectionable album or video, discuss it and analyze what the words say and what the music conveys. Though your child will probably balk against such analysis, gently but firmly lead him forward. Help him to understand how this or that artist or group battles against his being a godly youngster, provokes discontent with school, encourages him to be critical of church, youth groups, and the Bible.

Push for some mutually agreed-on guidelines to apply to home listening and viewing. Set schedules and limits on leisure time so spent, and make sure to hold your child to it, enforcing compliance with grounding of privileges. Expect some initial outbursts, pouting or whining, but don't react, get angry, or feel compelled to defend your "house rules." Remind your child that it is your house, and you pay the bills so you are entitled to make the rules. Remind him or her of Proverbs 22:6. "Train up a child in the way he should go, Even when he is old, he will not depart from it." In time, your youngsters will adapt and may even learn to appreciate the limits you have set, seeing it as an expression of your concern and love, and experiencing a fuller and more productive lifestyle.

## Listen to Good Christian Music

Colossians 2:8 teaches "See to it that no one takes you captive through philosophy and empty deception, according to the tradition of men, according to the elementary principles of the world, rather than according to Christ."

The big question is what exactly is Christian music? The Bible tells us that we are to be "speaking to one another in psalms and hymns and spiritual songs, singing and making melody with your heart to the Lord." (Eph. 5:19). The real test of any "Christian" music is this: does it make us worshipful? Does it bring us closer to the throne of God where we can glorify and exalt Him? What may fill our hearts with love of Christ may not do it for a generation that follows us. But the least common aspect should be this: when the music ends, what message are we left with? Can we repeat some of the praises and holy words that have been sung, or are they just window-dressing to a basically worldly musical mood?

This becomes a very personal matter. I myself am inclined to traditional expressions—hymnal selections, praise songs from Maranatha Music, spiritual and Scriptural renderings by Andrae Crouch and other contemporary composers. Some of my friends prefer offerings sung by Keith Green and Amy Grant; still others enjoy tunes by Ralph Carmichael and The Spurlows.

There are some guidelines we can follow.

First, we know that Christians should dress themselves with some measure of decorum (see 1 Tim. 2:9; 1 Pet. 3:3). So suggestive, skimpy or sensual clothing is unsuitable. Second, Ephesians 4:29 teaches, "Let no unwholesome word proceed from your mouth." That tells us that Christian lyrics ought not to be mixed with scatology or coarse street words, for that would be an offense to the words of God. You should not mix holy things with pig slop, for the whole altar will be despoiled.

In a similar vein, can a Christian message be communicated if it cannot be heard? Some music is so loud or the singers so mangle their enunciation that it is virtually impossible to hear the words without liner notes or an interpreter.

So a good rule of thumb is that if we cannot hear the words of praise, the chances are God cannot—or will not—hear them either. The music *is* the message here, and glorifying God is just a means to an end—which is to enable loud groups to market to the "Christian" market. If your children *insist* on listening to their favorite grunge group, then better songs with Christian lyrics than Satanic ones.

## Try the "Christian Music Diet"

Al Menconi recommends you try a thirty-day Christian music diet in your home. He challenges Christian families to put aside all secular entertainment—including television, videos, board games, and recorded sounds—and replace these with nothing but Christian music, taped sermons, Christian videos, Christian reading material, prayer, devotional studies, and spiritual discussions with family and friends. After thirty days, evaluate your experience with your family.

Menconi guarantees it will be a life-altering experience, particularly for those families who presently enjoy very little Christian electronic input. In short, he advises you try replacing electronic devilry with electronic worship.

## Check Out These Resources

While no single source has all the answers, several Christian music ministries help guide today's parents and their children through the treacherous waters of the contemporary music scene. Among them—

- Al Menconi Ministries
  P.O. Box 5003
  San Marcos, CA 92069
  Telephone: (619) 591-4696

This organization publishes a monthly newsletter on contemporary music called *Al's AnAlysis, Media Update* magazine which comments on music issues, and *Al's Advice* which offers recommended Christian albums at discounts.

- Steve Russo Evangelistic Team
  8768 Helms Avenue, Suite A
  Rancho Cucamonga, CA 91730
  Telephone: (909) 627-1122

This ministry for teens emphasizes evangelism, rock music evaluation, leadership, and other areas of interest. Literature and tapes available on request.

- Keith Day Enterprises
  P.O. Box 6544
  Orange, CA 92613-6544

The ministry publishes a quarterly magazine titled *Urgency, The Rock Magazine for Urgent Times.* This publication offers interviews with Christian rock musicians and reviews of albums and videos in the Christian field.

*Caveat:* Since this is a for-profit operation, which carries advertising, there is a danger of their recommending material that might not be as well-screened as one would like. I suggest you write and ask for a sample copy of the publication and review one of his recommended albums yourself to see if you agree with the evaluation.

There are also some Christian record clubs that offer albums, cassettes and CDs at affordable prices. These include:

- Family Record and Tape Club
  Division of Word DMS Inc.
  P.O. Box 11083
  Des Moines, IA 50381-1083

- Contemporary Christian/Gospel Division
  Columbia House
  1400 N. Fruitridge Avenue
  Terre Haute, IN 47811

# 10

# Movies! Movies!

*I don't think I can review movies much longer. It is an assault on the senses and an assault on the spirit.*

Michael Medved, film critic

Consider this quote from a notable: "When 'Question authority!' becomes the chief slogan of a culture, that culture is doomed because it won't be able to hang together. The cynicism has now gone too far. We are becoming what the history books tell us late Rome was like—mired in decadent self-absorption and lacking virtue."

No, the comment above did not come from Pat Robertson, Billy Graham, or even film critic Michael Medved; instead, that observation came from movie producer Oliver Stone, whose 1994 release *Natural Born Killers* was a virtual object lesson in "self-absorption" and violence. Noted film critic Stanley Kauffman underlined the self-serving hypocrisy of Stone's pious plaint about today's America and the fall of Rome in his *New Republic* review:

> "Oliver Stone's *Natural Born Killers* is mainly about itself. The subject . . . is coarse film-fodder: maniacal violence . . . another variation on the Bonnie-and-Clyde form . . . . Young Mickey and Mallory encounter each other when he comes to her family's home to deliver meat. Mallory's home life, with a lascivious father and a non-protective mother, makes her hungry for breakout and adventure. They begin by

drowning her father in a goldfish tank and incinerating her mother in her bed. Then they cut loose in a red roadster, killing blithely in diners and service stations and convenience stores. Fifty-two deaths in three weeks . . . ."

## Violence Begets Violence

The screenwriter for *Natural Born Killers* as well as the 1995 Academy Award nominee *Pulp Fiction* was Quentin Tarantino, who describes himself as a post-baby boomer raised on a cultural diet of video movies, MTV, and "reality-based" tabloid news shows. Tarantino boasts how he builds on the work of earlier violence "classics" like Brian De Palma's *Blow Out*, Terrence Malick's *Badlands*, and Martin Scorsese's *Taxi Driver*. "I prefer rude, rowdy stuff because that's one of the easiest ways to conquer an audience's disbelief. The more realistic the violence, the more likely you will be to forget you are watching a film."

Without doubt, the motion picture industry sets the tone for television, videos, and cyberspace, affecting in less obvious ways radio, print, and other media. From the onset of "talkies" in the 1920s, movies pioneered the era of electronic "reality." Even as other entertainment modes like radio and TV came in, movies still set the pace, defined and tested limits, and explored the outer frontiers of technology and innovation in seeking to create the ultimate illusory world.

## Ruled by Self Restraint

In the good old days, movie content was ruled by the industry's own restraints. The Hays Association was a voluntary group of the major movie producers who created a system of "self-censorship," with its Hays Office the highest court of appeal. Beginning with the material selected for film production to the elimination of dangerous or salacious scenes from completed projects, studios accepted the restrictions imposed by the "czar," avoiding novels, stage plays, and specific situations described that could offend audiences or challenge the social order. The Hays Code included the following restrictions—

CRIMES AGAINST THE LAW—

1. *Murder* (a) the technique of murder must be presented in a way that will not inspire imitation; (b) brutal

killings are not to be presented in detail; (c) revenge in modern times shall not be justified.

2. *Methods of Crime.* (a) theft, robbery, safe-cracking, and dynamiting of trains, mines, buildings, etc. should not be detailed in method; (b) arson must be subject to the same safeguards; (c) the use of firearms should be restricted to essentials; (d) methods of smuggling should not be presented.
3. *Illegal drug traffic* must never be presented.
4. *The use of liquor* in American life, when not required by the plot or for proper characterization, will not be shown.

### Sex

The sanctity of the institution of marriage and the home shall be upheld. Pictures shall not infer that low forms of sex relationship are the accepted or common thing.

1. *Adultery,* sometimes necessary plot material, must not be explicitly treated or justified, or presented attractively.
2. *Scenes of passion* should not be introduced when not essential to the plot. In general, passion should so be treated that these scenes do not stimulate the lower and baser element.
3. *Seduction or rape* (a) they should never be more than suggested, and only when essential for the plot, and even then never shown by explicit method; (b) they are never the proper subject for comedy.
4. *Sex perversion* or any inference of it is forbidden.
5. *White slavery* shall not be treated.
6. *Miscegenation* is forbidden.
7. *Sex hygiene* and venereal disease are not subjects for motion pictures.
8. *Actual child birth,* in fact or in silhouette, are never to be presented.

9. *Children's sex organs* are never to be exposed.

### VUGARITY

The treatment of low, disgusting, though not necessarily evil subjects, should be subject to the dictates of good taste and regard for the sensibilities of the audience.

### OBSCENITY

Obscenity in words, gesture, reference, song, joke, or by suggestion is forbidden.

### DANCES

Dances which emphasize indecent movements are to be regarded as obscene.

### PROFANITY

Pointed vulgarity or vulgar expressions, however used, are forbidden.

### COSTUME

1. *Complete nudity* is never permitted. This includes nudity in fact or in silhouette, or any lecherous or licentious notice thereof by other characters in the picture.

2. *Dancing costumes* intended to permit undue exposure or indecent movements in the dance are forbidden.

### RELIGION

1. No film or episode may throw ridicule on any religious faith.

2. Ministers of religion, in their character as such, should not be used as comic characters or as villains.

3. Ceremonies of any definite religion should be carefully and respectfully handled.

### NATIONAL FEELINGS

1. The use of the Flag shall be consistently respectful.

2. The history, institutions, prominent people, and citizenry of other nations shall be represented fairly.

REPELLENT SUBJECTS

The following subjects must be treated within the careful limits of good taste—

1. *Actual hangings*, or electrocutions as legal punishments for crime. 2. *Third Degree* methods. 3. *Brutality* and possible gruesomeness. 4. *Branding* of people or animals. 5. *Apparent cruelty* to children or animals. 6. *Surgical operations.*

An industry committee checked every film for content expressing blasphemy, filthy language, explicit eroticism or perversion, superfluous violence or brutality, ethnic slurs, or anti-American sentiment—and made sure the offensive material were edited out or that movie would not achieve general release to the public . Some of you younger readers may raise your eyebrows and ask, "What kind of good drama could possibly pass that sort of scrutiny?" A fair question—and the answer may surprise you.

Most all of what filmland now considers "classic films" were produced within the Hays Office limitations, including such time-honored titles as *All Quiet On The Western Front, Grand Hotel, The Story of Louis Pasteur, The Great Ziegfield, Mr. Deeds Goes to Town, The Good Earth, Boys Town, Good-bye, Mr. Chips, Stage Coach, The Philadelphia Story, Kitty Foyle, The Grapes of Wrath, Sergeant York, Yankee Doodle Dandy, It Happened One Night, Mutiny on the Bounty, Life of Emile Zola, You Can't Take It with You, Gone with the Wind, Rebecca, How Green Was My Valley, Citizen Kane, Watch on the Rhine, The Song of Bernadette, For Whom the Bell Tolls, Gaslight, Mrs. Miniver, Casablanca, Lost Weekend, Mildred Pierce, A Tree Grows in Brooklyn, The Best Years of Our Lives, The Razor's Edge, Gentlemen's Agreement, Miracle on 34th Street, Hamlet, Johnny Belinda, Treasure of Sierra Madre, Key Largo, All the King's Men, Letter to Three Wives, Cyrano de Bergerac, Born Yesterday, All About Eve, The African Queen, A Streetcar Named Desire, A Place in the Sun, An American in Paris, High Noon, Come Back, Little Sheba, Viva Zapata, Stalag 17, From Here to Eternity, On the Waterfront, Marty, East of Eden, Giant*—and that's just some of many more that could be named.

# The New Wave

Then in the 1950s, new wave "existential" films from Europe stretched the limits with nudity. Though Hays Office standards still prevailed for domestic movies, "art houses" began showing these mostly French exports to a growing audience. As the 1960s rebellion set in, the Hays Office was dissolved and replaced by nothing beyond a new spirit of *laissez faire*. From then on, like third-graders testing the resolve of their substitute teacher, film makers began a relentless assault against the barricades of traditional morals, virtue, and faith. Hollywood's war against middle America began with language, inspired by the "filthy speech" movement spawned on the Berkeley campus.

## Profanity and Mayhem Take Over

Movie makers introduced profanity first as "black dialect" in the "blaxploitation" films of the late sixties. Movies like *Cotton Comes to Harlem, Black Caesar, Shaft,* and *Superfly*—which has been called "the most anti-black film made in America since D. W. Griffith's *Birth of a Nation*—were filled with four-letter words. But because they involved blacks cursing and killing blacks, they gained a kind of general acceptance. But, in time, these same cursewords and obscene expressions were introduced into mainline movies until, word by word, smut gradually became accepted as bold, "reality-based" dialogue.

Author Claude Brown (*Manchild in the Promised* Land) accurately points out that "profanity is the language of violence. Saturday night knifings and shootings in the black ghettos are almost all preceded by outbursts of profanity." And, I would add, in white neighborhoods as well. The filthy words, nudity, blood, and all other kinds of in-your-face outrages became the mainstay of modern film making. With television providing free entertainment at home, Hollywood felt it had to offer moviegoers themes and subject matter they could not get over the air.

With industry demographic studies showing that their main audience were the under-thirties crowd, this kind of marketing research approach resulted in self-fulfilling projections. Making movies for young, rebellious fans—many of whom were obsessed with challenging the traditions of their parents—theaters were forced into relatively limited choices. Today we find even the Disney Company producing such movies as *Bound by Honor*, which glorifies gang violence, and *The*

*Program,* extolling youthful drunkenness and death-defying stunts. The first film sparked gang warfare with three deaths after a screening in Los Angeles, while the second inspired teenagers in Pennsylvania and Long Island to imitate the movie hero by laying in the middle of a highway at night to prove they had nerves of steel. Unlike the actor, one was killed, and two others crippled for life by the ensuing accidents.

The two Menendez brothers, Lyle and Erik, revealed they were inspired to kill their parents for their inheritance by a made-for-TV movie called *The Billionaire Boys Club*. An attempted murder of actress Jodie Foster was sparked by the perpetrator's obsession with the movie *Taxi Driver*. In England, the film *Silence of the Lambs* was cited as stirring up a wave of child and teenage killers, and in Israel "snuff films," which depict the deliberate torture and murdering of victims for "entertainment," were blamed for inducing two teenagers to butcher a taxi driver "just for fun."

## Magnifying the Bizarre

Aside from violence, today's movies compete with one another to glorify the sensational, bizarre, and decadent aspects of modern life. Even when Hollywood remakes so-called "historical" films, directors and writers inject the more recently acquired tastes in "relativistic" morality, nudity, cruelty, and perverse views of social and sexual relationships. Virtually every adult film today contains unneeded nudity, obscenity, graphic sex, and toilet humor. From a pragmatic point of view, it is easier to hold someone's attention by shock and shlock than by imaginative writing. In fact, most of today's young screenwriters (and only the young ones get hired) are ignorant of the world's literary classics, and many are functional illiterates.

A prime example of the new wave was the 1993 film *Indecent Proposal*. This slick "new morality" tale was built around a happily married couple (Woody Harrelson and Demi Moore) who are offered $1 million by a super-rich bachelor (Robert Redford) to let him spend the night with the man's wife. "The night would come and go," coos Redford, "but the money will make you comfortable for a lifetime." Naturally, as the screenwriter and director wrote it, the money wins out over virtue. Even more regrettable, the film itself made money.

And who will forget the furor back in 1988 when Universal Studios gave Martin Scorsese $50 million to make a movie that not only outraged Christians, Catholics and Jews alike, but triggered an outpouring of negative sentiment outside the Universal Studios complex in Studio City, California. I was among some 50,000 well-behaved protesters (reported as 25,000 by the local media) who picketed, listened to protest speeches, sang hymns, and left feeling good about ourselves—though, of course, nothing had changed. The film *The Last Temptation of Christ* flooded into general release, was enthusiastically reviewed everywhere, and, thank the Lord, bombed at the box office, bringing back a paltry $7 million domestically.

You might think Hollywood would learn something from that. But no, producers continue to challenge religious faith and outrage American sensibilities at every turn. In fact, the young turks who make films these days are convinced it is their sacred duty to assault society's most cherished beliefs—their "art" demands no less. A few decades ago, following outcries and protests from Americans outraged by Hollywood's relentless assault against traditional morality, the film industry established a ratings system to inform audiences about a movie's language, possible nudity, or "adult situations and content." Still, anyone who has attended a theatrical movie lately knows that the published rating designation does not necessarily describe its true content.

## The Farce of Film Ratings

For example, the Robin Williams film *Toys* was advertised as "PG-13," that is, suitable for children accompanied by their parents—in short, family fare. Yet if you took your kids to see that movie, you would have been stung by a scene where female lead Robin Wright wriggled out of her blouse and bra, then climbed into bed with the mild-mannered hero after no more than a casual greeting. Another recent release, *Home Alone 2*, got a "PG" rating which recommended it for kids to view alone. Yet this sequel to the successful *Home Alone* contained superfluous violence and cruelty, along with questionable behavior as the young hero uses his father's credit card to indulge himself in hotel luxury and spendthrift whims.

## Self-Appointed Culture Leaders

A box-office hit and Oscar nominee in 1993 was the critically acclaimed *A Few Good Men*, directed by Rob Reiner. Promoted as a patriotic Marine movie, the storyline strongly criticized the Corps' code of honor and presented a Bible-quoting Christian officer as the real villain of the film. In an interview with the *Los Angeles Times,* Reiner displayed his real feelings about traditional beliefs "This . . . . right wing, Moral Majority [types] are destroying the country. They get people twisted around with ideas about how morality should be . . . . If they really believed in what they were preaching, if they really believed in what Jesus Christ said, they wouldn't be promoting family values."

Other than exhibiting a convoluted logic, Reiner's comments typifies the mindset of the Hollywood elite. Their enemies are those who are deemed the true enemies of the *artiste,* "the people" who in former times and different contexts were called the *bourgeoisie.* In other words, those who believe that they alone, and not society, are responsible for their choices and their deeds, good or ill. That is *not* a popular view among the Hollywood set. And that is an attitude they are determined to change.

Make no mistake about it, those who make films are fully aware of the power movies have to affect behavior. In fact, at most Hollywood parties, awardfests and power meals, film makers openly discuss what needs to be done to move America in the direction they know it is best for us to go. Civilians—those outside their rarefied sphere of insight—are simply sheep who need to be led. And who better to lead us than themselves?

While preparing this chapter, I talked to a naturalized Scot who worked as a distributor for Universal Film Corporation. When I first mentioned the current state of social decay and the old Hays Office, he snarled his contempt. Under the old code, he reminded me, if an unmarried couple were shown on the same bed, one of the pair's feet had to rest on the floor. How silly could you get? But as we went on to discuss the themes of this book and its findings, he gradually began to moderate his views until, by the time our ten-minute conversation had ended, the former champion of "new morality" was now lamenting the "sad state of American culture," concluding we had "gone past the point of no return." Is that true? Is there no longer the possibility that Hollywood will repent, recant, and start making films that foster healthy, Judeo-Christian values?

## Is Hollywood Out to Seduce the People?

In late 1994, the Center for the Study of Popular Culture organized a conference around the theme "Hollywood and American Culture," held at the Century Plaza Hotel in Los Angeles. While many liberal spokespeople for the film-industry were invited to defend the premise "Is Filmland in Sync with America?", few showed up. So the conservatives present presented their case that Hollywood was indeed out of touch with mainstream America, that its images were too violent and too sexual, and its main targets for attack were the cornerstones of society—religion, the family, and capital business.

Former Delaware Governor Pete du Pont railed against the "misrepresentation of culture by its elites. What you see on the screen is out of touch with the lives of most people." Canadian Broadcasting producer Tony Thomas charged that "The language of the gutter has become the *lingua franca* of the screen." In response, one of the few Hollywood elite present, Fox Inc.'s vice-president George Vradenburg, denied the charges. "We produce what will get audiences," he argued. "We tend to reflect shared values. We're told we put out too many R-rated movies when G movies are more profitable. But it's not true. R-rated movies are significantly more profitable. If movies are out of touch with America, why do Americans watch them?"

What is the truth? Are Americans really supporting Hollywood in the only way Hollywood cares, in the bottom line of bodies and bucks? In fact, *fewer* Americans are going to the movies every year, as the following table shows:

| YEAR | # of U.S. Admissions | Average Ticket Price |
|---|---|---|
| 1993 (5-mos. projection) | 906 million | $5.10 |
| 1992 | 964 million | $5.05 |
| 1991 | 981 million | $4.89 |
| 1990 | 1,056 billion | $4.75 |
| 1989 | 1,132 billion | $4.45 |
| 1988 | 1,084 billion | $4.11 |
| 1987 | 1,088 billion | $3.91 |
| 1986 | 1,017 billion | $3.71 |
| 1985 | 1,056 billion | $3.55 |
| 1984 | 1,199 billion | $3.36 |
| 1983 | 1,196 billion | $3.15 |
| 1982 | 1,175 billion | $2.94 |

When confronted with these numbers, some industry executives blame the recent downturns on the recession. Others ascribe the decline to rising ticket prices while another group cites the theory that young people thirteen to twenty-five, who historically formed the core of the movie-going public, are just not going to the movies as often as they once did.

Young moviegoers who typically attend movies twelve times a year are no longer the biggest segment of the audience for theatrical films. They are now outnumbered by baby-boomer moviegoers, ages twenty-five to fifty, who average just four movies a year.

Looking at the trend, *Daily Variety* box-office analyst Art D. Murphy concluded, "If you follow that demographic line, you'll eventually follow an industry into Forest Lawn." Murphy points to the fact that young people as a group stay away from theaters. "In 1983, youngsters accounted for 55 percent of all tickets sold—way above their proportion of the population. In 1992, they accounted for just 38 percent of tickets sold."

Producer Joe Roth, former head of Twentieth Century Fox, believes that young people today are simply *different* from previous generations. "You can only count on them as part of the overall audience for the big hits. This is the first generation that has lost the tribal rite of going to the movies every weekend. They see the video rental market as their weekend activity. This is the first generation that grew up with video games."

## The New Loners

Roth has put his finger on a most important, even revolutionary trend. Since their beginning, movie theaters acted as the bonding arenas for former generations of Americans. Sitting in the dark with eyes wide, youngsters shared communal Saturday afternoon adventures with hundreds of other kids watching the big-screen thrillers, chillers, and killers. Movies helped us to socialize, enabling us to hang out with large groups of peers with whom we laughed, hooted, hid our eyes during the scary parts, booed during the kisses, and cried during the tragic scenes. In that way, movies played a similar role for young Americans as theater-in-the-round played for ancient Greece.

Today, the center of action is shifting to home entertainment centers. There, families or friends gather in small groups to watch the latest rented or purchased videos. Youngsters arrange video parties at houses where—optimally—no parents will be home to monitor the action. In that setting, drugs, alcohol, or "huffing" inhalants becomes part of their viewing experience, along with the traditional popcorn and pizza. Often, obscene or even pornographic titles are shown in mixed company.

Where once the former tribal gatherings in movie theaters acted to limit such dangerous behavior, today's movie parties are small "gang" affairs, where inhibitions are harder to control and a single strong personality can easily dominate the others, inducing them to take part in risqué, lewd, and morally destructive acts. So what can we do to counter it?

## FIGHTING BACK

### Stay Away

Since the vast majority of Hollywood films are really not worthy fare for people who care about what they allow into their minds, the safest approach is to just stay away. Producers, distributors and exhibitors make that option more and more attractive, as rising costs and resulting inflated ticket prices put the price of a family movie day a luxury event that few budgets can afford very often. There still remains the crucial question of determining which movies, if any, are worth the time and money.

### Review the Reviewers

Following the reviews in local newspapers or covered by television critics is a risky business, because invariably these "guardians of good taste" are themselves answerable to the film industry. These reviewers attend free previews, eat, drink, and are entertained by those very hosts whose product they will evaluate for the rest of us. The pressures to protect the producers' multi-million dollar investment prompts the critics to lean over backward not to pan a movie as it usually most richly deserves. So, in most cases they look for things to praise. If a reviewer should, heaven forbid, consistently publish negative judgments, they soon find themselves not being invited to screenings and industry events.

Finally, major reviewers have already gone through a selective process of "socialization," pre-screened to agree in most important ways with the philosophies and perspectives of the film makers themselves. Very few are politically or socially conservative, and even fewer hold strong religious or biblical views. In short, the prospective moviegoer in search for clear guidance needs to regard all commercial movie reviews with, not merely a grain but a shaker full of, salty skepticism.

## Prescreen All Movies and Videos

Most of us have had the painful experience of paying good money to take our families to what we believe is "fare suitable for family viewing," only to later find out how badly we were duped. Either we take our family by the hands and lead them out in a silent and ineffective protest—since they have already pocketed our money—or we just grit our teeth and pray that the rest of the movie will not contain even more embarrassing scenes, words, and attitudes. So, aside from throwing up our hands and boycotting *all* films—which some families have chosen to do—how can we make reasonably sure that, when we pay for our tickets, we will get what we think we are paying for?

The only sure way is to pre-screen it yourself. That is obviously impractical, even assuming you had the time and money to watch ten movies each and every week, and then pay a second time—and watch a second time—with your family. If you do that, beyond making sure the movie is free from obscene words and pictures, you will want to ask yourself these questions: what is this film saying? What is its basic message? Many movies may charm you and make you feel good with pretty little songs, but the action teaches belief in cultic and new age religion. Some family films encourage childhood rebellion and disrespect for parents. Remember, it is not just the art but the heart and soul of the film that communicates values to you and your family.

Assuming you cannot act as your own reviewer, the logical alternative is to have someone else do it for you—someone whose interests, values and faith in God reflect your own. But who?

## Use Screening Resources

I suggest you try two sources that, over time, have proved themselves.

*Christian Film & Television Commission.* Headed by Ted Baehr, this organization publishes the bi-weekly MovieGuide, which reviews movies from a Christian perspective. Subscriptions are $40 a year.

*Write to*

*MovieGuide*
P.O. Box 190010
Atlanta, GA 31119
Telephone: (800) 899-6684.

*Focus on the Family.* The organization headed by Dr. James Dobson publishes a monthly magazine called *Parental Guidance.* Available for a suggested donation of $20 a year, this publication reviews the latest movies and television aimed at young people.

*Write to*

*Parental Guidance*
Focus on the Family
Colorado Springs, CO 80995
Telephone: (719) 531-5181

## Be Vigilant

The good news is that, if our youngsters are typical of their age group, they will be attending fewer theatrical films today than did past generations. That means we will have fewer choices to monitor. But there is another side to that equation—because of the degraded content of most contemporary movies, responsible parents will need to be even more vigilant to protect our kids from the garbage.

Be sure of this one thing—whenever a movie gets the full-court press of media publicity, our kids—not to speak of our friends and ourselves—will feel pressured to see it. In 1993, for example, it was *Jurassic Park* that got all the hoopla. In 1994, it was *The Lion King*, and in 1995, it was *Forest Gump.* When your children ask to see these films, and they will, you need to know about them. You will want to know what they are about—the sorts of "messages" they preach, the pictures they show, and the words and content they contain. That is precisely the purpose of the two resources we cited above; investing in them will be money well spent.

## Watch and Question

More than likely, your children and family will be watching videos, comprised almost exclusively of movies that have earlier been in general theatrical release. That constitutes both a blessing and a danger. It is a blessing because more time has elapsed to evaluate them. But it is a danger because with so many thousands of choices, there is more of a chance that the kids might view some undesirable titles at their friends' homes or even in your own house when you are absent. So take the time to arm yourself.

Most video rental stores offer title lists, usually containing about two hundred recent films, along with booklets that tell what they are about. In addition, all the major motion picture companies will, on request, send out catalogs of their films currently available on videotape. Send for them, so at least you will have a source to check a title against, along with their published rating. There are growing numbers of fine Christian videos available, on biblical themes and real-life dramas as well. Movies like *The Hiding Place* and *Norman* come to mind here. Moody Bible Institute offers a variety of fine videos, including a ten-part series called *Moody Science Classics* that present an entertaining, informative, and biblical view of God's creation.

Finally, make it a point to know what your children watch or plan to watch. When they name a movie you know is not appropriate, either from its R-rating or from personal research, explain why they cannot see it. Tell them how what they watch and read and hear affects the kind of person they are and the way they grow up.

When they go over to a friend's house for a video party, first find out what they plan to watch. If there are no strong reasons to veto the title, then ask them to write a review of it afterwards. You might make out a little form for them to fill out, with appropriate spaces. Who was the hero or heroes? Who was the villain or "bad guy" and why? What was the story about? How did the film measure up to Biblical standards? Would Jesus want you to watch this video? If not, why not—what were some bad things about it? This is an approach that works well for younger children in elementary school, particularly those in the lower grades.

## Make the Effort

It will take time and extra effort to defend yourself and your family against the inroads of the world. It will cost you some money, too. But it will be time, energy, and money well spent. After all, is your family not worth it?

# 11

# The Cyberspace Invasion

*The most profound technologies are those that disappear. They weave themselves into the fabric of everyday life until they are indistinguishable from it.*

Mark Weiser,
Xerox computer scientist

"Turn up the volume, Harry!"

Dutifully, the forty-something husband points his remote at the screen and pushes the "VOL-^" button until the intimate whispers of passion grow decipherable. They watch transfixed as the action begins to turn graphic and, just as modesty prompts them to avert their eyes, the scene fades to black, then swirls back to the inevitable next-morning kitchen scene, with the young woman humming happily as she leans over the cooktop preparing bacon and eggs.

"Where's Bobby?" the husband asks. "I haven't seen hide nor hair of him since supper."

"He's in his room," she replies.

"What's he up to?" the man wonders. "Teenagers are geniuses at getting in trouble."

"Not our Bobby," she rejoins. "He's busy at his computer, working on his history term paper."

"Hey, that's great," his dad enthuses. "Even if that computer did cost an arm and leg, if it keeps his nose on his studies, it's worth every cent."

"You're a blankety-blank, Ken!" the onscreen actress screeches. "As far as I'm concerned, you can drop dead right now and the world will be a better place!"

They turn their attention back to the miniseries as the action heats up, and all is well in their home sweet home. Or so they think.

Upstairs, seated before another cathode-ray screen, young Bobby is equally engrossed with his onscreen action. But these riveting graphics have nothing to do with history, geography, or any other kind of schoolwork. In fact, what the miniseries downstairs had censored out, young Bobby's photos—downloaded from the Internet—reveal in all their shocking, pornographic detail. Bobby's "innocent, hardworking computer" doubles as a secret gateway to corruption and perversion.

## Cyberspace Defined

The whole truth is that so-called "cyberspace," even as our flesh-and-blood world, is likewise populated by sinful human beings, perhaps well-intentioned or even knowingly evil. But what exactly is "cyberspace?"

Cyberspace—also known as the "information highway"—starts with a computer terminal or a PC as its basic door-of-entry. Linked to the computer, either inside or outside, is a modem, which uses telephone lines to connect that computer potentially to *every other* computer in the world. Using their modems, computers are ready to go "on line."

Going on-line means linking up with other computers, usually through a central distributing network. This could be a local "bulletin board" or a national or international service like America Online, CompuServe, and the Internet. Any home or office user simply subscribes to the service, then dials an access telephone number through the modem and, in a matter of seconds, that computer's screen fills with a menu of choices. These can range from the latest business news and stock quotes to news from U.S. and overseas newspapers, movie and restaurant reviews, encyclopedias and other research archives. You can shop using colorful product catalogs, play the latest computer game, "download" software programs for your home computer, take part in "forums," and exchange "electronic mail"—email—with people all over the world.

## Communicating with Others

Communicating with others in cyberspace is its most popular—and arguably its most controversial—feature. The old "mail order" bride has its own counterpart in the e-mail world. Using e-mail, popular talk-show host Rush Limbaugh met and courted the woman who shortly thereafter became his wife. When New York computer programmer David Alsberg was killed by a misdirected robber's bullet on Times Square, his online forum members all over the country held a cyberspace wake that went on for weeks, with messages, poetry, and reminiscences acting to console hundreds of friends who had never actually met Dave Alsberg face to face.

While the Soviet Union was disintegrating a few years ago and the world's major news media was caught blissfully unawares, blow-by-blow reports appeared almost hourly over the *Internet*, relayed by highly placed Russians with access to computer modems. So computer buffs at home, in the office or at universities, were far better informed than international news organizations.

As proof that cyberspace is now a vital new way people communicate, the White House conducts daily on-line discussion forums, while U.S. government agencies run a huge cyberspace library, offering all sorts of exotic information ranging from technical research to electronic browsing through the Library of Congress holdings to forms and instructions on how to apply for government grants, all available for downloading.

People interested in investments can check the price on listed stocks just a few minutes behind Wall Street's ticker or they can join online "chat groups" that trade late-breaking market intelligence. When Philadelphia-based financial director Edward Shrager lost his job, he went online to CompuServe and Prodigy where he posted his updated resume and checked out job listings. Within five months, Shrager had a new job he first spotted in cyberspace.

Hollywood and the record industry run online fan clubs, where consumers of movies and music interact with producers and artists. Remote rural residents in Northern California have formed their own online "cybertown," where people can order blackberry jam from a food store, browse through art gallery photos, find out what's playing at the local moviehouse or debate President Clinton's timber policies with their neighbors—all without leaving their isolated houses. Besides the big online subscription services, there are over 53,000 dial-up "bulletin boards" that serve such specialized interests as real estate property listings, stock photo galleries used by ad agencies, and model agencies offering motion-picture auditions of their top clients.

## Internet, the Global Town Hall

The ultimate online network, though, is the planetary Internet. Imagine 25 million home, office, military, scientific, and university computers all over the world linked by their modems to a local telephone line. First created by the major world industrial powers, the Internet hookup is still maintained and funded by the various sponsoring governments. It regularly links chat groups located in London, Singapore, Tokyo, Los Angeles, Cairo, and almost any other big city across the world who then take part in "real-time," not recorded, exchanges in give-and-take discussions. In this way, research physicists, artists, ministers, or just ordinary computer buffs separated by many thousands of miles frequently hold the sort of free-wheeling bull sessions one remembers from college days. *Christianity Today* reported how a college sophomore in Ohio linked to a user in Seattle led him to the Lord during an Internet chat session.

Anyone with a home computer and modem can access the Internet and its dazzling overload of communication choices. Because of its academic traditions, information is traded freely in the pursuit of truth, and censorship of any kind—other than self-restraint—is forbidden. Such a no-holds-barred environment offers enormous advantages, the most important one being the unimpeded flow of ideas and information, irrespective of any "political correctness." The other side of that coin is that, since anything is acceptable, the worst sort of human degradation and deviltry gets to share shelf space with philosophers, theologians, and noble thinkers.

## Corruption Via Email and Sex Forums

One of the easiest paths to juvenile corruption is through e-mail or chat groups. There, twelve-year-old girls have been found exchanging sexually explicit messages with absolute strangers of both sexes, young, old and in-between. I'll quote here from a recent letter to Ann Landers: "I am in my late teens and very much concerned about my twelve-year-old sister. I was looking for something in her desk and found a bunch of pornographic letters written to 'Margie' from some man across the country on the on-line computer network my parents subscribe to. These letters are not merely suggestive; they are sexually explicit. This man is in college, and I'm sure he has no idea my sister is 12 years old. What should I do?" Beyond the unbridled eroticism this encourages, since anyone else in the world can read these letters, electronic "peeping Toms" have access to those originating the correspondence and can potentially trace their whereabouts.

But where e-mail requires effort and some writing skills, plugging into a "sex" address on the Internet Usenet allows anyone to download articles describing all sorts of abnormal behavior, from bondage to exhibitionism, fetishes, multiple partners, voyeurism, and "watersports." Other outlets offer "successful pickup lines," "prices for prostitutes in cities around the world," and the latest dirty jokes.

Besides the articles, Internet discussion groups trade graphic sex stories, gay groups and transvestites freely promote their bizarre lifestyles, and "intergenerational" advocates describe the "joys, problems, and theories" relating to boy-man and girl-woman relationships. For those bored by mere words, users can download various kinds of pornography "divided by subject area," and "the sounds of sex in stereo" to be played through sound cards.

One hopeful note is that access to Internet's pictorial filth is barred from most major gateways, such as CompuServe, America Online or Prodigy (though accessible through Delphi, academic, and commercial services). That means in most homes, the kids will not be able to view this material unless they subscribe to local "bulletin boards" (BBS) that specialize in pornographic films and photography. Even so, the print porno is universally available and requires diligence to avoid and monitor for household youngsters.

## Cyberspace Burglary

More intriguing for many teenagers—and certainly for thieves, mischief makers, and corporate spies—are the opportunities cyberspace offers for penetrating computerized accounts and secret files. A whole mythology has grown up around the term "hacking," which simply means breaching computer security codes. Once inside these private networks, criminal hackers tap police investigation files, infiltrate credit-card lists, and use account information to charge goods and services, electronically transfer money from the banking records of others to their own accounts, or invade corporate data banks and steal industrial secrets which they then sell to competitors.

One imaginative cyber swindler, Justin Tanner Petersen aka "Agent Steal," broke through radio station phone lines and rigged them to win contests and award himself prizes ranging from new cars to luxury vacations in Hawaii. Other cyber-criminals filed over 25,000 fraudulent electronic tax returns with the IRS, claiming and receiving refunds they never earned. Cyber investment hustlers buy up "penny stocks" and tout them on bulletin boards with false claims of an impending merger or huge earnings report. Trusting buyers acquire the stocks at high prices, producing a windfall for the phonies at the expense of the unsuspecting patsies.

The legendary Kevin Mitnick hacked for years while evading arrest under the code-name "Condor." Pulling such stunts as breaking through the North American Defense Command computer in Colorado Springs and leaving mocking messages, he also became a skilled "phreaker," able to manipulate the telephone system to pull pranks on friends and enemies. One of his stunts involved disconnecting service to his favorite Hollywood stars, and he pulled the plug on his former probation officer just as she was preparing to revoke his probation. Unlike most other hackers, Mitnick never used his skills to enrich himself illegally, which endeared him to a generation of more innocent if rebellious computer users.

The usual offense committed by these young hackers is probing and gaining unauthorized access and use of remote computer systems, "just for the fun of it." This is a common temptation to teenagers who are still testing limits during the awkward years of struggle leading to adulthood. Most of them mean no harm, but the penalties for online intrusion can be harsh. The F.B.I. now has an entire department dedicated to tracking down and prosecuting anyone using cyberspace for illegal purposes.

## Hate and Terror Forums

Even more troubling is the free ride cyberspace offers to bigotry, terror, and hate messages. Just before the Oklahoma bomb explosion that killed nearly two hundred people, a twelve-year-old boy built a bomb after downloading an Internet formula for napalm bombs using gunpowder, gasoline, and foam chips. Fortunately, his father discovered the device before it detonated. Freely available Internet material includes such how-to tomes as "The Terrorist Handbook" and "How to Pick a Lock."

In Chicago, the "Minuteman" bulletin board posts inflammatory attacks against homosexuals, with one cartoon showing a gorilla snarling how he was infected with AIDS by a black man. Those who deny the Holocaust distribute free videos on the Internet "proving" that inmates of the Auschwitz concentration camp swam for relaxation in an Olympic-sized swimming pool and any claims of gas chambers were just "Jewish lies."

The Institute for Historical Review, top Holocaust denier in the U.S., maintains a worldwide Internet "store-front" headquarters where anti-Semitic literature is offered at no charge. And neo-Nazis use the Internet to promote dozens of computer hate games, including the popular Austrian game KZ (Concentration Camp) Manager. These groups publish anti-Nazi "hit lists" and provide detailed online lessons on how to build and blow up bombs.

## The CD-ROM Connection

There is even a CD-ROM disc on the market titled "Forbidden Subjects" that shares the inside dirty secrets of cyberspace counterculture—hacking, phreaking, tone box invasions, anarchy, subculture, magic, Internet and computer security secrets, confidential F.B.I. and police files, UFOs, the occult, and virus coding. For readers whose only experience with CDs (compact discs) involves playing recorded music, computer CDs use digital laser technology to store information on a compact disc. A low-power laser head "reads" the pits on the disc and translates them into print, sound, and pictures on a computer screen. Because the laser only "reads" the disc and does not "write" to it, it is called CD-*ROM*—with the ROM standing for "Read Only Memory.

Computer stores and other retail outlets sell all kinds of CD-ROM discs, which hold large quantities of information, recorded specifically for use on CD-ROM drives. Full encyclopedias like Grolier's, which used to occupy a full home-library bookshelf, now take just one CD-ROM disc featuring—besides text—voice-narrated articles and full-color photos to illustrate the entries. There are sports CDs, home medical CDs, World Atlas CDs, and multi-version Bible CDs complete with maps, commentaries, and concordances in Hebrew and Greek.

But, as with the Internet, there is a dark and seedy side to CD-ROMs. Playboy Enterprises sells a CD-ROM disc called *Interactive Pets and Playmates*, which allows computer users to control the action by manipulating video, sound, text, and graphics. Buyers of this disc can choose one of several dozen Playmates, then use the keyboard to command "Dominique" to pump iron or dance seductively or sing a song or strip naked on an ottoman couch.

Interotica Corp.'s read only disc titled *Nightwatch* allows the "player" to snoop around a plush singles resort using a control room filled with security cameras monitoring the guest suites. Another release, *Dream Machine*, features an onscreen female guide who helps the player choose from a variety of erotic fantasies, with the guide then assuming scenarios based on the viewer's selections. Other pornographic producers offer such interactive read only discs as *Night Watch Interactive* or *Heavenly Bodies Volume 3.*

When the O.J. Simpson murder trial was in progress, a CD-ROM disc hit the stores titled "The People vs. O.J. Simpson, An Interactive Companion." Divided into various "folders" headed "The Murder," "The Victims," "The Arrest," etc., the buyer simply clicked on subjects of interest to bring up pertinent videos, still photos, news coverage with narration, and free instant hookup to CompuServe's O.J. Forum.

Strongly signaling that CD-ROM discs are a wave of the entertainment future, Paramount Pictures now distributes "interactive" movies on compact discs. One title, based on the popular Mighty Morphin Power Rangers show, lets kids choose among various settings, control the action, and designate the outcome. In a very real sense, these interactive scenarios have closed the gap between dramatic entertainment and the interactive video games that marked the coming of age for today's "Generation X."

## Fostering the Illusion of Control

One possible consequence of interactive entertainment is the powerful illusion such discs foster that the player can control reality. With cyberspace technology growing more sophisticated, their ability to counterfeit real people and life events strikes uncannily at the core of thought and action. For example, interactive pornography conveys the notion that men can command women to do their bidding simply by pressing the "right button." Action discs teach the player that by using the right environment, kicks, and punches, he can always beat up or destroy the "enemy"—whomever that might be—in real life.

Interactive cyberspace is the logical stepchild of the stick-controlled video games first introduced in the 1970s—themselves the offspring of flashing-panel pinball machines of an earlier generation. About twenty years ago, kids began playing paddle pong and PacMan! in the arcades. Then Nintendo put these games on cartridges and sold devices to play them on a TV set. Now they can be played on computers using diskettes and read-only discs.

## Video Games Explored

Whether on TV or on the computer screen, it did not take very long for video-game manufacturers to learn how embedded gore, exploded flesh, and corpses strewn about made their game more addictive and so sold more of their products. Violent games like *Street Fighter* and *Mortal Kombat!* became so wildly popular that movie producers turned them into equally popular theatrical films. More recently, the game *Doom* has birthed a movie as well as four books of fiction. The best indication of video-game acceptance is the fact that Americans spend over $6 billion a year on video games, more than they spend going to the movies. Sega and Nintendo, the two largest game manufacturers, are played in two out of every five American homes.

According to *Computer Game Review*, those who create these video games openly admit that they design them to be addictive. Programming violence and peak emotions into the action stimulates a rush of adrenaline that cries to be repeated. It does not take a Ph.D. to understand that the more addictive a game's format and characters are, the more demand there will be for sequels and repeat sales.

Research indicates that, just like the violence on television, video-game mayhem helps desensitize children to real-life brutality. Psychologist Parker Page, who heads the Children's Television Resource and Education Center, warns, "Some kids who have a steady diet of playing violent video games may be more at risk of either being more aggressive with other children in the real world, or more tolerant of the aggression around them."

# Virtual Reality

Although still in its infancy, "virtual reality" may be the most compelling innovation yet in the never-never world of cyberspace. However, it requires some exotic equipment to experience the VR world, starting with a headset containing two video screens that produce a three-dimensional landscape. That is augmented by stereo headphones, plus optional gadgets like finger sensors, push-button boards, or a laser device to interact with the action.

Once plugged in, the VR "traveler" can experience spring storms complete with lightning, thunder, and rain—or visit the beach where gentle waves roll in, ocean mist fills the air, sea gulls glide past, and ships pass in the distance. You can learn French the VR way, with a 3-D tour of Paris where you lunch at the Eiffel Tower or walk along the Champs Elysees while your French "friends" chat with you. More practically, it is applied by architects and engineers to preview projects before they are built, enabling them to "walk" the corridors, "ride" the elevators, evaluate design alternatives, and view built-ins from different perspectives.

When the residents of Dresden, Germany, set out to rebuild a landmark Baroque church destroyed in WW2, they hired Research Triangle Institute in North Carolina to create a virtual reality model they could show to donors. Donning the VR headset, Dresdeners could see the blue church doors open out to a full view of the ornate ivory-and-gold altar along with the original organ Johann Sebastian Bach played as church organist in 1736. Pure light flooding in through the edifice's windows illuminates oil paintings of the apostles, which the VR "tourists" can see close up by pushing a "fly-up" zoom button.

VR has also invaded the world of entertainment, where arcades feature interactive games that challenge the line between illusion and reality. In Las Vegas, for example, theater patrons put on 3-D glasses and sit on computer-driven seats moving in concert with onscreen action. Once in place, they experience the sights, sound, and motion of a space trip or a white-water raft ride. In Tel Aviv, Israel, arcade customers ante up $4 for a six-minute game, where the VR tripper finds herself in a stark desert, confronted by a black hulking robot. At the left she spots a maze where, she is told, the enemy is hiding in ambush. "Track him down and kill him—before he kills you!" the computer-generated voice commands. "The year is 2068, and justice is harsh on the frontier." The effect, users report, is not only "mind-blowing", it is virtually real!

Fox Television recently launched a prime-time show called "VR.5" that features as heroine a shy telephone-line employee who discovers that she can burst into people's subconscious minds and pull them into a psychedelic world by using her home computer and modem. At Pasadena's Virtual World theme park, players battle each other from the interactive cockpits of 3-story "walking tanks" or race hovercraft cars through the mining canals of Mars. In the years ahead, the technology will offer ever more sophisticated and astounding cyber reality that will make everyday life seem colorless and boring by contrast.

## So What's the Harm?

We need to answer this question: Do these trips in cyberspace do any harm? The answer is a qualified yes. First of all, like all technological advances, computer consciousness is becoming so widespread that it becomes part of our lives without our really noticing.

One glance around your house will prove the point. From your CD player to your coffeemaker, garage-door opener and microwave oven, mini-computers run the show. As home computers and their limitless applications become all-pervasive, they will invade our privacy, run our lives and increase our dependence on them. Just listen to the projection made by Bertrand Cambou, Motorola's computer-chip scientist:

"Welcome to the world of 2006," he writes. "Miniature computers implanted into the human body are saving lives by automatically monitoring and controlling blood pressure, temperature, heart rate and cholesterol levels. Glasses and contact lenses are obsolete because implanted semiconductors reshape visual signals received from defective eye tissue. Pocket-sized devices combine audio, video, graphics and text, allowing you to compute, video-conference, create, access, store and transmit date, and network with other such devices anywhere on Earth.

"Your kitchen appliances understand the spoken word. Your car, with its hybrid gas-electric engine, drives itself and uses a global positioning indicator to tell you where you are and how best to arrive at your destination. Under-the-hood electronic systems control everything from the fuel-air ratio of your engine to the tilt of your steering wheel. Your world is now doing things that is indistinguishable from magic." Our greatest fear will be that power outages, brown-outs, or battery failures will "kill" our ability to communicate and function.

Beyond the loss of self-reliance, privacy will become an archaic oddity, with a host of outside intruders from cable and phone companies to banks and other computer modems able to monitor us on a daily basis.

## The Factoid Factor

Neurologist Dr. Richard M. Restak, in his book *The Modular Brain,* details how our world of easy-access information—factoids—has numbed our minds. Factoids are the ten-second sound "bytes" we ingest through electronic media, like a news anchor's leadline, a commercial's nonsense lyric, or a politician's six-word slogan.

Factoids require no analysis or independent thought, no intellectual perplexities. "This is a society that glorifies and overloads on factoids," Restak notes. "Factoids are the nibbits of nothing, the junk food of information." Included under the factoid umbrella are such mind-numbing, if popular, activities as trancing out with television or getting preoccupied with Internet forums on the philosophy of dress styles. This silliness becomes more important than such complex concepts as honor and personal integrity. As more people surrender to meaningless activities, it becomes socially and even morally acceptable to go back on your word or be rude, annoying, and vulgar.

## Computer Addiction

Arguably, the greatest danger stemming from involvement with cyberspace is the growing phenomenon of *computer addiction.* Even at tender ages, children show some of the same traits in relation to their video games as drug users to their substance. They quickly grow bored with the milder games and seek new releases that move faster, smash things, and destroy people more realistically. No longer satisfied with merely watching video characters slug it out, they crave games that put the player into the action as a participant. As Al Menconi of *Media Update* observes, "These features fill the mind and make these games so addictive."

At New York University, some 2,000 students a day—5 percent of the student body—cram into four computer labs where they sit for hours staring at a screen, laughing and talking to someone who cannot hear them. The great attraction there is the Internet where, by logging on to a news group, they can "talk" with thirty other people simultaneously about the latest movies, the psychology of body art, and Rush Limbaugh bashing.

Net addicts enjoy instant friendships with cybermates in England, Africa, and Australia, by logging into the address "soc.penpals." For youngsters raised on fast music and fast food, the Internet is a perfect cybermatch. But "surfing cyberspace" (browsing around the various chat groups and text downloads) for up to ten hours daily can cause carpal-tunnel syndrome and a plunging grade-point average. Some students become so connected to the computer cosmos that they "disconnect" from their own world. They give up friends, drop out of sports and other school activities, and may even lock themselves into their rooms to avoid being separated from their obsession.

And cyber addiction is not restricted to the young. Take Reid Miermaster, former computer teacher and graphics consultant in Kansas City. His $4,000 home computer not only provides his livelihood but has become the center of his life. He uses it to play CDs, control his television set, and his phone system. "I can sit at the computer and watch TV, listen to music, send and receive faxes and e-mail," he says.

When his marriage of sixteen years broke up, a major issue was the time he spent with his computer. As Miermaster explains, cyberspace was his escape from marital stresses. "I would spend time on the computer because the computer didn't scream at me," he recalls. "And then that got to be a problem because I was spending all my time on the computer." Though he now claims he does not run away from problems into cyberspace any more, he still admits he spends "about ten hours a day" with the machine for work and relaxation.

Stanford University professor Andre Bacard, who researches the social effects of technology, offers a sobering warning to those who may be addicted to computers. "There are people who, after they work on computers all day, go home and do it all night long, too. They may belong to computer networks, and they log on to one after another. Their entire social world is vicarious. I think," he concludes, "that it both encourages and cultivates psychosis in many people."

Nor are psychiatrists themselves exempt from such addiction. Dr. James Donley, medical director of outpatient psychiatry at the University of Kansas Medical Center, believes the potential is always there. "My wife tells me I'm computer addicted sometimes," he admits. "But I think the issue is that time can go by pretty fast when you're on a computer. And the activity is certainly inherently self-centered." Which is precisely the answer an addicted cocaine user might offer in defense of their weakness.

## FIGHTING BACK

### Bulletin Boards, On-line Services and the Internet

*Using Technology for Christ.* There is always a danger of blaming technology for the abuses people subject it to. The same printing presses that churn out tawdry novels and pornography also produce Bibles and Christian commentaries.

A similar principle applies to cyberspace. CompuServe online, for example, offers Christian Interactive Network (CIN), a user group that equips Christians for ministry through discussion groups, swapping research files and resources among participating Christian organizations and individuals. America Online and Prodigy online maintain several bulletin boards with Christian "born again" chat groups discussing questions of biblical history or doctrine, as well as sharing prayer requests.

And the Internet itself offers a rich variety of biblical and Christian resources, from online Bible programs in various languages that can be downloaded to your home computer to biblical quiz games and timelines available at the click of a mouse button. World-wide Christian discussion groups engage in lively exchanges, pastors and leaders share mutual problems and solutions, and missionaries separated by thousands of miles share experiences and network for special needs. An elaborate collection of Christian resources—including mailing lists, home pages of Web churches, music, sermon outlines, and much more—are freely available for reading and downloading.

*Anti-Social Uses.* To safeguard your family from sexually explicit material freely available on the Internet, Surfwatch Software of Los Altos, California, sells a program ($49.95 retail) that automatically blocks off more than 250 newsgroups that contain sexually graphic words and pictures. Beyond such undesirable material as pornography, punk forums or cult-religion advocacy, I see two online practices as particularly dangerous both for youngsters and adults alike, namely *Hacking and Phreaking,* and *Hate and Terror Forums.*

1. *Hacking and phreaking*. As earlier described, hacking involves bypassing computer security to "break in," for the purpose of snooping, writing to files, infesting it with a virus or creating other mischief, or—at its worst—to steal trade secrets, access credit lines, or transfer money to the hacker's own account. *Phreaking* means breaking telephone-company security to charge the phreaker's personal calls to the accounts of others.

First, there are some relatively painless ways the prudent computer user can prevent others from hacking their machine.

- *Passwords.* Use a mixture of letters and numbers. Choose a combination you can easily remember and do not write it down. Change it as often as practical, and do not ever share it.

- *Encryption.* Consider using built-in encryption features of programs like PCTools or Norton Utilities. Some of these programs will "shred" files you want to delete so they cannot be recovered. If you do not own that software, using Pkzip or another archiving program will offer some protection.

- *Screensavers.* Install a password-protected screen saver so your system will hide your work and lock itself if you leave your computer for awhile. If you use it in your office, install a program like Norton's "Disklock" which prevents unauthorized persons from gaining access to your computer's hard drive.

- *Backups.* Backing up data on tape or other storage devices helps security, because if your computer is stolen or important files corrupted because of hacking mischief, you can easily restore them.

- *Digital signatures.* Since electronic mail is easily forged, someone else can use your name without leaving a trace. RSA Data Security offers a free program on the Internet called "RIPEM/SIG" which authenticates information and verifies who sent an electronic expense account, document, or sales form by affixing a non-forgeable electronic signature. To get it, just request it from "rsaref@rsa.com" by e-mail.

- *Just Disconnect.* Without doubt, the most effective way to protect any computer from outside interference or tampering is simply to disconnect the phone line from the back of the machine and lock the door to your office or room.

Second, to determine if someone in your house is hacking, check your telephone bill. Look for lots of called numbers you cannot identify. This is a particularly strong indicator when a long stretch of time is logged against those unidentifiable numbers. Then talk with your computer-using children about these calls. If they own up to hacking, explain why it is a serious matter and how the F.B.I. now prosecutes people who hack.

Phreaking is harder to uncover, since you will not see any noticeable changes on your phone bill. You need to keep alert to your children's telephone habits. One telltale sign that your kids might be involved with charging calls to strangers is when you hear them talking to out-of-town or out-of-country friends or family, and the charges never show on your next billing. Confront them, and once sure they have been phreaking, read them the riot act. Take away privileges and do whatever else is necessary to stop them from stealing phone use. This is a serious crime with serious punishments attached.

2. *Hate and terror forums.* A Missouri teenager was turned in to the police after his father found a bomb in his basement made by his son, following instructions downloaded from the Internet. Short of waiting until you discover some disaster waiting to happen, parents do have the means to monitor whether your child might be "surfing" in such polluted waters.

Whenever a youngster signs up with the service, he or she will be asked to enter a credit-card number that the service will verify at that time. So watch for any new entries on your credit-card bills, looking particularly for charges from CompuServe, America Online, Prodigy, Delphi or any other firm that affords a pathway to the Internet.

If your household already has an Internet-accessible service, the carrier offers the option of blocking a child's passage to specified areas. So you need to research which Internet resources you wish barred and register those electronically with your service.

Finally, be alert to signs of extremist propaganda, such as downprinted hate articles, pamphlets, decals, or T-shirts imprinted with racist slogans. Very often, the same organizations that propagate hate messages also distribute material calling for armed actions and acts of terror.

There is an organization called "SafeSurf" devoted to helping parent's control their children's access to the underworld of cyberspace—erotic and pornographic material, anti-social forums, and pages encouraging intimacy with strangers. SafeSurf has its own page on the World Wide Web at: "http/www.safesurf.com/wave/" where they provide information about safe educational and entertainment Internet sites suitable for youngsters. SafeSurf also publishes an online newsletter called Internet Lifeguard that offers advice to parents on safe "surfing."

## CD ROMS

*Screen selections.* CD-ROM discs are themselves the most reliable indicator of whether or not they are appropriate for you and your family. Computer magazines like *Personal Computing* or *ComputerLife* review new releases and make recommendations that provide some guidance for the Christian family. Of course, you will need to screen selections further because many secular themes, while not obviously objectionable, still convey ideas and world views that compromise the biblical Christian perspective.

*Check it out.* It would be wise to check out the discs in your children's computer library. While most discs explain themselves on their jacket notes, some others—particularly the pornographic releases—tend to hide behind cryptic (for example, *fao* meaning "for adults only" or *T&A* designating nudity or *The Maxx* for "anything goes"). New age interactive discs are recognizable by their doom and gloom titles, but even when the label seems innocuous, the only real safeguard is to check it out yourself. So the key here as in all questionable areas is: when in doubt, check it out!

## Video Games

*Check the ratings.* Makers of video games use voluntary rating systems to warn buyers of any graphic violence or sexual content in their product.

One set of ratings, the ISDA system, applies to games played through devices linked to television sets. These manufacturers—including Nintendo, Sega, Atari and other producers—use labels to describe the age group for which the game is designed. "Adults Only—ages 18 and older" designates extremely graphic violence or sexual themes. "Mature—17 and older" games could feature graphic Mortal Kombat-type violence, "Teen—13 and older" releases would contain graphic violence with minimal bloodshed, as in Street Fighter, while "Children to Adults—6 and older" would have cartoon-type violence and "Early Childhood Ages 3+" games would contain no objectionable content, with characters like Barney the Dinosaur.

The other system, SPA, applies to games played on personal computers. This system uses a "barometer" symbol with numbers ranging from 1 to 4, designating the levels of violence, sex, and language. For example, a 2-rating for violence warns of the "destruction of living things," while a 4 indicates "wanton or gratuitous violence; torture; sex crimes." Other measures signify the degree of "nudity/sex—revealing attire" and "language—mild or coarse expletives" contained. The mildest rating is "ALL—suited for all audiences" which means the game contains "benign aggression, with some damage to nonliving things, but with no sex, nudity, profanity, or offensive slang."

Limit playing time. Treat video games just like you do television. Set a limit on the amount of time your children can play, optimally no more than an hour on school days

Look for alternate games. Help your children look for and choose from a whole range of video-game products. Try to substitute more educational games for the purely violent action/adventure titles. For a list of recommended games, you might want to contact Children's Television Resource and Education Center, San Francisco, CA

Christian homes will want to try games that use biblical characters as their heroes. For example, Exodus moves the players through mazes and Bible quizzes to help Moses defeat the Egyptians with the Word of God. Another called Super 3-D Noah's Ark uses food as a lure to restore order among the animals in a restless ark. Wisdom Tree, who manufacturers Christian video games for Nintendo and Sega systems, also markets such titles as King of Kings, Bible Buffet, and Bible Adventures, all available through Christian book stores.

Play games with your children. Your youngsters will get a big kick out of teaching you how to play their games, and this will give you a better chance to evaluate the content of their favorite titles. Since you'll be spending considerable time in this activity, choose video games you will enjoy playing, just as you used to enjoy some of the board games in the pre-video days.

Set limits and provide guidance. Just as you do not allow your children to rent overly violent or erotic movies at the video stores, apply the same principle to video games. Go shopping with your kids and help them make their selections. To do so wisely means you need to read the ratings stickers and game details on the package. When you are really not sure about a particular game, do not buy it; rent it from your local video store and give it a test run at home.

## Six Rules For Online Safety

The National Center for Missing and Exploited Children has published a useful pledge you can offer your children and post at the computer as an ongoing reminder.

1. I will not give out personal information such as my address, telephone number, parents' work address/ telephone number, or the name and location of my school without my parents' permission.
2. I will tell my parents right away if I come across any information that makes me feel uncomfortable.
3. I will never agree to get together with someone I "meet" online without first checking with my parents. If my parents agree to the meeting, I will be sure that it is in a public place and bring my mother or father along.
4. I will never send a person my picture or anything else without first checking with my parents.
5. I will not respond to any messages that are mean or in any way make me feel uncomfortable. It is not my fault if I get a message like that. If I do, I will tell my parents right away so that they can contact the online service.
6. I will talk with my parents so that we can set up rules for going online. We will decide upon the time of day that I can be online, the length of time I can be online, and appropriate areas for me to visit. I will not access other areas or break these rules without their permission.

## Combatting Addiction

As we previously saw in chapter 7 dealing with television, all sorts of research prove beyond any doubt that obsession with computer cyberspace presents all the defining characteristics of *any* addiction, including that to tobacco, drugs, or alcohol. To review, these include a mind-numbing effect that allows one to escape the stress of daily realities, a powerful compulsion to repeat the experience, and telltale withdrawal symptoms whenever the addicted person tries to cut off the addicting behavior.

1. The first step to break free is to admit the problem. Before we can change undesirable practices, first we have to own up that they *are* undesirable. We need to confess that fact to ourselves as well as others. In the case of cyberspace, we will want to clarify how exactly *we use* our computer and how our computer *uses us.*

2. Take a sheet of paper and draw a line down the center, creating two columns. In the first column, list all the ways you (or your children) use your computer as a work tool, a research library for tasks like reports or homework, for records keeping, and any other practical applications.

In the other column, list the ways you (or your children) use it for "entertainment"—to play games, browse bulletin boards and online services, to snoop on e-mail exchanges and chat groups, to download curiosity programs or pictures unconnected with any practical purposes, and any other cyberspace "surfing" you or your children enjoy.

3. Now tear off the left-hand column with the practical applications, and post the remaining column in reading distance of your computer or computers. That list will be your visual reminder for activities you and your children agree to commit yourselves to totally eliminate or at least limit drastically. You will want to discuss your decision with your husband, wife, or your children, so both you and they can be accountable one to the other.

4. Finally, pray for God's enabling power to give you and your children the victory over this pervasive electronic jungle we all now inhabit. And please read the final chapter titled "The Last Word."

## Conclusion

# The Enabling Power

*For the Son of Man has come to seek and to save that which was lost.*

Luke 19:10

These are indeed perilous times. It doesn't take a prophet to know it, even if an apostle-prophet first articulated it. Paul tells us in 2 Timothy 3:1 "In the last days, perilous times will come" (NKJV). These, my friends, are those last days. As the third millennium rushes up to greet us, time grows short for the promised return of Jesus Christ.

In the chapters that went before, we embarked on a pilgrimage through the treacherous trails and hidden pitfalls of our "new world" media jungle. Along the way, I offered you a broad range of weapons you can use to fight back on behalf of yourself and your family. The advice I offered is sound, tested, and proven workable.

But unless you are properly shielded, you are destined to fail. You may start out well, rightly analyze the ways the Media Jungle has penetrated your home, discuss the dangers with your husband or wife and children, and begin applying those tactics you determine are best suited to your family.

Sooner or later, though, you will weaken. You will begin to falter, struggle valiantly, but finally fail—unless you are empowered by the Holy Spirit. Then and only then can you be confident that you will remain strong.

The great question remains. Exactly how we can be sure of the Holy Spirit's enabling power? God's Word gives us the answer, in Ephesians 1:13. "In Him [Christ], you also, after listening to the message of truth, the gospel of your salvation—having also believed, you were sealed in Him with the Holy Spirit of promise."

The Holy Spirit *indwells* every believer who has been born again. He lives within no one else. Jesus Himself tells us, "Truly, truly, I say to you, unless one is born again, he cannot see the kingdom of God." (John 3:3). Our first birth is physical from our mother's wombs. We all know exactly when that happened; we call it our birth day. Even our driver's licenses testify to it.

In the same way, we must be born a second time—this time by the Spirit of God. That experience is our moment of salvation, when we pass from the dreadful sentence of separation from God into eternal life with Him. Those who have been born again know when that happened to them, and they call it their testimony. They know when it happened and how it happened.

If you, dear reader, do not know your re-birthday, then this Final Word is written specifically for you. Regardless of whether you call yourself a Christian or not, before you do anything else, please take a few minutes and "pay homage to the Son" of God. (Ps. 2:12). After you finish reading these last few paragraphs, close your eyes and in your own words, tell Jesus that you believe He is the Son of God who, in the fullness of time, was sent to earth by His Father to suffer and die on the cross to pay in full for all your shortcomings.

Tell Him you believe He died and rose again on Resurrection Sunday, and even now He stands in Heaven at the right hand of God the Father. Tell Him you know how much He loves you, so much He died for you, so that He could make you His child. Tell Him you love Him back because He first loved you, and tell Him now your heartfelt desire is to serve Him and Him alone all the days of your life.

Tell Jesus those things with a sincere heart, and the Bible promises you that not only will the angels in Heaven rejoice, but Jesus Himself will write your name in His precious Lamb's Book of Life. "Today, if you hear His voice, do not harden your hearts." (Heb. 4:7). "Behold, now is the acceptable time, behold now is the Day of Salvation" (2 Cor. 6:2).

If you do that, my friend, you will be born again. You will at once be empowered by the Holy Spirit who will come and make His home in you. And you will have that very special Enabling Power who alone gives you the victory, both now here on earth and later in His kingdom to come.

# Notes

## Introduction

*Page ix, lines 6–9* Thomas Stearns Eliot, *The Wasteland.*

*Page x, lines 17–18.* The term "coalition of 51 percent" is taken from David Chagall, *The New Kingmakers* (New York and London: Harcourt Brace Jovanovich, 1981), 51. For a more detailed analysis of targeting voters matching human personality traits to voting tendencies, see pp. 333–34.

*Page xi, lines 2–6.* R. B. Choate, "The Selling of the Child," report before the Consumer Subcommittee of the Committee of Commerce, United States Senate, New York (Feb. 27, 1973).

*Page xi, lines 10–15.* Television commercial for "New Skin" Liquid Bandages from Medtech Labs.

*Page xii, line 28, to page xiii, line 29. Los Angeles Times* (Feb. 23, 1994), A1, A16; *Los Angeles Times* (Feb. 24, 1994), A1, A10–11; Los Angeles *Daily News* (Feb. 24, 1994), 1 and back page.

*Page xii, lines 32–35. Journal of the American Medical Association* (June 1992) portion of research report conducted by Dr. Brandon Centerwall, University of Washington.

*Page xiii, lines 36, to xiv, line 6.* Ibid.

*Page xiv, lines 7–10.* Ibid.

*Page xiv, lines 11–18.* Cited in Los Angeles *Daily News* (Oct. 10, 1993).

*Page xiv, lines 19–26.* Lee Margulies, *Los Angeles Times* (Oct. 14, 1993) reporting on incident occurring in Moraine, Ohio, on Oct. 8, 1993.

*Page xiv, lines 27–33. Journal of the American Medical Association* (June 1992).

## Chapter 1: The Magic of Music

*Page 3, line 11, to page 4, line 28.* David Chagall, "How Music Affects Health," *Family Weekly* (July 3, 1977).

*Page 4, line 32, to page 5, line 15.* Quoted from the liner notes citing *Newsweek* (date not specified); recording issued by Capitol Records (1974, Toshiba EMI Ltd.).

*Page 5, lines 16–25. Prevention* (June 1990), 16–17.

*Page 6, lines 1–6.* Muzak Corporation Research Archives.

*Page 6, line 21, to page 7, line 4.* Personal interviews with Tony Asher (June 1979), "The Music Manipulators," *Oui* (Oct. 1979).

*Page 7, lines 32–34. Advertising Age* (1977 annual issue) and 1994 interview.

*Page 7, line 37, to page 8, line 4.* Tony Asher interview.

*Page 8, line 5, to page 9, line 27.* Cited by Muzak Corporation's Director of Marketing Leslie Ritter in personal interview (July 11, 1993), Muzak Research Archives.

*Page 9, line 37, to page 10, line 9. Los Angeles Times* (Aug. 29, 1994).

*Page 10, lines 11–29.* "Loud Music at Gym Can Impair Hearing," *L. A. Life* (Nov. 27, 1994).

*Page 10, line 31, to page 11, line 4.* "The Music Manipulators," *Oui* (Oct. 1979).

*Page 11, line 6, to page 12, line 30.* Leslie Ritter interview.

*Page 12, line 32, to page 13, line 29.* "The Music Manipulators," 132–33.

*Page 13, lines 30–36. L. A. Life* (June 12, 1993).

*Page 13, line 38, to page 14, line 12.* Interview with Eddy Manson (June 1979), *Oui* (Oct. 1979).

*Page 14, lines 25–34.* Ibid.

*Page 14, line 36, to page 15, line 11.* Los Angeles *Daily News* (Oct. 14, 1993) and *Los Angeles Times* (Oct. 14, 1993), A1 and A30.

*Page 15, lines 29–37.* Dr. Hajime Murooka, "Lullaby from the Womb," Capitol Records (EMI).

*Page 18, lines 3–39.* Ronald Allen and Gordon Borror, *Worship* (Multnomah Press, 1983), 157–64.

## Chapter 2: Signs and Portents

*Page 21, lines 21–30.* Donald P. Myers article, *Newsday* (June 25, 1993), cited by *Los Angeles Times* (June 27, 1993), E2.

*Page 21, lines 31–38.* Ibid.

*Page 22, lines 2–8.* Ibid.

*Page 22, lines 17–24.* Ivan P. Pavlov, *Conditioned Reflexes* (London: Oxford University Press, 1927; reprint edition, Dover Books, 1988).

*Page 22, line 25, to page 23, line 7.* Arnold Gessell, *Infant Development* (New York: Harper Brothers, 1952); also B. F. Skinner, *Verbal Behavior* (New York: Appleton-Century-Crofts, 1957).

*Page 23, lines 32–38.* Arnold Gessell, *Studies in Child Development* (New York: Harper Brothers, 1948).

*Page 25, lines 9–22.* F. Birren, *Color and Human Response* (New York: Van Nostrand Publishers, 1978).

*Page 25, lines 27–31. Thousand Oaks News-Chronicle*, Starsheet edition (May 6, 1993).

*Page 25, line 32, to page 26, line 2.* Birren, *Color and Human Response.*

*Page 26, lines 3–10.* Chuck Shepherd, *Thousand Oaks News-Chronicle*, Starsheet edition (Oct. 21, 1994).

*Page 26, lines 11–27.* F. Birren, *The Symbolism of Color* (New York: Carol Publishing Group, 1988); also *The Columbia Encyclopedia*, s.v. "color," (Morningside Heights, N.Y.: Columbia University Press, 1956), 425.

*Page 27, line 24, to page 28, line 1.* F. Birren, *Selling Color to People* (New Hyde Park, N.Y.: University Books, 1956).

*Page 28, lines 21–29.* Cited by T. V. O'Brien, "Psychologists Take a New Look at Today's Consumer," *Journal of Advertising Research* (August-September 1970).

*Page 28, lines 36–39.* Arnold Gessell, *Studies in Child Development*, 1948.

*Page 29, lines 2–9.* F. Birren, *The Symbolism of Color.*

## Chapter 3: Sex and Other Furies

*Page 32, lines 5–10.* L. Cheskin, *The Secrets of Marketing Success* (New York: Trident Press, 1967).

*Page 33, lines 6–10.* J. A. Dyal, "Response Strength as a Function of Magnitude of Perceived Incentive," *Perceptual and Motor Skills Journal* (1960).

*Page 33, line 10, to page 34, line 5.* Interview, Dr. Robert Stoller, U.C.L.A. School of Psychiatry (June 12, 1994).

*Page 34, lines 6–10.* "Sex in America," *U.S. News & World Report* (Oct. 17, 1994).

*Page 34, lines 11–29.* *Advertising Age* (Sept. 12, 1976), 9.

*Page 34, line 30, to page 35, line 7.* Ibid.

*Page 36, lines 10–18.* Purina dog food study conducted by Haug Associates, Los Angeles (Roper Research West), June 1977. For a detailed study into how emotions trigger and drive behavior, see P. T. Young, *Motivation and Emotions* (New York and London: John Wiley & Sons, 1961).

*Page 37, lines 1–31.* "The TV Spot: If You Enjoy It Maybe You Shouldn't Run It," *Advertising Age* (Dec. 3, 1975).

## Chapter 4: The Lifestyle Trap

*Page 41, lines 1–31.* Psychographic profile prototypes drawn from research findings of a psychographic study, "Life Style Portraits" (*Los Angeles Times* Research Department, 1983).

*Page 44, line 15, to page 45, line 20.* Consumer Opinion Research report, "Personality Plus: Marketing Beyond Demographics," National Advertising Bureau, New York (1973); updated in interviews with Jonathan Robbin, executive director (Nov. 17, 1980), and David Kalosis, Data Analysis director (July 17, 1995), Claritas Research, Rosalyn, Virginia.

*Page 45, lines 21–41.* "Personality Plus: Marketing Beyond Demographics."

*Page 46, lines 19–33.* Daniel Yankelovich report, "The Treacherous Waters of Social Change," National Industrial Conference Board annual meeting, New York City (Nov. 1973).

*Page 47, lines 18–27.* Bruce Horovitz, "More Advertisers Are Tailoring TV Spots to Ethnicity of Viewers," *Los Angeles Times* (May 3, 1994), D1, D3.

*Page 47, line 35, to page 49, line 35.* David Kalosis, Data Analysis director, Claritas, Inc., Arlington, Virginia (July 17, 27, 1995); "PRIZM, Cluster Narrative," "PRIZM, Cluster Matrix," "PRIZM, Cluster Highlights," Claritas (1994); and "UPDATE: Precision Demographics, vol. 2, no. 1," Claritas/NPDC Inc., Arlington (1993).

*Page 50, lines 14–17.* David Chagall, *The New Kingmakers* (New York: Harcourt Brace Jovanovich, 1981).

*Page 50, lines 17–18.* Interview, Democrat Party media consultant Eli Bleich (Nov. 12, 1992).

*Page 50, line 35, to page 51, line 3.* "Personality Plus: Marketing Beyond Demographics."

## Chapter 5: Pied Pipers of Kiddieville

*Page 54, line 7, to page 56, line 16.* David Chagall, "The Child Probers," *Television Today*, Robert Cole, ed. (New York, Toronto, Melbourne: Oxford University Press, 1981), 113–19.

*Page 56, lines 26–28.* Ibid., citing consistent Nielsen television measurement studies.

*Page 56, lines 31–35.* Institute of Child Development study, University of Minnesota, Patricia Bauer, project director (Knight-Ridder Tribune News Wire, Aug. 1994), published in *L.A. Life*, Los Angeles *Daily News* (Aug. 16, 1994), 8.

*Page 56, line 36, to page 57, line 2.* Advertising and spending estimates, *Advertising Age* roundup issue (June 1994).

*Page 57, lines 15–20.* "Off–the-record" interview, executive for major research firm involved with juvenile studies (March 1995).

*Page 57, line 22, to page 58, line 31.* Chagall, "The Child Probers."

*Page 58, line 33, to page 59, line 15.* Citing article "Kid2Kid Puts Youth Market in Focus," *Advertising Age* (Oct. 10, 1994), 30.

*Page 59, lines 16–22.* Lendon Smith interview, Chagall, "The Child Probers," 119.

*Page 60, lines 3–16.* Ellen Creager, "Their Bodies Scream Grown-Up, but Emotionally, They're Still Kids" (Knight-Ridder Tribune News Wire), *L.A. Life*, Los Angeles *Daily News* (April 9, 1995), 16.

*Page 60, lines 19–38.* Jane M. Healy, "The Brown University Child and Adolescent Behavior Letter" and "Does Video Reshape Your Brain?" *American Teacher* (1992).

*Page 61, lines 1–14.* "TV Addiction Blunts Attention, Conversation," *The Jerusalem Post* (Sept. 3, 1994).

*Page 61, lines 25–35.* Nancy Imperiale, "New Generation of Sing-Alongs Has Marketers Singing Happy Tune," *Orlando Sentinel* (July 1, 1993) and *L.A. Life*, Los Angeles *Daily News* (July 7, 1993), 8.

*Page 62, lines 12–15.* Glenn Collins, "Shoppers Again Finding Mighty Few Morphins," *The New York Times* (March 15, 1995).

*Page 62, lines 15–20.* Lynette Rice,"Power Rangers in Live Stage Show, *L.A. Life*, Los Angeles *Daily News* (Nov. 27, 1994), 4.

*Page 62, lines 21–34.* Lynette Rice, "Kicking Up a Fuss," *L.A. Life*, Los Angeles *Daily News* (Nov. 27, 1994), 4.

*Page 62, line 35, to page 63, line 6.* Ibid., 5.

*Page 63, line 10, to page 64, line 17.* "Kids' *Daily News*," Los Angeles *Daily News* (Jan. 17, 1995), 1–2.

*Page 64, line 26, to page 65, line 12. Los Angeles Times* (April 1, 1993; Oct. 15, 1994); *Associated Press Wire Services* (June 9, 1993); *Reuters Wire Services* (Oct. 19, 1994).

*Page 65, lines 17–20. New York Times* Syndicate release, Los Angeles *Daily News* (Aug. 11, 1993).

*Page 67, line 37, to page 68, line 13.* Harry Cheney, "Saturday Morning Cartoons," *Focus on the Family Magazine* (March 1993).

*Page 68, lines 13–16.* "Nickelodeon Expanding Its Lineup," *Los Angeles Times* (Oct. 21, 1994), F28.

*Page 68, lines 16–19.* "Children's Cable Network Planned," *Los Angeles Times* (Feb. 14, 1995), D1, D4.

## Chapter 6: Mind Control in the Livingroom

*Page 69, lines 4–16.* Redramatization, Christmas season network TV commercial for BankAmericard. (1978—ca. 1985).

*Page 70, line 31, to page 71, line 4.* H. J. Kupper, , "Psychic Comcomitants in Wartime Injuries," *Psychosomatic Medicine Journal* (1945), 22.

*Page 71, lines 9–28.* For more detailed analysis of enhanced perceptive abilities in hypnotic states, see C. S. Moss, , *Hypnosis in Perspective* (New York: The Macmillan Company, 1965).

*Page 71, lines 32–34.* For a systematic development of defining the hypnotic state, see A. Salter, *What Is Hypnosis. Studies in Auto and Hetero Conditionin* (New York: Smith Press, 1944).

*Page 72, lines 9–14.* From Moss, *Hypnosis in Perspective*, 86.

*Page 72, lines 25–38.* J. A. Dyal, "Response Strength as a Function of Magnitude of Perceived Incentive," *Perceptual and Motor Skills Journal* (1960).

*Page 73, lines 10–20.* Corn-Belcher, Welch and Fisichelli, "Conditioning Factors Underlying Hypnosis," *Journal of Abnormal Social Psychology* (1949).

*Page 73, lines 21–27.* Ibid.

*Page 73, line 29, to page 74, line 4.* W. I. Halpern, "Sensory Overkill in Sesame Street," report to the American Association of Psychiatric Services For Children," annual meeting (1973).

*Page 74, lines 5–16.* T. X. Barber, "Hypnotizability and Personality Traits," *Journal of Clinical Experimental Hypnosis* (1956).

*Page 74, lines 17–30.* For detailed analysis of inducing the hypnotic state, see Kubie and Margolin's article "Hypnotism and the Nature of the Hypnotic State,"*American Journal of Psychiatry* (1944); also Ernest S. Hilgard, *The Experience of Hypnosis* (New York: Harcourt Brace & World, 1968).

*Page 75, line 28, to page 76, line 20.* Redramatization, network TV commercial, Tic Tac Breath Mints (late 1970s—ca. 1985).

*Page 76, lines 21–34. Pediatrics Journal* (Feb., 1993) cited by Rita Rubin, Kerry Hannon, and Margaret Mannix, in "News You Can Use," *U.S. News and World Report* (Feb. 22, 1993), 68.

*Page 76, line, 36, to page 77, line 4.* Drs. Howard D. Tawney and Ben Benson, *Hypnosis and You* (New York: Fawcett Publications, 1956), 64–65.

*Page 77, lines 22–28.* Ibid., 70.

*Page 78, lines 2–9.* Ibid., citing 138–140.

# Chapter 7: Television—The Phantom Reality

*Page 81, lines 4–5.* Stephen Bertman, "Modern Values and the Challenge of Myth," *Imprimis*, vol. 22, no. 3 (March 1993), 3.

*Page 82, lines 26–32.* Rick Du Brow, "Has TV Lost Touch with Its Audience?" *Los Angeles Times* (Nov. 26, 1994), reviewing S. Robert Lichter, Linda S. Lichter, and Stanley Rothman titled "Prime Time: How TV Portrays American Culture," (1994).

*Page 82, line 34, to page 83, line 7.* Study Thomas Skill, James Robinson and Colleen Kinsella, University of Dayton Communications (1992), cited by the Associated Press wire services published in the Los Angeles *Daily News* (Dec. 27, 1994), 8–9.

*Page 83, lines 8–15.* "Hostile Hallways: The AAUW Survey on Sexual Harrassment in America's Schools," conducted by Louis Harris and Associates (1994) and commissioned by the American Association of University Women Educational Foundation.

*Page 83, lines 16–20.* Mona Charen, "New York Has Become One Bad Apple," Los Angeles *Daily News* (July 15, 1993), 19.

*Page 83, lines 20–23.* Rena Pederson "This Is No Way to Treat a Young Lady," *Dallas Morning News*, republished Los Angeles *Daily News* (March 31, 1993), 15.

*Page 83, lines 23–25.* Ibid.

*Page 83, lines 26–29.* Charen, "New York Has Become One Bad Apple."

*Page 83, line 36, to page 84, line 3.* "Daytime Dial," Los Angeles *Daily News* (Sept. 1994—March 1995).

*Page 83, line 21, to page 86, line 32.* D. Chagall, "Can You Believe the Ratings?" *Television Today*, Robert Cole, ed. (Oxford, New York, Toronto, and Melbourne: Oxford University Press, 1981), 197–209.

*Page 84, lines 1–30.* "Daytime Dial," Los Angeles *Daily News* (Sept. 11, 1994); "The Soaps," *Los Angeles Times* (Oct. 3, 1994); also "Star Watch," *Thousand Oaks News-Chronicle* (Aug. 5, 1993).

*Page 87, lines 36–39.* Howard Rosenberg, "Tuning into the Mixed Messages Children Get," *Los Angeles Times* (Aug. 16, 1993), F1, F11.

*Page 88, lines 5–15.* U.S. Center for Disease Control, Atlanta, Georgia, study compiled, Alan Guttmacher Institute; published *New York Times* (April 1, 1993).

*Page 88, graphs.* "TV Hours Per Day" line-chart drawn from data compiled by the A. C. Nielsen Company, 1960–1990; "Divorces Per 1,000 Married Women" line-chart drawn from data compiled by the National Center for Health Statistics, (1960–1990).

*Page 88, lines 26–29.* Cecelia Goodknow, "Teen-Age Girls Come of Age in a Hostile Environment," *Seattle Post-Intelligencer* republished in "L.A. Life," Los Angeles *Daily News* (April 4, 1995), 16.

*Page 89, lines 3–5.* Los Angeles *Daily News* (Feb. 14, 1995), 14, citing data compiled by U.S. Census Bureau and United Nations statistics.

*Page 89, lines 9–16.* Goodknow, "Teen-Age Girls Come of Age."

*Page 89, lines 16–19.* "Hour of Decision," "L.A. Life," Los Angeles *Daily News* (Feb. 26, 1995), 4–5.

*Page 89, lines 23–27.* "Big World—Small Screen," study commissioned American Psychological Association (1992), *Journal of the American Medical Association* (June, 1992); and cited by A.M.A. trustee Dr. Pamela Formica in the Los Angeles *Daily News* (June 8, 1993).

*Page 89, line 27, to page 90, line 4.* "TV Violence under Attack," Los Angeles *Daily News* (May 23, 1993), 1, 8–9.

*Page 90, lines 5–16.* Ibid.

*Page 90, line 16–31. Journal of the American Medical Association* (June 1992).

*Page 90, lines 32–35.* "French Media Officials Sued in Bomb Death," Los Angeles *Daily News* (Sept. 2, 1993).

*Page 90, line 35, to page 91, line 11.* Data through 1991, Centers for Disease Control and Prevention, Atlanta, Georgia, reported in the *Los Angeles Times* (Nov. 2, 1994), A13; school data, U.S. Department of Education, in *Insight* magazine (Sept. 13, 1993), 28.

*Page 91, lines 11–29. U.S.A. Weekend* (Aug. 13–15, 1993), 5; *U.S.A. Weekend* (Oct. 22–24, 1993), 4.

*Page 91, lines 30–36.* Associated Press newswire release (Jan. 20, 1994).

*Page 92, lines 4–27.* "A Kinder, Gentler Hollywood," *U.S. News and World Report* (May 9, 1994), 39–44.

*Page 92, lines 29–32.* "Harvard Researchers Start Nationwide Anti-Violence Campaign," Los Angeles *Daily News* (April 14, 1994).

*Page 92, lines 32–35.* "Psychologists Urge Intervention to Reverse Rising Youth Violence," *Los Angeles Times* (Aug. 11, 1993).

*Page 92, line 36, to page 93, line 3.* "Healing Our Mean Streets," *Christianity Today* (July 18, 1994), 47.

*Page 93, lines 6–10. Los Angeles Times* poll (March 23, 1993).

*Page 93, lines 11–19.* "TV Violence More Restricted Overseas," Los Angeles *Daily News* (July 27, 1993), 3.

*Page 93, lines 27–30.* Los Angeles *Daily News* (May 7, 1994), 7.

*Page 93, line 35, to page 94, line 4. Imprimis,* vol. 23, no. 11 (Sept. 1994).

*Page 94, lines 28–35.* Gini Graham Scott, *The Truth about Lying* (San Francisco: Smart Publications, 1994), 8–9.

*Page 97, lines 15–24.* S. Robert Lichter, Stanley Rothman, and Linda S. Richter, *The Media Elite* (Bethesda, Md.: Adler & Adler, 1986), 39–51.

*Page 98, lines 4–9.* "Hour of Decision," "L.A. Life," Los Angeles *Daily News* (Feb. 26, 1995), 4.

*Page 98, line 29, to page 99, line 8.* Ibid., 4–5.

*Page 99, lines 12–16.* 15-year survey, Gallup Report (1994), Gallup Research Center, Princeton, N. J.; and the Barna Report (1992–93), Glendale. Calif.

*Page 99, lines 17–27.*"Religious Faith Inching into Prime Time, Study Finds," Los Angeles *Daily News* (May 7, 1994), 16.

*Page 99, lines 28–38.* "Monitoring Group Finds TV Still Ignores Religion," *Los Angeles Times* (April 7, 1995), F2.

*Page 100, lines 1–8.* "Religious Faith Inching into Prime Time."

*Page 101, lines 5–15.* For a detailed analysis of how habits and addictions are formed, see J. C. Eccles, "The Neurophysiologic Basis of Man" (New York: Garland Press, 1988).

*Page 101, line 32, to page 102, line 15.* Marie Winn, *The Plug-In Drug* (New York: Viking Press, 1977), 223–226.

*Page 102, lines 16–24.* Ibid., 226 (with author's license, adding the Disney Channel and a Christian show for other uplifting examples).

## Chapter 8: All The News That's Fit To View

*Page 105, lines 7–17.* S. Robert Lichter, Stanley Rothman, and Linda S. Richter, *The Media Elite* (Bethesda, Md.: Adler & Adler, 1986), 29.

*Page 105, lines 18–25. Imprimis,* vol. 23, number 11 (Nov. 1994), 5.

*Page 105, line 28, to page 106, line 14.* Ibid., 3.

*Page 106, lines 16–36.* Mona Charen, Los Angeles *Daily News* (May 11, 1995); also in the SWBC Leadership Newsletter, West Covina, Calif. (May, 1995), 4.

*Page 107, lines 2–10.* The Gallup Report, annual issue, (Princeton, N. J., 1989) *The New Republic* (Sept. 12, 1994), 23.

*Page 107, lines 20–39.* The author worked for *TV Guide,* 1976–1987, as a reporter and contributing editor, focusing on research and investigative stories.

*Page 109, lines 11–15.* de Tocqueville quoted by National Public Radio commentator Steven D. Stark, "When You Live By The Culture," *Los Angeles Times* (Feb. 8, 1995), M1, M6.

*Page 110, line 5, to page 111, line 12.*David Chagall, "Only As Good As His Skin Tests" *TV Guide* (March 26, 1977), 5–10.

*Page 111, line 18, to page 112, line 17.* Paul H. Weaver, "News and the Culture of Lying: How Journalism Really Works," *The Free Press* (New York, 1994); also discussion on "Booknotes," C-Span, transcript of interview with Paul H. Weaver by Brian Lamb (Sept. 4, 1994), 8.

*Page 112, lines 21–36.* Marc Gunther, "Video Can Inform, Deceive," Los Angeles *Daily News* (Oct. 7, 1993).

*Page 112, line 38, to page 113, line 14.* Transcript of interview with Paul H. Weaver by Brian Lamb"Booknotes," C-Span (Sept. 4, 1994), 9–10.

*Page 113, lines 15–24.*Thomas B. Rosenstiel, "Postus and the Posties," *Los Angeles Times Magazine* (May 16, 1993), 21.

*Page 113, lines 25–31.* Joe Logan, "CNN Denies Staff Made Calls During 'Live' NAFTA Debate," Los Angeles *Daily News* (Nov. 12, 1993).

*Page 114, lines 3–6.* Eric Mink, "Deception Just Another Facet of Today's TV News Coverage," New York *Daily News* (Feb. 16, 1994) as sited in "L.A. Life", Los Angeles *Daily News* (Feb. 17, 1994), 9.

*Page 114, lines 10–15.* Rick du Brow, "NBC Crash Has Impact on Viewers," *Los Angeles Times* (March 27, 1993), F1, F13.

*Page 114, lines 15–21.* John Leo, "Spicing Up The (Ho-Hum) Truth," *U.S. News & World Report* (March 8, 1993), 24.

*Page 114, lines 22–31.* Mona Charen, "Duping Viewers Has Gone on for Many Years," Los Angeles *Daily News* (June 14, 1993), 13.

*Page 114, lines 32–40.* Ibid.

*Page 115, lines 1–9.* "WNET Calls WWII Documentary 'Flawed'," *Los Angeles Times* (Sept. 9, 1993), F3.

*Page 115, lines 12–22.* Mona Charen, "Racial Spoils System Takes Over at Justice," Los Angeles *Daily News* (Sept. 12, 1994), 15.

*Page 115, lines 24–37.* David Shaw, "Alar Panic Shows Power of Media to Trigger Fear," *Los Angeles Times* (Sept. 12, 1994), A19.

*Page 116, lines 2–11.* Data from the National Center for Health Statistics, Centers for Disease Control, Marsh and McLennan.

*Page 116, lines 20–24.* David Robiek, quoted in David Shaw, "RISK: Unbalanced Reports Can Widen the Reality Gap," *Los Angeles Times* (Sept. 11, 1994), A30.

*Page 116, lines 25–29.* Ibid.

*Page 116, lines 30–35.* Dr. Bruce Ames, quoted in, "RISK."

*Page 117, lines 1–6.* David Shaw, "RISK: Why Stories Make Us Fret about What We Eat, Drink," *Los Angeles Times* (Sept. 11, 1994), A.31.

*Page 117, lines 8–17.* Rita Beamish, "Voters Rate the Coverage by News Media as Mediocre," *Los Angeles Times* (Nov. 20, 1992), A13.

*Page 117, line 18, to page 118, line 3.* Data derived from "The Times Poll," (conducted March 6–9, 1993), cited in the *Los Angeles Times* (March 31, 1993), A16.

## Chapter 9: The Top-40 Nightmare

*Page 122, lines 20–22.* Dr. Mary Carskadon, Brown University, professor of psychiatry, *Sleep* (Spring 1993) as cited in Kathleen Doheny, "Personal Health," *Los Angeles Times* (April 27, 1993), E3.

*Page 123, lines 9–26.* Background on The Sex Pistols, Al Menconi with Dave Hart, "Today's Music" (Elgin, Ill.: David C. Cook Publishing, 1990), 62–63.

*Page 125 to page 126.* MTV programming charted by the author, viewing during the period April 2–15, 1995 via "MTV," Los Angeles.

*Page 126, lines 28–41.* Ibid., Analysis based on direct viewing, April 2–15, 1995.

*Page 127, lines 1–26.* Analysis based on direct viewing; also citing older incidents described in David Kronke, "Just Boys or Civilization Destroyers?" *Los Angeles Times* "Calendar" (Sept. 12, 1993), 73.

*Page 127, lines 27–33.* Bob DeMoss, "Do You Know What Your Kids Are Watching?" *Focus on the Family Magazine* (August 1994), 2.

*Page 127, lines 34–39.* Bruce Horovitz, "Retailing: The Delicate Side of Beavis and Butt-Head," *Los Angeles Times* (Nov. 9, 1993),D6.

*Page 128, lines 1–13.* DeMoss, "Do You Know What Your Kids Are Watching?"

*Page 128, lines 16–19.* Terence Trent D'Arby, Q&A interview by Robert Hilburn, *Los Angeles Times*, (July 6, 1993), F3.

*Page 128, lines 19–22.* Heidi Siegmund, "Nine Inch Nails Hit It with the Moshers," *Los Angeles Times* (March 11, 1994), F6.

*Page 128, line 22–25.* 700 Club's "Fact Sheet," "Today's Rock Music: Intoxicating Teens with Violence," *700 Club Newswatch* (June 29, 1994).

*Page 128, lines 25–27.* Glenn Danzig quote cited in Steve Hochman, "He's No Walk in the Park," *Los Angeles Times'* "Calendar" (Oct. 9, 1994), 7.

*Page 128, lines 27–29.* Cannibal Corpse and Pantera lyric, 700 Club's "Fact Sheet," "Today's Rock Music."

*Page 128, lines 31–33.* Chuck Philips, "Gangsta Rap: Did Lyrics Inspire Killing of Police?" *Los Angeles Times* (Oct. 17, 1994), F2.

*Page 128, lines 33–36.* Ibid., F5.

*Page 128, lines 22, to page 129, line 2. 700 Club "Fact Sheet,"* "Today's Rock Music: Intoxicating Teen with Violence," *700 Club Newswatch* June 29, 1994.

*Page 129, lines 4–5.* "Boy Planned to Kill Father, Ambush Police," *Los Angeles Times* (Feb. 24, 1994), A1.

*Page 129, lines 7–11.* "Video Inspired Boy in School Hostage Plot," Los Angeles *Daily News* (Oct. 10, 1993), 7.

*Page 129, lines 11–13.* 700 Club "Fact Sheet," "Today's Rock Music."

*Page 129, lines 13–15. Media Update,* vol. 14, issue 3 (May/June 1995), 3.

*Page 129, lines 15–16.* 1994 sales figures for rap music from Recording Industry Association of America, "L.A. Life," Los Angeles *Daily News* (March 22, 1995), 7.

*Page 129, lines 22–31.* For a more detailed analysis of violence in rap music and a profile of Death Row publishers, see the article "Songs of Violence Top the Charts," *Los Angeles Times* (April 3, 1995), A1, A18.

*Page 129, line 34, to page 130, line 13.* "Ready for MC Mickey?" *Los Angeles Times* (Sept. 15, 1994), F1, F6.

*Page 130, lines 26–34.* Lynette Rice, "Not Just for Sundays Anymore," "L.A. Life," L .A. *Daily News* (April 23, 1995), 4–5.

*Page 131, lines 23–34.* Steve Lewis, "A Crash Course On," *Media Update,* vol.14, issue 2 (March/April 1995), 4.

*Page 131, lines 18–23.* Lynette Rice, "Not Just for Sundays Anymore."

*Page 131, lines 24–32.* P. K. Mitchell quotes *Urgency,* vol. 1, issue 4 (Fall 1994), 1–3.

*Page 131, line 33, to page 132, line 3.* Ibid., Malicide interview, 7–9.

*Page 132, lines 4–14.* "Alice Cooper: The Last Temptation," in *Urgency,* vol. 1, issue 4 (Fall 1994), 17–18.

*Page 132, lines 30–38.* John Dart, "The Spirit Moves Them," *Los Angeles Times* (Feb. 26, 1995), B1, B5.

*Page 132, line 39, to page 133, line 2.* Don Lattin, "Rebel Priest Changes Religion, Goes Underground with 'Rave Mass'," Los Angeles *Daily News* (April 23, 1994).

## Chapter 10: Movies! Movies!

*Page 141, lines 5–9.* Oliver Stone, quote from interview by Nathan Gardels, *Los Angeles Times* (Feb. 26, 1995), M5.

*Page 141, line 14, to page 142, line 2.* Stanley Kauffman's review titled "Apocalypse Now," *The New Republic* (Oct. 3, 1995), 26–27.

*Page 142, lines 4–13.* Hilary de Vries, "A Chat with Mr. Mayhem," *Los Angeles Times* "Calendar" (Sept. 11, 1994), 45.

*Page 142, line 31, to page 145, line 10.* Hays Office Code, Edward F. Dolan, "A History of the Movies" (New York: Bison Books, 1983), 300–02.

*Page 145, lines 21–36.* "The World Almanac and Book of Facts 1991" (New York: Pharos Books, 1989), 340–341.

*Page 146, lines 14–32.* For a fine analysis of the introduction of profanity through Black exploitation films, see Claude Brown, "The Language of Violence," *Los Angeles Times* (March 24, 1994), B9.

*Page 146, line 39, to page 147, line 3. Bound By Honor* citation Gus Frias, "We're Teaching Our Children How to Kill," *Los Angeles Times* (June 14, 1993), B.7.

*Page 147, lines 3–6.* Bob Strauss, "'Program' Re-Edited Following Teen Death," Los Angeles *Daily News* (Oct. 20, 1993), 1, 6.

*Page 147, lines 7–9.* Alan Abrahamson, "TV Movie Inspired Killings, Menendez Prosecution Claims," *Los Angeles Times* (Aug. 20, 1993), B1, B9.

*Page 147, lines 11–12.* David Gritten, "Film, Street Violence Has Brits Talking," *Times of London*, as cited by *Los Angeles Times* (March 19, 1993), F1, F18.

*Page 147, lines 12–15.* Liat Collins, "Education Chief Declares War on TV Violence" *Jerusalem Post* (Jan. 21, 1995), 11.

*Page 147, lines 28–35.* Douglas Armstrong, "Slick, Quick Fable Is Truly Indecent Sort of Proposal," "Starwatch," *Thousand Oaks News-Chronicle* (April 29, 1993).

*Page 147, line 36, to page 148, line 7.* Michael Medved, "The Last Temptation of Hollywood," *Christianity Today* (March 8, 1993), 29.

*Page 148, lines 21–31.* Michael Medved, "And What about Hollywood Films These Days?" *Focus on the Family Magazine* (March 1993), 4.

*Page 148, line 33, to page 149, line 7.* Ibid.

*Page 149, line 37, to page 150, line 18.* Irene Lacher, "Is Filmland in Sync with America?" *Los Angeles Times* (Oct. 9, 1994), F1, F5.

*Page 150, lines 23–35.* Table on U.S. Movie Admissions derived from data provided by the Motion Picture Association of America, for years 1982–92; also first five-months projection figures for 1993 based on box-office grosses from Entertainment Data Inc.

*Page 150, line 36, to page 151, line 21.* David J. Fox, "Honey, They Shrunk the Movie Audience," *Los Angeles Times* (June 8, 1993), F1, F6.

*Page 152, lines 20–30.* I attended many of these film "previews," where he was treated to fancy food, flattery, and even free souvenir gifts and momentos, all intended to influence a favorable review. And the Christian movie industry is not exempt from such shananigans. When the movie *Born Again* was about to be released, I was invited to a preview screening where the same sorts of inducements were distributed, including personal interviews with the author, Charles Colson.

## Chapter 11: The Cyberspace Invasion

*Page 158, lines 4–6.* "Limbaugh Meets Wife Through Compuserve," *Thousand Oaks News-Chronicle* Enterprise (June 17, 1994), 1.

*Page 158, lines 6–11.* Peter H. Lewis, "Strangers, Not Their Computers, Build a Network in Time of Grief," *New York Times* (March 8, 1944), A1, C18.

*Page 158, lines 12–17.* Allison Kaplan Sommer, "Hooked on Internet," *Jerusalem Post* (May 14, 1994), 12.

*Page 158, lines 19–24.* Lawrence J. Magid, "D. C. Gets On-line with the Public," *Los Angeles Times* (July 9, 1994), D4, D13. Since Internet "Home Pages" change rather swiftly, the reader can determine which officials and departments are online only by logging on to the current White House Internet Page.

*Page 158, lines 28–31.* "An Electronic Job Hunt," in *U.S. News & World Report* (March 28, 1994), 72–73.

*Page 158, lines 32–33.* Daniel Cerone, "Hollywood Online," *Los Angeles Times*/Calendar (April 17, 1994), 7– 8, 82–83.

*Page 158, lines 34–39.* Marie Gravelle, "Welcome to Cyberville," *Los Angeles Times* (May 15, 1994), A3, A30.

*Page 158, line 39, to page 159, line 3.* Anne Gregor, "Dialing Up the Bulletin Board," *Los Angeles Times* (May 22, 1994), D3.

*Page 159, lines 17–19.* Timothy C. Morgan, "Cyber Shock," *Christianity Today* (April 3, 1995), 78.

*Page 159, line 34, to page 160, line 6.* Ann Landers column, Los Angeles *Daily News* (March 16, 1994), 13.

*Page 160, lines 10–22. The Internet Yellow Pages,* compiled by Harley Hahn and Rick Stout, 2nd ed., (New York: Osborne McGraw-Hill, 1995). This 810-page tome lists all sorts of information sites, arranged by areas of interest. While those with sexual content constitute a small portion of the listings, they are the "busiest," often denying entry because too many users are trying to access them.

*Page 160, line 32, to page 161, line 4.* For a well-reasoned and (mostly) factual discussion of the kinds of people who make up the "hacker" community, see the article "Hackers Convene in Texas for HoHoCon '93" by Damien Thorn, published in *Nuts & Volts Magazine* (March, 1994), 100–102, 133–135.

*Page 161, lines 5–8.* John Johnson, "Hacker in Hiding," *Los Angeles Times* (Oct. 30, 1994), B1, B4; also, for a dramatized account of the legendary hacker called "Dark Dante," see Jonathan Littman, "The Last Hacker," *Los Angeles Times* Magazine (Sept. 12, 1993), 18, 20, 22, 24, 64.

*Page 161, lines 8–10.* Robert A. Rosenblatt, "Electronic Filing Fraud Costing IRS Millions," *Los Angeles Times* (Feb. 11, 1994), A1, A17.

*Page 161, lines 10–14.* Walter Hamilton, "Hustlers Hit On-line Computer Services," Los Angeles *Daily News* (July 1, 1994), Business Section, 1-2.

*Page 161, lines 15–25.* John Johnson and Julie Tamaki, "Authorities Again Seek Legendary Hacker," *Los Angeles Times* (July 10, 1994), B1, B6; also Howard Breuer, "Computer Hacker Step Ahead of the Law," Los Angeles *Daily News* (July 5, 1994), 3.

*Page 161, lines 31–33.* Gordon Witkin, "Wanted, in Cyberspace," *U.S. News & World Report* (March 14, 1994), 71.

*Page 161, line 35, to page 162, line 4.* Report by Wisconsin U.S. Senator Herb Kohl, delivered to the Senate Subcomittee on Terrorism, Technology, and Government Information of the Senate Judiciary Committee (May 12, 1995).

*Page 162, lines 5–18.* Rabbi Abraham Cooper, "Cyberspace Bigots Getting a Free Ride," *Los Angeles Times* (Dec. 18, 1994), M2.

*Page 162, lines 20–24.* I received a four-color glossy brochure from a firm called "The Profit Group" in Tucson, Arizona, offering CD-ROM discs featuring "adult fare," shareware, and the disk titled "Forbidden Subjects" with a red-flagged label reading "WARNING! This Disc Contains Information No One Wants You To Know About," exactly the sort of caveat that attracts young people and emotionally immature adults.

*Page 162, line 34, to page 163, line 2.* "The Ultimate CD-ROM Home Reference Library," Advertising Supplement to Ziff-Davis' *Personal Computing* (December 1994), 34.

*Page 163, lines 4–17.* Amy Harmon, "The 'Seedy' Side of CD-ROMS," *Los Angeles Times* (Nov. 29, 1993), A1, A26–A28. This coverage was provided to the author by Maryam Kubasek, Director of Communications at the National Coalition Against Pornography.

*Page 163, lines 18–24.* Yardena Arar, "Cyber Potatoes Can Get Latest on Simpson Case," "L.A. Life," Los Angeles *Daily News* (Oct. 10, 1994), 5.

*Page 163, lines 26–29.* Amy Harmon, "Paramount Leaps into the Interactive Fray," *Los Angeles Times* (Feb. 24, 1994), page D1.

*Page 163, line 38, to page 164, line 2.* Harmon, "The 'Seedy' Side of CD-ROMS."

*Page 164, lines 16–18.* "Combating Kombat," "L.A. Life," Los Angeles *Daily News* (Sept. 14, 1993), 8.

*Page 164, lines 19–20. Media Update* (March/April 1995), vol. 14, issue 2, 7.

*Page 164, lines 20–24.* David Wharton, "Video Legions," *Los Angeles Times* (Nov. 18, 1994), F10.

*Page 164, lines 25–28. Media Update* (March/April 1995), vol. 14, issue 2, 7.

*Page 164, lines 34–38.* Rip Rense, "Joy of Mayhem," *Los Angeles Times* (Nov. 5, 1993), E12.

*Page 165, lines 2–18.* I interviewed software manufacturers and several print sources for his overview of "Virtual Reality," including Glenn Russell of Pacific Softworks, Camarillo, California; the *Superlife* brochure from Zygon International, (May 1995); Daniel Howard Cerone, "V.R.5 Steps Into Critical Real World," *Los Angeles Times* (March 23, 1995), F1, F11; and Penny Star, "Virtual Reality Games Come to Tel Aviv," *Jerusalem Post* (June 11, 1994), 16A.

*Page 165, lines 19–27.* "Virtual Reality Raises Dresden Church from Rubble," *Los Angeles Times* (June 11, 1994),B12; also Julianne Basinger, "Virtual Reality Likeness to Guide Reconstruction of Dresden Church," Los Angeles *Daily News* (July 9, 1994),12.

*Page 165, lines 28–33.* Jennifer Pendleton, "Providing a Whirl on Motion Simulators," *Los Angeles Times* (Feb. 14, 1995), F3, F9.

*Page 165, lines 33–40.* Penny Star, "Virtual Reality Games Come to Tel Aviv," *Jerusalem Post* (June 11, 1994), 16A.

*Page 166, lines 1–10.* Daniel Howard Cerone, "V.R.5," see the article "V.R.5 Steps into Critical Real World," *Los Angeles Times* (March 23, 1995), F1, F11.

*Page 166, lines 13–38.* James Coates, "The Invisibility Factor," *Chicago Tribune* release, Los Angeles *Daily News* (April 20, 1994), 15–16.

*Page 167, lines 6–17.* Kristina Sauerwein, "The Flake Factor," *Los Angeles Times* (March 27, 1995), E1, E3.

*Page 167, lines 30–32. Media Update,* vol.14, issue 2, (March/April 1995), 7.

*Page 167, line 33, to page 168, line 14.* Amy Wu, "Lost in Cyberspace: Pitfalls of Easy Access to Internet," Op-Ed article, *Los Angeles Times* (Nov. 20, 1994),A12.

*Page 168, line 15 to page 169, line 3.* "Addiction to Computers Stirring Worries," (Dec. 26, 1994).

*Page 169, lines 7–28.* I conducted extensive searches through the online services described in this section, *Using Technology For Christ,* and would encourage readers with online access to do likewise, if they haven't already done so.

*Page 170, lines 10–36.* Robert Lee Hotz, "Paranoia Your Password? Ok, But Don't Tell Anyone," *Los Angeles Times,* Computer Supplement. (April 11, 1994), 25.

*Page 171, lines 16–18.* Report by Wisconsin U.S. Senator Herb Kohl, delivered to the Senate Subcomittee on Terrorism, Technology, and Government Information of the Senate Judiciary Committee (May 12, 1995).

*Page 172, lines 12–20.* An anonymous file of offbeat cyberspace terms offered on the Internet. Called the "Jargon" file, it can be accessed at: "Address: ftp.std.com" and "Path: /obi/Nerd.Humor/webster/jargon".

*Page 172, lines 25, to page 173, line 11.* Jeff Leeds, "Video Game Makers Unveil Consumer Rating System," *Los Angeles Times* (July 30, 1994), page A16; and Jeannine Aversa, "Computer, Video Games to Be Rated" (July 29, 1994).

*Page 173, lines 20–28.* Bernie Mixon and Michsael A. Lev, "Religious Figures Do Battle in Video Game World," *Chicago Tribune* release, "L.A. Life," Los Angeles *Daily News* (Feb. 26, 1995), 14.

*Page 174, lines 3–30.* "Child Safety on the Information Highway," furnished by the National Center for Missing and Exploited Children, 2101 Wilson Boulevard, Suite 550, Arlington, Virginia 22201–3052 (telephone 1–800-843-5678).